ST. MARY'S COLLEGE OF MARYLAND LIBRARY
ST. MARY'S CITY, MARYLAND

W9-BWL-934

FACTIONAL POLITICS IN AN INDIAN STATE

33783

FACTIONAL POLITICS IN AN INDIAN STATE

The Congress Party in Uttar Pradesh

PAUL R. BRASS

UNIVERSITY OF CALIFORNIA PRESS

BERKELEY AND LOS ANGELES

1965

University of California Press
Berkeley and Los Angeles

Cambridge University Press
London, England

© *1965 by the Regents of the University of California*

Library of Congress Catalog Card Number 65-23109

PRINTED IN THE UNITED STATES OF AMERICA

For Linda

Preface

The field research for this study was carried out over a period of nearly seventeen months, between September, 1961, and January, 1963, in Uttar Pradesh. Throughout this time, I maintained a residence in Lucknow. From Lucknow, I made frequent field trips to the districts for two- and three-week periods. In addition, I made several trips to Delhi to interview members of Parliament (MPs) and to use the newspaper files of the All India Congress Committee Press Information Department. Before beginning the field work, I spent two months in London working on newspapers in the India Office Library.

Most of the material in this book is based upon personal interviews with more than 250 political leaders and other politically informed people in Uttar Pradesh. The majority of my interviews were with past and present officers of the District Congress Committees and with other prominent local Congressmen, with local opposition party leaders, with officers of local government and cooperative institutions, and with administrators, teachers, and journalists in the districts. I also visited several Block Development Office headquarters and spoke to the administrative officials at this level. I interviewed the panchayat presidents in some villages in Aligarh, Gonda, and Deoria districts. In Lucknow, I interviewed most of the senior ministers and ex-ministers in the state government, prominent state party leaders of the Congress and opposition parties, and many members of the Legislative Assembly (MLAs) from a number of districts in the state.

In addition to personal interviews, I benefited from first-hand observations of the 1962 General Election in Uttar Pradesh. I witnessed election meetings in Aligarh villages and in the mohallas of Kanpur City. I also worked in the election offices in five districts, copying out polling station statistics for the 1957 and 1962 elections. The election officers in all the districts were invariably helpful.

vii

The third major source of information was newspaper reports. At the India Office Library in London, I used the back files of the *Leader* and the *Pioneer*. In Delhi, I used the excellent Press Information Department files of the All India Congress Committee on the Uttar Pradesh Congress. These files contained clippings from the major English and Hindi papers in India since 1946. I want to thank Mr. C. L. Sharma, who heads the Press Information Department, and his staff for permitting me to use the files for several weeks. During my stay in Uttar Pradesh, I kept my own clippings from the *Statesman* (Delhi), from the *National Herald*, and from *Aj*. In Kanpur, Mr. S. P. Mehra gave me access to the files of his newspaper, the *Citizen*. I also used the Kanpur supplement of the *Hindustan Times;* I owe thanks to Mr. T. V. Venkataraman for making the files available to me.

Other sources of information are mentioned in the study where appropriate.

In describing events in district politics, I have used two kinds of statements—those concerning the subjective perceptions of the politicians about political affairs and those which actually describe political events in the districts. I have tried to indicate in the footnotes whenever my descriptions of both subjective perceptions and of objective events are based upon interviews. In trying to construct a description of actual events in district politics, I was often faced with the problem of conflicting versions of reality. I have treated as "facts" those descriptions of events in district politics which I have been able to confirm from different kinds of sources (e.g., both newspaper reports and interviews), or those which opponents agree upon, or those which I have received from informed neutral observers. Unfortunately, it is not possible in many cases to give the identities of my informants.

My preparation for field work in India was begun in 1959 under the guidance of the members of the Committee on South Asian Studies at the University of Chicago. I was first attracted to Indian politics as a research field in course work with Dr. Myron Weiner. Dr. Weiner guided my research both at Chicago and in India. It was my good fortune to be in India while Dr. Weiner was there and so to be able to talk over my problems with him. I owe a special debt also to Miss Maureen Patterson, who was my first instructor in Hindi, my guide to library resources, and a personal friend.

Field research for the study was made possible by a Foreign Area Training Fellowship granted by the Ford Foundation. I am grateful to the Ford Foundation for their generous grant and to the staff of the Foundation for the sympathetic attention which they always gave to my requests.

Many people in Uttar Pradesh willingly gave me their time and their help. Dr. Trilokinath Srivastava, of the K. N. Government College, Gyanpur, introduced me to the intricacies of Uttar Pradesh politics in conversations in London. In Uttar Pradesh, I very often visited people uninvited and unexpected. I was always received with friendliness and hospitality. For reasons of propriety, it is not possible to thank those in politics and in government service who were helpful to me. However, I must thank those who aided my work by providing me both help and hospitality: Mr. Arthur Grice and S. P. Mehra in Kanpur; Anand Singh and the late Raghvendra Pratap Singh in Gonda; Nazir Hyder, of the Aligarh Muslim University; and Dr. Mohendra in Padrauna. I owe a great debt for help in many ways to Hayat Ahmad and to Zarina Bhatty.

I am grateful to those who read all or parts of the manuscript and made helpful suggestions and criticisms: Dr. Grant McConnell, Dr. Duncan MacRae, Jr., Maureen Patterson, Dr. Myron Weiner, Professor Fred G. Bailey, and Dr. Bernard S. Cohn. I benefited also from discussions in Professor Bailey's seminar at the University of Chicago. However, I am solely responsible for any errors and for the conclusions and interpretations presented.

The editors of the *Economic Weekly*, *Asian Survey*, and Dr. Myron Weiner, the editor of the book *Indian Voting Behaviour*, have kindly granted me permission to reproduce material verbatim or in revised form. The maps were drawn by Richard D. DePuma.

My greatest debt is to my wife, who read the manuscript piece by piece at all hours of the day and night, whenever I needed her support.

Contents

FIGURES

TABLES

Fig. 1. The districts of Uttar Pradesh.

I.

Introduction

In the adaptation of modern institutions of representative government to traditional societies, political parties play the decisive role. In every modern polity, and in every polity which aspires to modernity, political parties are an indispensable link between the society and the institutions of government. In traditional societies undergoing modernization and political development, political parties have the double task of providing stable government and of bringing new groups of people into the political process while orienting them toward the political and economic goals of the modern state. The ability of former colonial countries to make a successful transition from foreign bureaucratic rule to democratic self-government depends very much upon the capacity of the political parties to perform these tasks.

The capacity of the ruling party in a new state to perform these tasks in turn depends upon how successful it is in the years after independence in transforming itself from a nationalist movement to an effective political party.[1] In the period of transformation, there is an inevitable process of disintegration. Ideological and communal differences which were submerged in the movement for independence develop into internal conflicts, leading to defections and splits. New conflicts develop over the distribution of positions of power and status in the new government. The ruling party is faced both with opposition from outside and conflict within the organization.

In some of the new states, the political parties have failed to check the

[1] This conception of the problems of transition from movement to party is based upon Myron Weiner's analysis of the stages of development of national movements in South Asia in *Party Politics in India: The Development of a Multi-Party System* (Princeton: Princeton University Press, 1957), pp. 12-16, and *Political Change in South Asia* (Calcutta: Firma K. L. Mukhopadhyay, 1963), pp. 36 ff.

1

processes of disintegration, have proved incapable of providing stable government, and have been replaced by military governments. Another common pattern of political development in the new states has been the emergence of one-party systems. In these cases, the leadership of the ruling parties have successfully checked the process of disintegration by prohibiting external competition and suppressing internal conflict. Few political parties in the new states have been able or willing to imitate the pattern established by the Indian National Congress. The Congress party in India has attempted to prevent the disintegration of its organization by competing with opposition parties for popular support and by managing internal conflict, rather than suppressing it.

This book is an analysis of the transition of the Congress organization in one Indian state, Uttar Pradesh, from a mass movement to an effective political party. It is a study of the processes of disintegration and integration in a modern political organization operating in a traditional society. It is an examination of the problem of the adjustment and adaptation of a modern political party to the traditional order.

Political parties which failed to make a successful transition from movement to party failed largely because they did not establish firm roots in the traditional societies. The ruling parties in the one-party states have been unwilling to compromise with traditional attitudes and loyalties in their eagerness to transform their societies. The Indian National Congress has adopted many measures which strike at the traditional order, including land reform and social reform measures, but the party organization has not taken upon itself the task of attempting to bring about a total and rapid transformation of values and attitudes in the traditional society. The Congress has chosen to make adjustments and accommodations, to interact with rather than transform the traditional order. In India, modernization is not a one-way process; political institutions modernize the society while the society traditionalizes institutions.

An important aspect of the transition of the Congress from movement to party has been the devolution of power from the center to the states. In the post-Independence period, the Congress increasingly has become a coalition of semi-autonomous state parties. Central control continues to be exercised, particularly in the arbitration of internal conflict, but conflict and controversy in state politics center around state issues and state personalities.

Within the states, there is an interaction between state politics and politics in the districts. As the Indian National Congress is a coalition of state parties, the state parties are themselves coalitions of semi-independent district party organizations. It is in the districts that the Congress organizations interact with the traditional societies. In the districts, the forces of disintegration are most directly felt.

The working of the Congress organization in Uttar Pradesh will be studied at the state and district levels because the two levels of organization are integrated in important ways. However, the main concern of the study is with the effectiveness of the local, district Congress organizations in organizing popular support and in maintaining internal unity. Five districts have been selected for case studies. Each district has been selected because it represents in a very distinct way a particular kind of problem with which the Congress must deal and a particular kind of environment in which the Congress must operate. Each district is untypical of the state as a whole because no single district can be typical in a state so large and so diverse, but each district is typical of a regional kind of environment or a problem which is statewide in scope.[2]

The general argument of the book can be stated briefly. The problem of maintaining internal unity has been a much more serious concern for the Congress party in Uttar Pradesh than the organization of popular support. Like most political parties in India, the Congress party organizations in Uttar Pradesh are riven by factional conflicts. In fact, the faction is the basic unit of the Congress party in Uttar Pradesh. Yet the Congress has not split apart or become so disorganized as to be unable to provide stable government in the state. The ability of the Congress organization to maintain itself despite incessant factional struggle has much to do with the character of the factions themselves. The factional structure of the Congress party in Uttar Pradesh reflects the adaptation of the organization to the traditional society, for the faction belongs to the traditional order. The Congress, the agent of modernization in rural Uttar Pradesh, has become traditionalized. The traditionalization of the Congress organization does not mean that it does not perform a modernizing function in the society. Rather, there is a two-way interaction; the Congress performs its modernizing role through traditional social organization, the faction, which in turn adapts itself to modern party organization. In this two-way interaction, both the modern party organization and the traditional society are undergoing change.

The role of factions in the Congress party organization is thus not disruptive only. Factions perform both integrative and disintegrative functions for the Congress party organization in Uttar Pradesh. The dual role of factions and factional conflict will be demonstrated in the case studies.

Although the maintenance of internal unity is the primary concern of the Congress organization in Uttar Pradesh, the party must also organize

[2] The districts selected are described at the end of chap. iii. For the location of the districts, see fig. 4.

popular support. The ability of the Congress to organize popular support and to compete successfully with opposition parties will be analyzed in each district. In each of the districts selected for detailed study, opposition to the Congress takes different forms. In Gonda, opposition comes from Swatantra and the Jan Sangh; in Deoria, from the Praja Socialist Party (PSP) and the Socialists; in Kanpur, from the Communists; in Aligarh, from the Republicans; and, in Meerut, from independents. The variety of opposition parties which the Congress must face in these five districts is a measure of the diversity of the social and political environment in Uttar Pradesh. The fact that all the major opposition parties in Uttar Pradesh are represented in these districts makes it possible to examine the capacity of the Congress organization to compete with political parties which have different ideologies and social bases.

II.

Uttar Pradesh:
History, Economy, People, and Politics

THE ENVIRONMENT

Area and Population

The area of Uttar Pradesh is 113,654 square miles,[1] almost exactly that of the state of Arizona. The population, according to the 1961 census, was close to 74,000,000 [2]—a figure surpassed only by the largest and most populous countries of the world. In parts of the state, the land has passed beyond the point of population saturation—rural densities exceeding 1,000 persons per square mile in many districts—and yet the growth rate continues to increase. The decade from 1911 to 1921 saw the last population decline in this state. Since 1921, the population has increased decennially by 6.7, 13.6, 11.8, and, in the last decade, by 16.7 percent.[3]

The population of the state is overwhelmingly rural. Only 12.9 percent of the population of Uttar Pradesh live in urban areas.[4]

However, the urban population is unimpressive only relative to the total population of the state. The 1961 census lists no less than 244 cities and towns with a combined population of approximately 9.5 million people. Even excluding most of the small towns, which lack real urban characteristics, there are 17 cities with a population over 100,000, 7 containing more than a quarter of a million people, and 3 exceeding half a million.[5]

Administratively, Uttar Pradesh is divided into 54 districts, ranging in

[1] *Census of India, 1961, Paper No. 1 of 1962: Final Population Totals*, p. 348.
[2] *Ibid.*
[3] *Ibid.*, p. 349 and *Census of India, 1951*, Vol. II: *Uttar Pradesh*, by Rajeshwari Prasad, Pt. I-A (Allahabad: Superintendent, Printing and Stationery, 1953), p. 25.
[4] *Census of India, 1961, Paper No. 1 of 1962, op. cit.*, p. 349.
[5] *Ibid.*, pp. 236-244.

area from under 1,000 to over 4,000 square miles and in population from
100,000 to 2,700,000. Rural population densities range from 41 in the hill
district of Uttar Kashi to 1138 persons per square mile in Deoria district.
All districts, even those with large urban centers, are predominantly rural;
only Lucknow district is nearly evenly balanced between urban and rural
areas. Literacy varies from under 10 percent in Budaun district to close to
40 percent in Dehra Dun.[6]

Geographic and historical regions

In broad terms, there are three major geographical areas in Uttar Pradesh: the northern mountains, the central plain, and the southern hills. Most
of the area and population of the state are concentrated in the plains—close
to 70 percent of the area and 90 percent of the population.

The northern mountain area, Kumaon, forms the central part of the central Himalayan range, with Himachal Pradesh on the west, Tibet on the
north, and Nepal on the east. Peaks vary from 5,000 to 8,000 feet in the
foothills to over 25,000 feet in the northern mountain range. The physical
geography of Kumaon sharply separates it from the plains below, but the
sacred geography unites the area with the plains. The area has been for
long an important place of pilgrimage for Hindus of the plains, for it contains the headwaters of the Ganges. In modern times, the hill stations of the
region have become resort areas for the people of the plains during the
months of May and June. The region contains nomadic tribes who trade
across the borders with Nepal and Tibet. However, Kumaon is overwhelmingly Hindu; the entire region is dominated numerically, economically, and
politically by Brahmans and Rajputs, many of them originally immigrants
from the plains. The region has been the area in Uttar Pradesh least affected
by Islam; only in Dehra Dun and in the *tarai*[7] portion of Naini Tal district
are there many Muslims.

The northern mountains are an area for religious pilgrimage and a
haven from the heat of the summer. The southern hill and plateau districts,
in contrast, contain no important places of pilgrimage and have the most
unattractive climate in the state. In the pockets among the low hills, tem-
peratures rise to extremes of 115° to 120° in the hot months. The region is
a rocky area where agriculture is difficult and population is sparse. There
are five hill districts—Mirzapur on the southeastern tip of the state and
Jhansi, Jalaun, Hamirpur, and Banda on the southwest. The four southwest
districts belong to the region of Bundelkhand, the greater part of which
lies in Madhya Pradesh. The whole area lies on the fringe of the Vindhyan
mountain range which separates north India from the Deccan. With only

---

[6] *Ibid.*, pp. 348-351.
[7] The tract of marshy and jungly land between the Himalayas and the plains.

rare exceptions in India's imperial ages, Bundelkhand has been largely a battleground among petty local chiefs or between northern and southern empire-builders. The region takes its name from the Bundelas, a Rajput clan which rose to prominence here between the fifteenth and seventeenth centuries.

All of the central plains area of Uttar Pradesh forms part of the Gangetic basin, but there are some important geographic differences within the area. Spate divides the area into two portions—the Upper Ganges Plain, comprising all of the western and central plains districts, and the Middle Ganges Plain, which is made up of the eastern districts of the state and is more like the plain of Bihar.[8] However, another division is possible, which considers both geographic and historical differences. Following Crooke, the plains can be divided into a southern and northern portion—the Ganges-Jumna Doab on the south and the area between the Ganges and the Nepal *tarai* on the north.[9]

Spate has pointed out the great significance of the Doab and particularly of the Delhi-Agra axis in Indian history, the latter an area of warfare where empires have been founded and destroyed.[10] Three of the state's five great cities are located in the Doab, each representing a different civilization. Agra, in the northern part of the Doab, was the capital of the Mughal Empire during its greatest period; Kanpur, further down, a modern industrial city, was created by British entrepreneurs in the late nineteenth century; finally, Allahabad, at the confluence of the Ganges and the Jumna, is the oldest city of the three and one of the most sacred of Hindu cities. In terms of physical geography, the area has a light rainfall, is irrigated by the canal systems of the Ganges and Jumna rivers, and is primarily a wheat-growing area, with sugar an important cash crop in the northern districts.

The northern plains area must be further subdivided into four parts: Rohilkhand, Oudh, Gorakhpur, and Benares. Rohilkhand includes seven districts in the west—Bijnor, Moradabad, Rampur, Budaun, Bareilly, Pilibhit, and Shahjahanpur. The region takes its name from the Rohilla Afghans who rose to dominance here in the eighteenth century. Rohilkhand has the heaviest concentration of Muslims in the state; in three of the districts, the proportion of Muslims is over a third of the total population. Rampur district remained an autonomous Muslim princely state until 1949. The region contains no important cities, but Bareilly has a population of over a quarter of a million and three other towns—Moradabad, Rampur, and Shahjahanpur —have populations over 100,000.

[8] O. H. K. Spate, *India and Pakistan: A General and Regional Geography* (2d ed.; London: Methuen and Co., Ltd., 1957), pp. 495-521.

[9] W. Crooke, *The North-Western Provinces of India: Their History, Ethnology, and Administration* (London: Methuen and Co., 1897), pp. 27 ff.

[10] Spate, *op. cit.*, p. 150.

Oudh, the central portion of the northern plains tract, contains twelve districts—all, except Gonda and Bahraich, on the southern side of the great Ghagra river. Oudh is the area in Uttar Pradesh with the longest historical identity. The borders of Oudh have fluctuated throughout its history, the twelve districts being the last to be annexed by the British in 1856. Oudh was an important province under both the Delhi Sultanate and the Mughal Empire. The annexation of Oudh in 1856 and the land settlement which antagonized the *talukdars* were among the most important causes of the spread of the Mutiny of 1857. Lucknow, the last capital of Oudh, is now the capital of Uttar Pradesh. Agriculturally, the twelve districts are transitional from the western wheat-growing area to the eastern rice-growing region.

Finally, on the eastern borders of the state are the predominantly rice-growing regions of Gorakpur and Banaras, part of the Middle Ganges Plain which merges into Bihar. The Gorakhpur region was sometimes part of Oudh, sometimes part of the old province of Bihar under the Mughal Empire. The Benares region has more historical individuality. Jaunpur, in this area, was the seat of an independent Muslim kingdom which challenged the authority of the Delhi Sultanate in the fourteenth century. Later, the area became part of Oudh; but, by the time of the British arrival, the Raja of Banaras had become effectively independent of Oudh. The city of Banaras is the most important center of Hindu pilgrimage for all of India.

Uttar Pradesh is largely a collection of geographic and historical regions. Yet, for the most part, the differences between regions are shadings rather than sharp breaks. Moreover, the borders of the state are in hardly any respects natural. On all sides, Uttar Pradesh merges into the physical and cultural environment of its neighboring states and countries. Kumaon merges into the central mountain belt, Bundelkhand into Madhya Pradesh, the eastern districts into the plain of Bihar. Even the northern boundary of the state is artificial, for there is *tarai* on both sides of the Nepal border. The Jumna forms a natural boundary between Uttar Pradesh and the Punjab in the northern districts of the Upper Doab, but the same river cuts the districts of Mathura and Agra in half. The desert of Rajasthan encroaches on the tip of Agra district.

Historical: The formation of Uttar Pradesh

The boundaries of present-day Uttar Pradesh (with the exception of the states of Tehri Garhwal and Rampur) were formed by the British gradually, by conquest and annexation, over a period of 76 years (fig. 2). British influence was firmly established in the area as early as 1764, when the forces of the Nawab of Oudh were defeated at Baksar. However, the British did not begin to acquire formal sovereignty over any of the territory of the

Nawab until 1775, when they forced the cession of the province of Banaras. For a time, the British remained content to consolidate their power in north India, using Oudh as a buffer state against the Marathas, Sikhs, Jats, and Afghans, whose forces were active to the west and northwest.

The period of greatest territorial acquisition by the British in the area

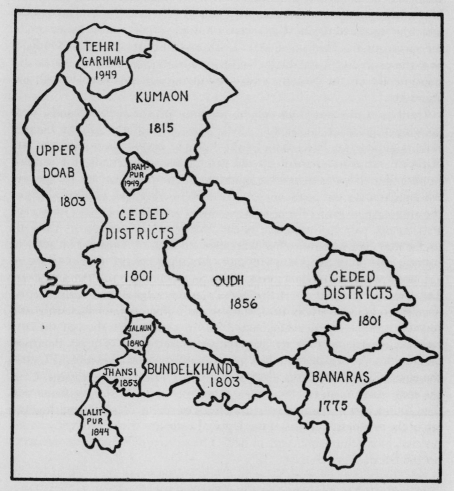

Fig. 2. The formation of Uttar Pradesh.

of Uttar Pradesh occurred in the first years of the nineteenth century, during the governor-generalship of Wellesley. Wellesley ended the policy of using Oudh as a buffer state and forced the cession from the Nawab of the Gorakhpur region in the east and the lower Doab and Rohilkhand on the south and northwest. Oudh was thus reduced to an enclave surrounded and "protected" by the British on all sides except the north, where the Himalayas separated Oudh from Nepal. The acquisition of the lower Doab and Rohilkhand brought the British in direct confrontation with the Maratha chiefs, Sindhia and the Peshwa. The Anglo-Maratha War of 1803 brought the Upper Doab into British possession; in the same year, the British acquired most of Bundelkhand from the Peshwa by treaty.

Kumaon, except for Tehri Garhwal, was added to the British domain after the Anglo-Nepalese War of 1815. The three enclaves of Jalaun, Lalitpur, and Jhansi in Bundelkhand were acquired by the doctrine of "lapse," in the case of Jalaun and Jhansi, and by treaty with Sindhia in the case of Lalitpur. Finally, in 1856, the remainder of the old province of Oudh was annexed.

Until 1834, the territories acquired by the British in North India were administered from Calcutta. For a brief period, from 1834 to 1836, the new territories, with the exception of the Banaras region, were raised to the status of a separate presidency, with headquarters at Allahabad. However, in 1836, partly for reasons of economy and partly as a result of a struggle for control over the patronage of the new province, the administration of the area was reorganized. The new provinces were reunited with the Bengal Presidency, were renamed the North-Western Provinces, and were put under the administration of a lieutenant-governor.[11] In other words, the status of the North-Western Provinces remained inferior to that of the established presidencies of Bombay, Madras, and Bengal. In 1856, Oudh was added to the North-Western Provinces, but was administered separately by a chief commissioner. In 1877, the separate chief commissionership was given up and the region came under the direct administration of the lieutenant-governor. In 1902, the integration of the North-Western Provinces and Oudh was formalized and the two provinces were renamed the United Provinces of Agra and Oudh. The state was given its present name, Uttar Pradesh (which means "northern province"), after independence was achieved. In 1949, the two princely states of Tehri Garhwal and Rampur were integrated with the provincial government.

The Land
Zamindars and Talukdars.—The gradual process of acquisition by the British of the United Provinces, and the continual changes in administrative structure which were introduced, made for considerable diversity in administration. This diversity was particularly marked in the area of land

---

[11] The struggle for control of the patronage of the new territories among the officers of the East India Company and the reasons for the changes in the administrative structure in this period have been analyzed in Dharma Bhanu, *History and Administration of the North-Western Provinces (Subsequently Called the Agra Province), 1803-1858* (Agra: Shiva Lal Agarwala and Co. Private Ltd., 1957), chaps. iv and v.

settlement and revenue administration. It is often difficult to tell to what extent differences in administration from region to region grew out of differences in the local patterns of land rights or out of differences in the approach of British administrators to various proprietary classes. Moreover, it was some time before the British fully understood the complexity and variety of Indian land tenure systems.[12]

It would be out of place to discuss all the variations in land rights and in the land settlements which were made in the United Provinces. One distinction is, however, of considerable political importance, that is, between the *mahalvari* settlement in the North-Western Provinces and the *talukdari* settlement in Oudh.

Under the *mahalvari* system, the local village authorities or *zamindars* (of one or more or parts of one or more villages) were recognized as the landlords of their *mahals* or estates and paid the land revenue directly to the state. Under the *talukdari* system, the local village authorities were generally ignored and the *talukdar*, who was responsible for the collection of revenue usually from a number of villages, was recognized as the landlord of an entire *taluk* (revenue collection area). Both the *zamindar* and the *talukdar* were intermediaries between the cultivator and the state, although the smaller *zamindars* might cultivate some land of their own. In the North-Western Provinces, the *talukdars* were generally eliminated from the revenue administration. In Oudh, the *talukdars* were recognized as the sole proprietors and the *zamindars* were reduced to the status of tenants generally. In the North-Western Provinces, the settlement was overwhelmingly with the *zamindars*; in Oudh, the settlement was predominantly with the *talukdars*. That is, in the North-Western Provinces, no important *talukdars* retained effective control over their *talukas*; in Oudh, however, some *zamindars* became landlords. In the North-Western Provinces, the *zamindars* might be single owners of estates or coparcenary holders of estates. Some of the *zamindars* owned estates as large as those of the *talukdars* of Oudh.[13] In each district, there were several thousand *zamindars*. In the whole of Oudh immediately after the *talukdari* settlement, there were only 256 *talukdars*.[14]

These two patterns of land settlement represented two different forms of political as well as economic control. In the North-Western Provinces, the system of joint *zamindari* proprietorship tended to preserve or reinforce the

[12] Walter C. Neale, *Economic Change in Rural India: Land Tenure and Reform in Uttar Pradesh, 1800-1955* (New Haven: Yale University Press, 1962), p. 56.

[13] A full description of the land settlements in Uttar Pradesh can be found *ibid.* Some of the definitions in this section have been taken from Neale's useful glossary.

[14] Rajkumar Sarvadhikari, *The Taluqdari Settlement in Oudh* (Calcutta: Thacker, Spink and Co., 1882), p. 146.

economic and political dominance of lineage groups of proprietors.[15] The
result is that, in most villages in the joint *zamindari* areas of Uttar Pradesh,
a "dominant caste" controlled the land and dominated political life. Where
a single *zamindar* collected the revenue or in the *talukdari* areas in Oudh,
an entirely different kind of local structure of political dominance developed. The big *zamindar* or *talukdar* retained some of the attributes of a
petty local chief. He acted not merely as a tax collector, but as a judge and
a policeman, a dispenser of loans and a giver of gifts. In all these roles,
except that of tax collecting, the large landed proprietor acted independently of the local official administration, although not necessarily or usually in conflict with it. Village political life was controlled by the large
landed proprietor through his under-proprietors or revenue agents, some
of whom had under-proprietary rights, while others were economically dependent upon the proprietor.

Zamindari abolition.—The entire system of intermediaries was abolished
by the Congress government of Uttar Pradesh in July, 1952, under the
terms of the Zamindari Abolition Act. Under the Act, the state collects the
revenue directly from the tenants. The tenants acquired the right to purchase from the state full rights of ownership to their land by paying a fee
ten times the amount of their annual land revenue. A uniform pattern of
land tenure was established throughout the state (except in the hill districts). There were now only two main classes of landholders—*bhumidhars*
and *sirdars*. *Bhumidhars* were those who acquired full rights of ownership
to their land (and a 50 percent reduction in their land revenue) by paying
10 times their land revenue to the state. *Sirdars* were those who did not
make this payment; *sirdars* acquired all rights of ownership except the right
to transfer their property.

Several observers have noted that *zamindari* abolition changed very little
either in the agrarian structure or the pattern of political dominance in
Uttar Pradesh. Since the *zamindars* were entitled to retain both grovelands
and lands, known as *sir* and *khudkhasht*, which they cultivated themselves
or which they traditionally managed directly, few of the *zamindars* were
actually dispossessed. Only 6 percent of the over 2,000,000 proprietors in
Uttar Pradesh held no *sir* or *khudkhasht* land;[16] these were mainly absentee
landlords. Most of the *zamindars* were small-holders, but it was not uncommon for the bigger *zamindars* and *talukdars* to retain a thousand or two
thousand acres of land by this provision. Moreover, those who became
bhumidhars after *zamindari* abolition were mostly ex-*zamindars*.[17]

[15] McKim Marriott, "Little Communities in an Indigenous Civilization" in McKim
Marriott, ed., *Village India: Studies in the Little Community* (Chicago: The University
of Chicago Press, 1955), p. 185.
[16] Neale, *op. cit.*, p. 218.
[17] *Ibid.*, p. 241.

In general, the absentee landlords and the big *zamindars* and *talukdars* were hurt most by the provisions of the Act, but because some were hurt does not mean that others gained. In effect, *zamindari* abolition merely confirmed all actual cultivators—whether *zamindars* or tenants—in the possession of their lands on a new legal basis.[18] The benefits to the holders of new legal titles were mainly psychological.[19]

Peter Reeves has shown how little was changed politically and socially by the Act. In villages where absentee landlords owned the land, "those who traditionally held sway, the high-caste tenant groups, continue to do so, while in the villages . . . where the zamindari body has remained in residence it has retained power or has conceded it only to the next-highest landholding group." [20] The bigger *zamindars* and *talukdars* retained their personal landholdings and their traditional influence over the political and social life of the villages formerly under their control.

Land ceilings.—In 1960, the Uttar Pradesh government passed another measure of "land reform." The Imposition of Ceiling on Land Holdings Act imposed a forty-acre limit on land holdings in the state. The Act was designed both "to provide land for landless agricultural labourers" and to bring about "a more equitable distribution of land." [21] Neither of these aims is likely to be achieved in any significant measure. A forty-acre ceiling, even if rigidly applied to all kinds of land, provides little surplus land in Uttar Pradesh; only 1.3 percent of the cultivated area would become surplus.[22] In fact, even less than this amount of land will become available under the Act, since grovelands and cooperative farms are excluded from the limit. Large landholders with foresight have for some time been preparing for this Act by converting their lands into mango, guava, and jack-fruit groves and by forming "cooperative farms" managed by their dependents. Finally, the ceiling applies to individuals, not to families, so that ex-*zamindars* with large families may still retain a substantial portion of their lands under foodgrains.

The Economy

In terms of per capita output, Uttar Pradesh is a region of agricultural stagnation and industrial decline.[23] In other words, although there has been

[18] P. D. Reeves, "Zamindari Abolition in Uttar Pradesh: An Investigation Into its Social Effects" (n.d.). (Mimeographed.)

[19] Neale, *op. cit.*, p. 245.

[20] Reeves, *op. cit.*, p. 15.

[21] The Uttar Pradesh Imposition of Ceiling on Land Holdings Act, 1960.

[22] Baljit Singh, *Next Step in Village India: A Study of Land Reforms and Group Dynamics* (Bombay: Asia Publishing House, 1961), p. 85.

[23] Government of Uttar Pradesh, Planning Department, *Third Five Year Plan*, Vol. I: *Report* (Lucknow, 1961), p. 6.

some increase in both agricultural and industrial output in this state in
recent years, "the rate of development has not been faster than the rate of
growth of population." [24] Per capita income in Uttar Pradesh for urban and
rural areas combined increased slightly from Rs. 260 in 1950-1951 to Rs.
269 in 1960-1961.[25] However, rural income per capita declined from Rs. 198
in 1949-1950 to Rs. 193 in 1958-1959.[26] The Five Year Plans in Uttar Pradesh have not been able to alter this condition of economic stagnation,
largely because of inadequate investment.[27] The Third Five Year Plan
offers no hope of improvement, unless there is a radical change in the rate
of investment, public and private; the Plan itself provides for a very low
per capita investment.[28]

Agriculture.—Aside from the basic and underlying problem of lack of
capital, agriculture in Uttar Pradesh suffers from two other difficulties—
backward agricultural technology and uneconomic holdings.[29] Technologi-
cally, agriculture in Uttar Pradesh (as elsewhere in India), suffers from
problems of soil erosion, lack of fertilizers, lack of adequate irrigation facilities, poor quality seeds, inefficient agricultural implements, and so on. To
help in the solution of these problems, a vast program of national extension
and community development has been in operation for the last decade and
a half. Most of the villages in Uttar Pradesh are now included in community
development blocks.

The problem of uneconomic holdings has been worse in Uttar Pradesh
than elsewhere in India. Close to 56 percent of the holdings in Uttar Pradesh,
according to a 1949 report, were under 2 acres; 81 percent of the holdings
were under 5 acres and 94 percent were under 10 acres.[30] Only 6 percent of
the population had holdings above the minimum which the Zamindari
Abolition Committee considered to be an economic holding.[31] Recent sur-
veys indicate that the holdings problem is as acute as ever.[32] Under such
conditions, it is not surprising that the ex-*zamindars* who have been able to
retain even 40 or 50 acres of land are able to maintain their economic and
political dominance in village life.

The eastern districts.—Uttar Pradesh's agricultural problems are most

[24] *Ibid.*, p. 5.
[25] *Ibid.*, p. 3.
[26] Baljit Singh, *op. cit.*, p. 38, citing Government of Uttar Pradesh, *Monthly Bulletin
of Statistics* (January, 1960), p. 128.
[27] Government of Uttar Pradesh, *Third Five Year Plan*, I, 6-9.
[28] *Ibid.*, pp. 15-16.
[29] Neale, *op. cit.*, pp. 148-154.
[30] *Report of the Congress Agrarian Reforms Committee* (2nd ed.; New Delhi: All-
India Congress Committee, 1951), p. 14.
[31] *Report of the United Provinces Zamindari Abolition Committee* (Allahabad:
Superintendent, Printing and Stationery, 1948), I, 24.
[32] Baljit Singh, *op. cit.*, p. 27.

pronounced in the eastern districts of the state. Here, population densities are over 1,000 persons per square mile, land holdings are extremely small,[33] and the resource base is very narrow. There are fewer industries here than in the west and much less urbanization; only three of the seventeen cities of Uttar Pradesh with a population over 100,000 are in this region—Allahabad, Banaras, and Gorakhpur. Unemployment is acute; villagers from the eastern districts go as far as Calcutta and Bombay for work. Heavy floods are an annual occurrence in much of the area and famine conditions are common.

Industry.—Large-scale industrialization offers little prospect for the foreseeable future in Uttar Pradesh of relieving the pressure on the land. Few new large industries have been established in Uttar Pradesh under the plans and those that have been established employ an insignificant number of people. In recent years, the Uttar Pradesh government has turned increasingly to industrial estates of medium- and small-scale industries to provide employment for those displaced from the land. Seventeen new urban industrial estates and twenty-three rural industrial estates have been planned for completion in the Third Five Year Plan;[34] the largest of these estates will provide employment for eight to ten thousand people.[35]

Two industries of long standing provide the major portion of this state's industrial base: the Kanpur textile industry and the statewide sugar refining industry. Neither industry is capable of much further expansion in Uttar Pradesh. Employment in the Kanpur textile industry long ago reached its peak; in 1953, it stood at 51,084.[36] In the last decade, employers engaged in retrenchment and rationalization so that employment is probably slightly less now. The sugar refining industry, with 70 factories spread over the state, employed 55,121 people in 1961.[37] Total factory employment in Uttar Pradesh in 1960 for all industries was only 314,454.[38]

The political implication of these economic conditions is that Uttar Pradesh is *not* a society which is experiencing the disruptive impact of rapid economic change. There is no doubt that economic change is taking place, but it is not the kind of change which is leading, in the short run at least, to new economic bases for political conflict.

[33] For example, in Basti district, the Zamindari Abolition Committee reported that 51 percent of the cultivating population of the district held less than one acre of land, in *Report of the United Provinces Zamindari Abolition Committee, op. cit.*, I, 25.

[34] Government of Uttar Pradesh, *Third Five Year Plan*, I, 34.

[35] *Development of Industries in Uttar Pradesh (Progress Review), 1961-62* (Kanpur: Directorate of Industries, n.d.), p. 36.

[36] D. N. Majumdar, *Social Contours of an Industrial City: Social Survey of Kanpur, 1954-56* (Bombay: Asia Publishing House, 1960), p. 51.

[37] *Development of Industries in Uttar Pradesh, op. cit.*, p. 186.

[38] Government of Uttar Pradesh, Department of Labour, *Annual Review of Activities 1961* (Allahabad: Superintendent, Printing and Stationery, 1962), p. 93 n.

Caste and community

The population of Uttar Pradesh is divided into two large religious communities, Hindus and Muslims, each of which is in turn divided into many castes and thousands of "subdivisions" of castes. The 1891 census, the most comprehensive caste census for Uttar Pradesh, lists some 54,710 so-called "subcastes" of Hindus and Muslims in Uttar Pradesh.[39] The subcaste is often the effective local caste unit, which may be confined to a few villages or to a tahsil[40] or a district. Above these local units are the broader groups of castes, such as Brahmans or Rajputs. The broad caste group is the conventional "caste," but the local units do not necessarily identify with or are even necessarily aware of the existence of most of the other local units who form a caste group. This kind of identification with a larger caste group is, however, one which has been developing over the last hundred years with improved communications, with the formation of caste associations, and with the introduction of democratic politics. Politically, the subcastes tend to decrease in importance and the caste groups to increase in importance at higher levels in the political system.

The 1891 census lists 240 caste groups, of which 155 are Hindu and 85 are Muslim.[41] These figures still include many very small castes confined to small areas of the state. The 1931 census listed 14 large caste groups, which accounted for 62 percent of the population of both Hindus and Muslims.[42] For purposes of this study, only a few of the larger or more important castes need to be mentioned. It is convenient to divide the Hindu caste population into three overlapping categories—the agricultural castes, the professional castes, and the urban trading castes. This classification omits the vast numbers of artisan and specialist castes, who have little political importance at present. Muslims will be treated separately.

The agricultural castes must be further subdivided into the traditional landowning castes, the cultivating castes, and the castes which provide field laborers. Among the traditional landowning castes, the Thakurs and Rajputs are by far the most important. Before *zamindari* abolition, Rajputs and Thakurs owned the largest share of the land in most of the districts in Uttar Pradesh; in Oudh, Rajputs were the most prominent *talukdars* and owned more than 50 percent of the land in most districts. Rajputs and Thakurs

[39] *Census of India, 1891*, Vol. XVIII: *The North-Western Provinces and Oudh*, by D. C. Baillie, Pt. III (Allahabad: North-Western Provinces and Oudh Government Press, 1894), p. iii.

[40] A tahsil is a subdivision of a district.

[41] *Census of India, 1891, loc. cit.*

[42] *Census of India, 1931*, Vol. XVIII: *United Provinces of Agra and Oudh*, by A. C. Turner, Pt. I (Allahabad: Superintendent, Printing and Stationery, 1933), p. 535.

are associated with the traditional Kshatriya class, the ruling class in the classic Hindu social order. Many of the Rajput clans trace their origins to Rajputana, from where they migrated partly in search of territory and partly as a result of the Muslim invasions from the seventh century onward.

After the Thakurs, the Brahman castes have been the leading proprietary castes in Uttar Pradesh. In many districts before *zamindari* abolition, Brahman castes took second place behind the Thakurs as landowners, although Brahmans were only rarely the leading proprietors in a district. Conventionally, Brahmans are the priestly castes and the learned castes, but most Brahman castes have direct ties with the land.

Thakurs and Brahmans were important landowners in most areas of Uttar Pradesh. Three other important landowning castes have a regional distribution only—the Jats and Tyagis in the western districts of the state and the Bhuinhars in the eastern districts. The Jats and Bhuinhars are examples of the way in which Uttar Pradesh tends to merge into its neighboring states, for the Jats are the characteristic peasant-owner caste of the Punjab, whereas the Bhuinhars belong more to Bihar. The Tyagis are a localized caste, important in a few districts in northwestern Uttar Pradesh and the Punjab.

All of the landowning castes mentioned above have also been traditionally cultivating castes, in the sense that most of their members actually work on the land or have personal farms cultivated by laborers under their supervision. Thakurs and Brahmans have the reputation of being poor cultivators, but they held as tenants before *zamindari* abolition the major portion of the land in Uttar Pradesh. The dominance of Thakurs and Brahmans in the countryside thus had a double support; they were both proprietors and cultivators of the land. Bhuinhars, Tyagis, and Jats also cultivated land; only the Jats, however, have the reputation of being industrious and efficient cultivators.

The major cultivating castes, that is, those who cultivated the land as tenants but were not prominent landowners, are castes such as the Kurmis, Ahirs and Ahars, Lodhas, Gujars, and Gadariyas. Three of these castes, the Ahirs and Ahars, Gujars, and Gadariyas, are traditionally graziers, but most of the members of these castes are cultivators. Ahirs and Kurmis are both fairly widespread castes in Uttar Pradesh, but the main concentrations of these two castes are in Oudh, in the eastern districts, and in Bihar. The Lodhas and Gadariyas are smaller castes, but also have a broad distribution; the Gujars are confined largely to the western districts of Uttar Pradesh.

The laboring castes include castes like the Chamars, Pasis, and Koris. Of these, the most important are the Chamars, who are also associated traditionally with leather-working. Chamars form the largest single caste group in Uttar Pradesh, accounting for close to 13 percent of the total population of the state,[43] distributed in all districts except in the Kumaon hills.

There is an approximate correlation in the countryside between the status of a particular caste and its relation to the land. Here, the local caste unit again becomes decisive, for caste hierarchies change from place to place. However, broadly speaking, Brahman and Rajput castes tend to be elite castes. The status of the other landowning castes—Bhuinhars, Tyagis, and Jats—is also high in the local environment. The cultivating castes generally are of middle rank, corresponding to their economic position. Near the bottom in social status are the Chamars. However, the Chamar castes generally are in a process of upward mobility:[44] many have adopted a new name, Jatavs, and would be insulted if they were called by their old name, which is now considered demeaning.

The professional and trading castes are largely urban castes, with the exception of the Brahman priestly class which exists both in the countryside and in the cities. Another professional, predominantly urban caste is the Kayastha caste. Kayasthas were traditionally scribes and officials under the Mughals, but now, along with the Brahmans, they comprise the bulk of the lawyers, doctors, and teachers in the cities and towns. The trading castes include primarily the Vaishya or Bania castes, Agarwalas and Guptas, and the Khatris.

Numerically, the largest caste groups are the Chamars (12.7 percent), followed by the Brahmans (9.2 percent), Ahirs (7.8 percent), Rajputs (7.6 percent), and Kurmis (3.5 percent).[45] All the other castes mentioned above form only 2 or 3 percent or less of the total population of the state.

Muslims.—A similar division into castes could be made for Muslims, but it is not necessary to go into the details of Muslim caste for purposes of this study. The two important features of the Muslim population of Uttar Pradesh which should be pointed out, however, are the dispersion of Muslims throughout the state, on the one hand, and the relative concentration of Muslims in the cities and towns, on the other.

Muslims form approximately 15 percent of the total population of the state. In no district in Uttar Pradesh do Muslims form a majority of the population. The heaviest concentration of Muslims is in a broad northern band of districts, including the Upper Doab, Rohilkhand, and northern Oudh. In these northern districts, the proportion of Muslims is above their proportion in the population of the state as a whole, that is, from 15 percent

[43] *Ibid.*
[44] See Bernard S. Cohn, "The Changing Status of a Depressed Caste," in Marriott, ed., *Village India,* pp. 53-77.
[45] *Census of India, 1931, loc. cit.*

to nearly 50 percent in Rampur district. Altogether there are 20 districts in this northern belt and there is one other district, Agra, which is not in the belt but falls in the same Muslim population range. In the southern portion of the state, the proportion of Muslims ranges from 5 to 15 percent; ten districts have a Muslim population above 10 percent and 14 districts have a Muslim population between 5 and 10 percent. Only in Kumaon is the Muslim population negligible.

Like Hindus, most Muslims in Uttar Pradesh live in rural areas. However, the proportion of Muslims who live in the cities and towns is much higher than the proportion of Hindus—over 30 percent for Muslims and only 9 percent for Hindus. According to the 1941 census, close to 40 percent of the urban population of Uttar Pradesh was Muslim.[46] In Rohilkhand and western Oudh, almost all the principal cities have Muslim majorities; these include four of the 100,000-population cities of Uttar Pradesh—Moradabad, Saharanpur, Rampur, and Shahjahanpur. All other major cities and towns in the plains districts have large Muslim minorities, generally from 20 percent to 50 percent of the population. This concentration of Muslims in the cities and towns has been of great political importance in Uttar Pradesh. It has been in the cities and towns where the Hindu-Muslim communal riots have generally taken place. The towns are the centers of politics for Muslims even more than for Hindus. In the rural areas, the Muslim population is dispersed and politically ineffective. In the towns, many constituencies are completely dominated by Muslims.

In general, the demography of Uttar Pradesh reveals a tremendous diversity of peoples. This diversity is in addition to the geographical, historical, and economic diversities which exist in this state. That is, the various elements in the physical and social environment of Uttar Pradesh do not always reinforce each other. Geography and history divide the state in one way, the agricultural economy divides it in another way, and patterns of population settlement divide it in still other ways. The political significance of this kind of diversity is that there are no regional identifications within the state. Diversity is spread evenly throughout Uttar Pradesh: this is the most important environmental factor in Uttar Pradesh politics.

MODERN POLITICAL HISTORY

From the Mutiny to Non-Cooperation

The period between the Mutiny of 1857 and the first Congress Non-Cooperation movement of 1921 is of extraordinary importance in modern Indian history. It was during this period that English education began to

---

[46] *Census of India, 1941*, Vol. V: *United Provinces,* by B. Sahay (Delhi: Manager of Publications, 1942), p. 56.

flourish in Indian universities, that movements of social reform and religious revival developed, that new political institutions were introduced into India, and that the Indian National Congress was formed. The cultural, intellectual, and political life of north India in this period has been neglected by historians of modern India, partly because north India occupied a secondary role in the intellectual and political life of the late nineteenth and early twentieth centuries, compared to Bengal and Bombay. Yet the roots of many developments in twentieth-century Indian politics lie not in nineteenth-century Calcutta and Bombay, but in nineteenth-century Banaras, Allahabad, and Aligarh.

Nineteenth-century Banaras, Allahabad, and Aligarh represented the three different cultures which existed in modern India. Banaras, the traditional home of Hindu orthodoxy, became the center of Hindu religious revival under the leadership of Pandit Madan Mohan Malaviya. Malaviya's revivalism led almost inevitably to communal conflict, for in nineteenth-century Uttar Pradesh, there remained many vestiges of Muslim dominance in the life of the province. Thus, to support the Hindi language, Malaviya had to attack Urdu; Malaviya led the movement in Uttar Pradesh, which began in 1883, to change the court character from Persian to Devanagari, essentially a change from Urdu to Hindi.[47] Malaviya is best known as the father of the Banaras Hindu University. He was also a prominent leader of the Hindu Mahasabha, which gave organizational form to the politics of Hindu communalism, and presided over the 1923 session of the Mahasabha in Banaras.

In this same period, Muslim communal politics began to take form after the founding of the Anglo-Oriental College at Aligarh in 1875, under the leadership of Sir Syed Ahmad Khan. Although Sir Syed joined in pre-Congress nationalist politics,[48] by the time of the formation of the Indian National Congress, his attitude toward nationalist politics had undergone a change. In a statement in 1888, Sir Syed gave his objection to the Indian National Congress and "to every Congress in any shape or form whatever which regards India as one nation." [49] The Anglo-Oriental College later became the Aligarh Muslim University and the training ground of Muslim League leaders.

If Hindu communalism in Uttar Pradesh was born in Banaras and Muslim communalism at Aligarh, the secular tradition in Uttar Pradesh politics has its origins in Allahabad. Allahabad was, during the late nineteenth and early twentieth centuries, the capital of the United Provinces and the locus of

---

[47] Ram Gopal, *Indian Muslims: A Political History (1858-1947)* (Bombay: Asia Publishing House, 1959), p. 41.

[48] *Ibid.*, p. 48.

[49] Cited *ibid.*, p. 67.

the High Court; also in Allahabad was Muir Central College, a government institution where the first generation of Congressmen in Uttar Pradesh received their education. Allahabad was the home of Tej Bahadur Sapru, the famous Liberal leader, the "Hindu incarnation of John Stuart Mill." [50] More important, Allahabad was the home of the Nehrus. The secular tradition which Molital Nehru (and later Jawaharlal) represented probably grew out of two environments—the Muir College and High Court environment and the synthetic cultural environment of the Kashmiri Brahman community. Motilal Nehru and men like him were quite at home in the new institutions of government that were being established in India. Temperamentally, Motilal Nehru belonged to the constitutional wing of the Congress and he later led the Swaraj party in the legislatures, along with Chitaranjan Das from Bengal. However, Motilal, along with many others of different opinions, was swept into the movement of Non-Cooperation begun by Gandhi in 1920-1921.

From Non-Cooperation to Independence

The Non-Cooperation movement of 1921 brought to Indian politics a brief moment of unity which was never again recaptured. The movement meant different things to different people. It appealed to "the growing Hindu reaction against the dominance of Western civilization" and to Muslim religious resentment against the British because of the war against Turkey.[51] For liberal constitutionalists like Motilal Nehru, the movement was a protest against the atrocities of Jallianwala Bagh and the denial of civil liberties afterwards.[52] In Uttar Pradesh, the movement also had an economic content. In 1918, Purushottamdas Tandon had begun to organize the peasants in Oudh to fight for their rights against the *talukdars*. The peasant movement merged with the Congress movement in Uttar Pradesh, where there were "serious agrarian riots in the Oudh districts of Rae Bareli and Fyzabad." [53]

The most serious break in the political unity of the nationalist movement began with the outbreak of Hindu-Muslim riots. The rioting began with the notorious Moplah rising of 1921 in Malabar and was followed by an increase in communal tensions throughout the year 1922 in cities and towns

[50] Evan Cotton, "Some Outstanding Political Leaders," chap. x in John Cumming, ed., *Political India, 1832-1932: A Co-Operative Survey of a Century* (London: Oxford University Press, 1932), p. 192.

[51] L. F. Rushbrook Williams, *India in 1923-24* (Calcutta: Government of India Central Publication Branch, 1924), p. 243.

[52] Jawaharlal Nehru, "My Father," in S. P. and Preet Chablani, eds. *Motilal Nehru: Essays and Reflections on His Life and Times* (Delhi: S. Chand and Co., 1961), p. 18.

[53] Peter Reeves, "The Politics of Order: 'Safety Leagues' Against the Congress in the United Provinces, 1921-22" (1962), p. 3. (Mimeographed.)

throughout the country. In 1923, full-scale rioting broke out in north India; in Uttar Pradesh, there were riots in Moradabad, Meerut, Allahabad, Gonda, Agra, Rae Bareli, and the most serious of all in Saharanpur.[54] The riots of 1921-1923 led to the resurgence of both Hindu and Muslim communal politics. The Hindu Mahasabha became active again in 1923 and the Muslim League, which had been dormant during the Non-Cooperation movement, re-emerged as a political force in 1924.[55] The Congress Civil Disobedience movement of 1930-1931 was followed by another series of communal riots, culminating in the terrible Kanpur riot of 1931.

Despite this background of communal bitterness, Congress and League leaders in Uttar Pradesh formed an electoral agreement for the provincial elections of 1936.[56] Although the Congress contested only 9 of the 66 Muslim seats in Uttar Pradesh, the Muslim League won only 27 seats, the rest going to independent Muslim candidates.[57] Nevertheless, on the basis of the pre-election agreement, negotiations between the League and the Congress for a coalition Cabinet were begun. The negotiations failed and the Congress formed a government with the League in opposition. The failure of the Cabinet negotiations marked the final turning point in Congress-League relations in Uttar Pradesh. From 1937 on, the Congress and the League went separate ways. In the next provincial election in Uttar Pradesh in 1946, the League won 54 of the 66 Muslim seats,[58] exactly double the number of seats won in 1936, for the first time vindicating the League's claim to be the political spokesman for Muslims in Uttar Pradesh.

Hindu communal politics was less successful in Uttar Pradesh, largely because the Congress had become the political organization of Hindus in the state as the estrangement between Hindus and Muslims developed.[59] The Mahasabha devoted itself to unifying the Hindu community through social reform propaganda and to proselytizing among Muslims.[60] Yet the Mahasabha kept alive the tradition of militant Hinduism, which was taken up more effectively by the Jan Sangh after Independence.

The influence of Motilal and Jawaharlal Nehru remained the dominant one in the Congress party in Uttar Pradesh in this period. In the 1920s, Motilal Nehru formed the Swaraj party within the Congress to fight the provincial and national elections. In this period, Rafi Ahmad Kidwai and Pandit Pant rose to prominence in Uttar Pradesh politics. Kidwai and Pant

[54] *India in 1923-24, op. cit.*, p. 258.
[55] Ram Gopal, *op. cit.*, p. 162.
[56] *Ibid.*, p. 243.
[57] *Ibid.*, p. 247.
[58] *Ibid.*, p. 304.
[59] *Ibid.*, p. 132.
[60] *Ibid.*, p. 160.

and their associates, representing the constitutional tradition in the Uttar Pradesh Congress, dominated the first Congress government in 1937.

A new development in this period was the growth of ideological politics within the Congress. The Congress Socialist Party (CSP) was formed in 1934 as a party within the Indian National Congress. In Uttar Pradesh, the CSP was led by Acharya Narendra Dev. The Socialists generally worked with the peasant leaders in the Congress and provided the intellectual justification of the agrarian movement. The peasant movement under Tandon, however, retained a separate identity from the Socialists within the Congress organization.

The Congress before Independence was a movement, rather than a political party. It contained within it a wide diversity of political beliefs, excluding only the militant communalists.

The development of political parties after Independence

From a movement, the Congress after Independence became a political party. The importance of this change for the internal functioning of the Congress party in Uttar Pradesh will be discussed in the next chapter. Here, the development of opposition political parties both out of differences within the Congress and out of dissatisfaction of non-Congressmen with the Congress will be summarized.

It should, of course, be kept in mind that the most important development in the pattern of party politics immediately after Independence was not the formation of new political parties in opposition to the Congress, but the disappearance from Uttar Pradesh politics of the main opposition to the Congress, the Muslim League. After the partition, the Muslim League leaders in Uttar Pradesh left for Pakistan. With the departure of their political leadership and the end of separate electorates, Muslim political organization in Uttar Pradesh came to an abrupt end.

Communal politics in Uttar Pradesh did not, however, end with the departure of the League. Hindu-Muslim riots attended the news of partition in Uttar Pradesh, as elsewhere in India. The partition gave a new impetus to Hindu communal politics, for militant Hindus blamed the Congress equally with the League. The Hindu Mahasabha continued its activities, but more important for the future of Hindu communal politics in Uttar Pradesh was the entrance of the Rashtriya Swayamsevak Sangh (RSS) into politics and the formation of the Jan Sangh. The RSS, originally a non-political youth organization,[61] became active politically in the period between 1947 and 1951 when its workers provided assistance to Hindu refu-

[61] Myron Weiner, *Party Politics in India: The Development of a Multi-Party System* (Princeton: Princeton University Press, 1957) p. 178.

gees from Pakistan and "defended" Hindus in the communal riots of this period. The Jan Sangh was formed by RSS leaders in 1951 to fight the general elections.

The Jan Sangh was formed by people who had either no past association with the Congress or who had only slight associations with the Congress. The other main opposition parties in Uttar Pradesh, the Praja Socialist Party and the Socialist Party, developed out of splits from the Congress. The first split came in 1948, when the Socialists left the Congress in Uttar Pradesh under the leadership of Acharya Narendra Dev. The second split occurred in 1950-1951 when some defeated faction leaders in the Uttar Pradesh Congress left the Congress and joined Acharya Kripalani's Kisan Mazdoor Praja Party (KMPP). These two organizations merged after the 1952 general elections into the PSP. The Socialist Party arose in 1955 as a result of a split within the PSP.

The Jan Sangh and the Socialist parties provide the main opposition to the Congress in Uttar Pradesh. There are other parties which have strength in a few districts in the state. Swatantra has some influence among the ex-rajas and *zamindars* in a few districts; the Communists have some strength in some of the eastern districts and in the industrial city of Kanpur; the Republicans, descendants of the old Scheduled Caste Federation, have some strength in three districts in the western part of the state.

The party system in Uttar Pradesh may be described as a multiparty system with one party, the Congress, dominant. Table 1 summarizes the results of the Assembly elections by party in Uttar Pradesh for the last three general elections. The significant changes since 1952 have been the decline in the voting strength of the Congress and the increase in the strength of the Jan Sangh. It will be demonstrated in the rest of this study that the decline in Congress strength has much to do with internal factional conflict and does not necessarily show a trend that will lead to the disintegration of the Congress organization in the state. In fact, the decline of the Congress is partly due to a complacent tolerance of internal conflict based upon the justified belief among Congressmen that opposition parties do not represent a serious threat to their control over the state government.

THE CONGRESS PARTY IN UTTAR PRADESH: MEMBERSHIP AND ELECTORAL SUPPORT

Membership
It is difficult to draw a definite conclusion about the strength of the Congress from membership figures. Membership figures for the Congress in Uttar Pradesh are an index more of the intensity of internal factional strife than of external support. When internal conflict is great and when import-

ant organizational contests are expected, faction leaders in the Congress work to enroll primary members[62] in their localities. Charges are invariably raised by rivals that primary members enrolled by their opponents are "bogus." The implication of such a charge is that one's rivals have merely taken names from the voter lists at random and paid the membership fees out of their own pockets. The advantage in enrolling additional members is that the number of members on the Mandal Congress Committee,[63] the

TABLE 1
UTTAR PRADESH ASSEMBLY ELECTION RESULTS

Party	1952		1957		1962	
	Pct. of Vote	No. of seats	Pct. of Vote	No. of seats	Pct. of Vote	No. of seats
Congress	47.9	390	42.4	286	34.9	249
Jan Sangh	6.4	2	9.8	17	15.3	49
PSPa	17.8	20	14.5	44	11.9	38
Socialistsb	...	...	...	...	8.5	24
Communist	0.9	0	3.8	9	5.4	14
Swatantra	...	...	...	...	4.8	15
Republican	...	...	...	...	3.8	8
Others	27.0	18	29.4	74	15.3	33
Total	100.0	430	99.9	430	99.9	430

Source: *Indian Affairs Record*, VII (April, 1962), 117.

a The 1952 PSP vote is the combined vote of the old Socialist Party and the KMPP.
b In 1957, the Socialists ran as Independents and won 25 seats.

lowest unit of the Congress organization, increases in proportion to the number of primary members in the Mandal.

In 1959, the last year for which figures are available, the primary membership of the Uttar Pradesh Congress was approximately 2.4 million (see table 2). This figure was the highest since Independence, with the exception of 1950, when membership was free and 4.8 million members were enrolled. In general, the primary membership figures show a direct correspondence between the intensity of factional strife and the number of Congressmen enrolled. Although the high membership in 1950 is partly explainable in terms of the absence of a membership fee, it also reflects the great internal struggle in the Congress at the time. The contest between Acharya Kripalani and Purushottamdas Tandon for the presidency of the Indian National Congress, a contest which grew out of the internal conflict in the Uttar Pradesh Congress, took place in 1950.[64] In the years between 1950 and 1957,

[62] The categories of Congress members are described in the Appendix.
[63] See the Appendix for a description of the Mandal Congress Committee.
[64] This point is discussed in the following chapter.

quiet realignments were taking place within the Congress party in Uttar Pradesh. No important organizational contests occurred in this period and, consequently, enrollment declined. The rise in primary membership figures since 1957 reflects the growth of a new phase of factional conflict. By 1959, when membership reached its peak since 1950, the Congress party organization in Uttar Pradesh was in the midst of an internal conflict which ultimately led to a change in government leadership in 1960.[65]

Accurate active membership figures for recent years for the state as a

TABLE 2

CONGRESS MEMBERSHIP IN UTTAR PRADESH, 1950-1959

Year	No. of Members	
	Primary	Active
1950[a]	4,800,000	n.a.
1953[b]	1,800,000	50,000
1954[b]	1,100,000	9,361
1957[c]	643,274	9,156
1958[d]	1,250,000	n.a.
1959[e]	2,400,000	n.a.

[a] *National Herald,* June 23, 1950.

[b] *National Herald,* May 11, 1954.

[c] Indian National Congress, *Report of the General Secretaries: January, 1958 to December, 1958* (New Delhi: All India Congress Committee, 1959), p. 51.

[d] *National Herald,* January 24, 1959.

[e] *Hindustan Times,* January 29, 1959. The *Report of the General Secretaries: January, 1960 to December, 1960* (New Delhi: All India Congress Committee, 1961) of the Indian National Congress gives, on p. 33, the figures 161,501 and 4,208 for primary and active members respectively in 1959. However, these figures are based on an incomplete return from the Province as a result of an AICC inquiry into charges of fraudulent enrollments.

whole are not available to the author. An active membership of 50,000 in Uttar Pradesh (reached in 1953) would mean one active Congressman for approximately every 1500 people, about the number of people in a large village. However, Congressmen in the districts do not claim to have an active Congress worker in every village.

Even active membership figures exaggerate to some extent the number of people who are party "militants." Influential local party leaders often enroll and try to elect to party units all the adult members of their families and their trusted employees. Moreover, Congress membership is not spread evenly in the districts. The large towns may be over-represented in comparison with the villages. For example, Hathras tahsil in Aligarh district had

[65] The history of factional conflict in the Uttar Pradesh Congress is given in the following chapter.

a total population in 1951 of 206,201, of which 57,162 or 28 percent lived in the town of Hathras. In contrast, of the 113 active members of the Congress in this tahsil in 1959, 48 members or 42 percent of the total came from Hathras town. Also, some villages have more than one active Congress member, while many have none. Sixty-five active members of the Congress in Hathras tahsil came from villages or small towns, but there are 363 villages and three small towns in the tahsil.[66]

In general, two aspects of Congress membership should be stressed. First, fluctuations in both primary and active membership figures reflect changes in the intensity of internal factional conflict rather than changes in external support. The membership figures for the Congress in Uttar Pradesh are not an accurate measure of the strength of the organization. Second, the Congress does not have an active member in all villages in the state. In Hathras tahsil, the great majority of the villages have no active Congress members.[67]

Electoral support

Table 1 shows a sharp over-all decline of support for the Congress in Uttar Pradesh in the last two general elections. It was stated that the decline does not necessarily indicate that the Congress organization in the state is disintegrating. An analysis of the election results in the Assembly constituencies in each district gives results which indicate that many of the district Congress organizations are able to arrest electoral decline and increase their votes from election to election. Most districts, 44 of the 51,[68] do show a decline in the Congress vote from 1952 to 1962. Moreover, 25 of the 44 districts show a continuous decline from 1952 to 1957 and from 1957 to 1962. In only 7 districts has the Congress proportion of the total vote increased over the decade. However, in 15 districts, the Congress organizations increased their proportions of the total vote from 1957 to 1962.

Another way of looking at the election results in each district is by ranking them in terms of the proportion of total votes won by the Congress in

---

[66] The population figures come from the *Census of India, 1951, Uttar Pradesh District Population Statistics 6: Aligarh District* (Allahabad: Superintendent, Printing and Stationery, 1953); the membership figures come from the 1959 register of active members of the Aligarh district Congress, provided by the Congress office in the district.

[67] The figures for Hathras tahsil are given as an example only. Hathras tahsil is neither a "backward" nor a highly politicized area and is, therefore, a useful example. Data for a systematic study of Congress membership in other rural districts in Uttar Pradesh were not available to the author.

[68] Although there are 54 administrative districts, there are only 51 electoral districts. The three new defense districts of Uttar Kashi, Chamoli, and Pithoragarh are combined by the state election office with the districts of Tehri Garhwal, Garhwal, and Almora respectively, from which they were separated for defense purposes.

each district in each election. In 1952, the range was from 65.9 percent in Saharanpur district to 31.3 percent in Ghazipur district. In 1957, the Congress won without contest all the seats in Tehri Garhwal district and lost all the seats in Shahjahanpur district with a total vote of only 22 percent. In 1962, the range was from 64.1 percent in Tehri Garhwal to 21.2 percent in Etah district. The median district percentage has declined continuously over the three elections from 47 percent in 1952 to 43.5 percent in 1957 to 37.3 percent in 1962.

A comparison of the relative rank of each district from election to election shows that there is great variation in the consistency of the ranking of many districts in support for the Congress. Some districts have declined precipitously in rank. For example, in Aligarh district in 1952, the Congress polled 56.3 percent of the vote, the seventh highest vote in the state. In 1962, the Congress polled only 24.9 percent in Aligarh district, the third lowest vote in the state. Some districts have shown an equally sharp increase in support for the Congress. Thus, Tehri Garhwal district, which has been the strongest Congress district in the last two general elections, was the fifth lowest-support Congress district in 1952. The important point about such extreme fluctuations is that they indicate that factors are at work in such districts which cause a deviation from the statewide pattern of slow decline in support for the Congress.

Three factors are of particular importance in explaining extreme changes in the electoral position of the Congress in a district: internal party factionalism, sudden changes in the allegiance of a class of voters, and the acquisition or defection of powerful leaders (such as ex-rajas) who control large blocks of votes. Thus, the extreme decline of the Congress in Aligarh district resulted from a combination of a sudden change in the allegiances of a low caste group and of Muslims with intense internal factionalism.[69] The influence of these factors on the election outcome in Aligarh operated in a unique way in the district and did not reflect a statewide pattern. In Tehri Garhwal, an ex-princely state, the rise in Congress strength in the last two elections occurred because of the recruitment into the Congress of the former Raja, whose influence remains paramount in the district.

Not all of the 51 electoral districts show such sharp changes in support for the Congress. The results of the ranking of districts for the three general elections revealed that some districts were persistently above the median in support for the Congress and some were persistently below. Twenty-three districts were isolated which showed considerable stability both in their absolute percentages of support for the Congress and in their relative ranking. Twelve districts were consistently above the median in three

[69] See chap. v.

general elections and 11 were consistently below the median. Figure 3 shows the location of both the high- and low-support districts.

Attempts to correlate support for the Congress with various environmental factors yield few clear patterns. Figure 3 shows both regional differences and similarities between high- and low-support districts. Kumaon,

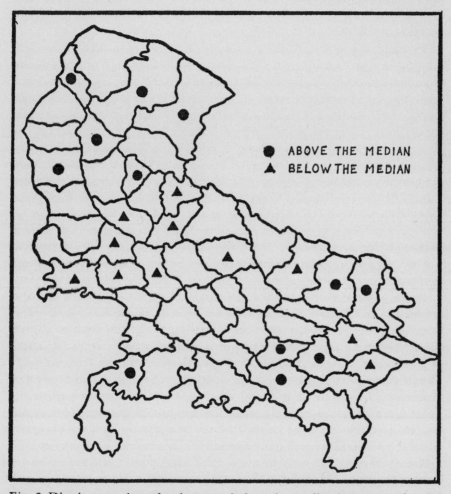

Fig. 3. Districts consistently above or below the median in support for the Congress in the 1952, 1957, and 1962 General Elections.

the northern Doab, western Rohilkhand, and the southern hill districts are the areas where the Congress has been persistently strongest. The central Doab and eastern Rohilkhand are the areas where the Congress has been persistently weakest. In Oudh and in the eastern districts, some districts have been persistently pro-Congress, others persistently anti-Congress.

Over the three general elections, there has been a marked shift in areas of Congress support. In the first General Election, the Congress was very strong in all of the northwestern districts, in most of Kumaon, and in parts of the central plains area. The Congress was weakest in the eastern districts and in the southern hills. By 1962, the areas of (relative) Congress strength had shifted away from the northwestern districts and the central plains to the southern hills and the eastern districts.

The regional distribution of Congress strength and the shift in areas of support over the decade both indicate that there is no apparent connection between poverty, economic decline, and opposition to the Congress. If anything, the distribution indicates exactly the opposite, that is, that the Congress is strongest and has been becoming (relatively) stronger in the most backward and poverty-stricken areas of the state. Kumaon, Bundelkhand, and the eastern districts are three areas which have been selected by the state government as the most backward areas of Uttar Pradesh and which are to receive special help in the Third Plan.[70] Although Kumaon has the lowest population density in the state and the eastern districts the highest, the problems of both areas relate to pressure on the cultivable land —a result of overpopulation in the eastern districts and a relative lack of cultivable land in Kumaon. In Bundelkhand, where population densities are also very low, agricultural productivity suffers from a severe shortage of irrigation facilities.

Because of the sharp contrasts in densities between the eastern districts, on the one hand, and Kumaon and the southern hill districts, on the other hand, there is no correlation between rural density and support for the Congress in the high-support Congress districts. Four of the 12 high-support districts were among the 12 highest density districts in Uttar Pradesh. An equal number were among the 12 districts with the lowest densities. The 11 low-support districts also show no correlation between rural density and Congress strength. Two of the 11 districts were among the 11 districts with highest densities; one was among the 11 with lowest densities. The evidence from the regional distribution of Congress strength and from the attempt to correlate rural density with Congress support is thus ambiguous. The regional distribution indicates a positive correlation between poverty and support for the Congress, but the district by district comparison indicates no correlation.

Variations from district to district in literacy rates also give ambiguous results when compared with the strong and weak Congress districts. The 12 high-support districts show no correlation; three districts are among

---

[70] Government of Uttar Pradesh, *Third Five Year Plan*, pp. 47-61.

the 12 highest in literacy and two are among the 12 lowest. However, the lowest support districts show a slight correlation; only one of the low-support districts is among the 11 districts with the highest literacy rates, but four are among the 11 districts with the lowest literacy rates. A scatter diagram shows only a very slight correlation.

Data from urban and rural constituencies indicate that Congress has greater strength in the few predominantly urban constituencies of Uttar Pradesh than it has in the rural areas. There are 21 wholly urban Assembly constituencies and 5 more which are predominantly urban.[71] In 1952, the Congress won in all urban constituencies, compared to 90 percent successes in rural constituencies. In 1957, the Congress won 21 of 26 urban constituencies or 81 percent, compared to 66 percent in the countryside. The figures for 1962 are 17 of 26 urban constituencies or 66 percent for the Congress, compared to 58 percent of rural seats. The Congress has thus done better in urban and predominantly urban constituencies in all three elections. However, support for the Congress has declined in the cities and towns, as it has in the countryside. Finally, the difference in support for the Congress in urban and rural areas narrowed considerably in the 1962 election.

No strong correlations exist between support for the Congress and the proportion of major caste and religious groups by district. The high-support and low-support districts are each approximately equally divided among districts with large and small Muslim populations. There is a slight correlation between support for the Congress and the number of Brahmans in each district, indicating the possibility of a tendency for Brahmans to be pro-Congress. The data on Rajputs and Ahirs indicate a slight correlation in the opposite direction, indicating the possibility of a tendency for these caste groups to vote against the Congress. However, for all three castes, the correlations both in district by district comparisons and in scatter diagrams are very slight.

For low caste groups, it is possible to compare the results in the constituencies reserved for these groups with the results from general constituencies. The results support the widely-held belief that the Scheduled Castes are strongly pro-Congress. In 1952, the election reports did not reveal the Scheduled Caste candidates. However, the Congress won 162 out of 166 seats in the double member constituencies[72] or 97.5 percent of the seats compared to 86.4 percent of the single member constituencies. In 1957,

[71] I have classified as "predominantly urban" only those constituencies which include towns with a population over 100,000. The average population in an Assembly constituency is between 150,000 and 200,000.

[72] In the double member constituencies, one seat was reserved for a Scheduled Caste candidate, one seat was unreserved.

the Congress won 68 of the 89 constituencies reserved for Scheduled Castes or 78 percent of the seats, compared to 64 percent of the general seats. In 1962, the Congress won 55 of the 89 reserved constituencies or 62 percent of the seats, compared to 57 percent of the general seats. The data suggest three statements about the vote for the Congress in Scheduled Caste constituencies. First, Congress successes have been persistently greater in the reserved constituencies than in the general constituencies; second, the percentage of seats won by the Congress has declined in both the reserved and general constituencies; and third, the difference in the proportion of Congress successes in reserved and general constituencies narrowed considerably between 1957 and 1962. The last point suggests that Congress strength among the low castes may be weakening.

In general, the detailed data by district and constituency show a general decline in support for the Congress by nearly every measure. However, the decline is not clearly related to any statewide environmental factors. The decline does not appear to derive from discontent in the poorest areas of the state, nor from the cities, nor from among the low castes. In fact, the data indicate the contrary, that the deprived and disadvantaged tend to support the Congress.

The absence of very sharp divisions in state politics is consistent with the description of the environment which has been given above. Differences in Uttar Pradesh politics, as in the social and economic environments, tend to be shadings rather than sharp divisions. The merging and mixing of regions and peoples in Uttar Pradesh combines with a lack of communication throughout the state among members of ethnic and other groups to produce a relatively complex politics without clear patterns. The factional character of internal Congress politics in the state also tends to produce a patternless politics. Districts which have been consistently strongly pro-Congress may suddenly become very weak Congress districts when the local organizations become divided by intense factional strife. Similarly, internal cohesion in a local Congress organization is often sufficient to stop a deterioration in Congress strength and to enable the Congress to increase its vote. These propositions will be developed in the case studies.

III.

The Congress Party in Uttar Pradesh:
The Growth of Factional Conflict

This chapter will be concerned with identifying elements of continuity
and change in Uttar Pradesh Congress politics. It will be argued that conflicts which developed in the pre-Independence period—particularly since
1937, when the Congress first came to power in Uttar Pradesh and other
states[1]—culminated in major internal crises in the post-Independence period,
crises which led to a change in the content of political debate and in the
character of political leadership within the Uttar Pradesh Congress. The
content of political debate changed from an internal discussion of the place
of language, culture, and region in the modern state and of the social and
economic goals of Indian democracy to a more mundane controversy over
the respective roles of party and government in the political system. Simultaneously, political leadership in Uttar Pradesh passed from the hands of
the prominent leaders of the nationalist movement from this state into the
hands of the second rank of party workers. The charismatic leaders, the
prophets of independence, whose positions in the movement depended
upon the esteem and awe in which they were held by the rank and file of
Congressmen, were replaced by "political" leaders—men whose positions
depend less upon their personal esteem than upon the political patronage
they distribute.

Personal politics and factional politics existed in the Uttar Pradesh Congress before Independence, alongside a politics of issues. Since Independence, personal and factional politics have come to dominate the internal
politics of the state Congress. This chapter will also describe the new sys-

[1] Congress Governments were elected in 1937, under the Government of India Act
of 1935, in Madras, Bihar, the Central Provinces, the United Provinces (Uttar Pradesh),
Bombay, and Orissa and were in power from 1937 until 1939.

tem of factional politics—the nature of factional alignments, the effect of factional politics on the stability of the state Government, and the inter-relations between state and district party factions.

PRE-INDEPENDENCE PATTERNS OF POLITICS AND CONFLICT IN THE CONGRESS PARTY

Looking back at the Congress party in Uttar Pradesh and at the men who ruled it in the pre-Independence period for indications of developments to come is at first appearance a fruitless task. The issues that existed then seem irrelevant to contemporary Uttar Pradesh Congress politics. Even more frustrating are the apparently complete and wholly inconsistent changes of political allegiance which later took place among the men who emerged from this early period to positions of importance in post-Independence state politics. Divisions between "modernists" and "traditionalists," "secularists" and "revivalists," which seemed important then, hardly occur within the Congress party today. Men who were, during this period, ardent believers in Marxism and scientific socialism saw no inconsistency later in giving allegiance to Purushottamdas Tandon, at one time the leading spokesman in both the state and the country of Hindu revivalism.

Two aspects of traditional Indian society can help to explain how such inconsistencies are tolerated or ignored by politicians in contemporary state politics. For one thing, a high value has always been placed in Indian society upon compromise and persuasion and upon men who are adept at the art of reconciling opposites. Nothing so confounds a Westerner as the facility with which Indians find correspondences where the former sees only incongruities and inconsistencies. The second (and the more easily comprehensible) feature of traditional Indian society which helps to explain the changing patterns of alliance and conflict in Uttar Pradesh Congress politics is the essentially personal character of political loyalties. For many (perhaps most) politicians in Uttar Pradesh, there is no internal conflict involved in following leaders whose viewpoints on important issues are different from their own or in switching allegiances from one leader to another, leaders whose personal ideologies are sharply at variance. A politician may join a "socialist" faction, not because he has any ideas about socialism, but because he admires certain characteristics of the leader of the faction—characteristics which have nothing to do with ideology.

For pre-Independence Uttar Pradesh politics, it is possible to construct a typology of political leaders. Two kinds of latent conflicts which existed in Uttar Pradesh before Independence and which culminated in open conflicts in the post-Independence period were between "modernists" and "traditionalists" on the one hand and between ideologists and virtuoso politicians on the other hand. A fifth kind of politician of considerable importance in the pre-Independence period and for some time afterwards was the arbiter. The arbiter did not participate in conflicts either of principle or of men. His role consisted in reconciling conflicting principles and in making enemies work together in a common cause.

It is useful to make this typology of political leaders not because it has any relevance to present-day Congress politics in Uttar Pradesh, but because it makes it possible to show how certain kinds of politicians have declined in importance and others have come to prevail. In brief, the "modernists," the "traditionalists," and the men of ideology were the first to disappear from state Congress politics, some into non-political activities, others into opposition. The next to go were the arbiters, those who were adepts in the art of compromise and reconciliation. In the end, the state Congress was left almost completely in the hands of the modern virtuoso politicians, men who understand both the traditional society in which contemporary Uttar Pradesh politics must operate and the modern machinery of party organization and government patronage.

The Modernist and the Traditionalist: Jawarharlal Nehru and Purushottamdas Tandon

No evidence has yet come to light that there was ever any personal antagonism between the Nehru family and Purushottamdas Tandon. Whenever Pandit Nehru spoke of Tandon or Tandon of Nehru, it was always in terms of the highest regard. Yet, in 1950, Purushottamdas Tandon forged an alliance with Sardar Patel in a struggle for control of the national Congress organization, a struggle which represented the only serious challenge which Pandit Nehru had to face against his power and his policies after Independence.

Except for Sardar Patel, who died before this conflict was finally resolved, every one of the principal actors in the contest for control of the national party organization came from or spent his political life in Uttar Pradesh. Although the 1950 presidential election of the Indian National Congress between Tandon and Acharaya Kripalani was primarily a struggle for political power in both Uttar Pradesh and national politics, it was widely interpreted and rightly so as a conflict over principles and ideologies as well. The events leading up to the presidential contest of 1950 at the national level, the victory of Tandon, his later resignation, and the assumption of the presidency by Pandit Nehru have been dealt with extensively elsewhere.[2] This analysis is concerned only with the interrelationship between this struggle and Uttar Pradesh politics.

[2] Myron Weiner, *Party Politics in India: The Development of a Multi-Party System* (Princeton: Princeton University Press, 1957), chap. iv.

Both Pandit Nehru and Tandon came from Allahabad. Both received an "English" education, Nehru in England and Tandon in Allahabad. Both became lawyers for a time early in their careers. And both belonged to the radical wing of the Indian National Congress in the sense that they early favored mass, peasant-based agitational movements to achieve the goal of independence. The similarities between the early careers of these two men are manifold, yet they represented two extremes of political attitudes in Indian life.

The major differences between Nehru and Tandon were not over ideology, although their attitudes toward socialism differed. Nehru never made a secret of his socialist principles and he often acted as the informal leader of the socialist movement within the Congress. However, he refused formally to lead or even to join the Congress Socialist Party (CSP).[3] Tandon was the leader of the peasant movements in Uttar Pradesh in the early 1930s. Although he was a radical revolutionary, he never espoused socialist ideology and he too refused to join the Congress Socialist Party. One of the anomalies of Uttar Pradesh politics that will be mentioned again later is that the most devoted followers of Nehru in Uttar Pradesh politics imitated his decision to remain aloof from the Congress Socialist Party, whereas most of Tandon's associates in the peasant movement joined the CSP.

The most important distinction between Nehru and Tandon was in their attitudes toward secularism and traditional Hindu values. The differences between the two men were never total. Nehru never rejected everything in traditional Hindu society, nor did Tandon ever openly oppose the idea of a secular state. Still, Nehru represented for many educated Indians the desire to be modern and "scientific" in one's outlook toward political and social problems, to be wholly secular in thought and action, and to consciously work against the triple evils which Nehru constantly castigated in his speeches—the evils of "casteism, communalism, and provincialism."

Tandon, on the other hand, represented Hindu "revivalism" and devotion to "Hindi, Hindus, and Hindustan." Although Tandon was considered a communalist by Muslim "revivalists" and has always been admired by Hindu communalists, it would be wrong to accept this view of Tandon. Tandon rather was the symbol in the Hindi-speaking areas of the kind of regional linguistic and cultural identification which became politically important after Independence. In the south, these cultural movements eventually developed into the often violent agitation for the linguistic reorganization

[3] The Congress Socialist Party was formed in Patna in 1934 as a party within the Indian National Congress. The reasons for the formation of the Congress Socialist Party and its later history are given *ibid.*, especially chap. ii and in Hari Kishore Singh, *A History of the Praja Socialist Party* (Lucknow: Narendra Prakashan, 1959), especially chaps. i-iv.

of states. In the north, where territorial unity is not a problem, the movement expresses itself politically in an identification of the Hindi-speaking areas as the "real" India and, sometimes, in the desire to impose this view of the "real" India upon the rest of the country.

By the time the contest for President of the Indian National Congress took place in 1950, Tandon and men who respected him as a symbol of Hindi and Hindu culture had become dominant in the Uttar Pradesh Congress. The Uttar Pradesh delegation gave a majority to Tandon. The success of Tandon, as Weiner points out, "was widely interpreted as a defeat not only for Kripalani but for Nehru as well." [4] Many who voted for Tandon no doubt felt that they were voting for Hinduism against secularism and for a more militant policy against Pakistan. Yet, only a few Congressmen in Uttar Pradesh look back upon this contest as a challenge to Nehru. Most Congressmen in Uttar Pradesh accepted both Nehru and Tandon as their leaders and saw no incompatibility between them. Congressmen in Uttar Pradesh intellectually recognized and accepted most of Nehru's political ideas as necessary for the development of the country, but it was Tandon who appealed to the emotional identification of Congressmen in Uttar Pradesh with their language, their culture, and their region.

The Ideologist and the Virtuoso Politician: Acharya Narendra Dev and Rafi Ahmad Kidwai

In the politics of Uttar Pradesh before Independence, there were many viewpoints and many different kinds of men to express them. All of the leading Congressmen of this period from Uttar Pradesh rose to national importance in one way or another. Acharya Narendra Dev was one of the early leaders of the Congress Socialist Party and an important Indian socialist thinker. He continued to hold positions of national importance in the socialist movement after Independence until his death in 1956. Rafi Ahmad Kidwai was a very different sort of person. He was devoted not to an ideology, but to a man and to politics itself. Throughout his life, he was Pandit Nehru's political right-hand man. Although far from being anybody's shadow or lackey, Rafi Ahmad Kidwai remained devoted to the Nehru family from the early 1920s, when he became private secretary to Motilal Nehru, until his death in 1954. These two men, Narendra Dev and Kidwai, represented two entirely different kinds of political styles; only one kind survived for long in the Congress party in Uttar Pradesh after Independence. It is another one of the curious anomalies of Uttar Pradesh politics that, although Acharya Narendra Dev helped to defeat Kidwai and to remove him from Uttar Pradesh politics, the style of politics of which Kidwai was the

[4] Weiner, *Party Politics*, pp. 71-72.

master became dominant in the Uttar Pradesh Congress very soon after Independence.

Acharya Narendra Dev intellectually was the leading exponent in the socialist movement in India of Marxism, as opposed to democratic socialism or Gandhian "socialism." [5] In practice, on specific policy issues, he tended to be moderate. Whatever his personal opinions, however, he always submitted to decisions taken by the party leadership even though often it took great political courage for him to do so. In a word, he placed loyalty to party and to the socialist movement above personal interest. Unlike Socialist leaders in other states, where the Congress Socialist Party had little importance in the Congress party organizations, Acharya Narendra Dev was always recognized as a leading member of the Congress in Uttar Pradesh and the Congress Socialist Party was the largest political group in the state Congress. In 1937, when the Congress formed governments in seven states and when the Congress Socialist Party officially opposed Cabinet-entry by its members, Narendra Dev personally favored participation in the Congress government, but declined an invitation to join the Uttar Pradesh Cabinet in deference to the official decision of the CSP.[6] Again, in 1948, when the Congress Socialist Party decided to withdraw from the Congress, Narendra Dev was reluctant.[7] When he took the decision to withdraw, however, it was again an act of political courage. At the time, the Congress Socialists were in control of the party machinery and had a group of forty or fifty members in the Congress state legislature party. Narendra Dev had a difficult choice to make. He and his followers could simply resign from the Congress and cross the floor of the House or they could resign from the legislature altogether and contest for their seats again in bye-elections against the Congress. Narendra Dev chose the latter course, with the result that only twelve legislators went with him, all of whom, including Narendra Dev himself, were defeated in the bye-elections by Congress candidates.

Acharya Narendra Dev was a man who was loyal to principle and to party, whatever the cost might be to his personal political career. Rafi Ahmad Kidwai was equally steadfast in his particular political style. If Narendra Dev was loyal to principle and to party, Kidwai was loyal to men—both to his leaders, Motilal and Jawaharlal Nehru, and to his followers, the motley band of district leaders who loved him and worked with him throughout his career.

More than any other political leader from Uttar Pradesh and as much as

[5] *Ibid.*, p. 35.

[6] On this point, see Sampurnanand, *Memories and Reflections* (Bombay: Asia Publishing House, 1962), p. 83.

[7] Raghukul Tilak, "Acharya Narendra Deva as I Knew Him" (Publication details not known). (Mimeographed.)

any leader in all of India, Rafi Ahmad Kidwai has become a legend. Wherever one travels in the districts of Uttar Pradesh, one has only to mention the name of Kidwai to hear a new story of Kidwai's loyalty to his friends and of his generosity to his enemies. Kidwai was the master politician, the prototype of the modern faction leader in Indian politics. He was also a great administrator, the man who is remembered for his decisiveness and his efficiency in solving India's food crisis when he was Minister for Food and Agriculture in the central government from 1952 to 1954.

Kidwai was the major election organizer and financer of the Congress election campaigns in Uttar Pradesh from the early 1920s when he organized the campaign of Motilal Nehru's Swaraj party through the 1937 and 1946 elections. After the successful Congress election campaign in Uttar Pradesh in 1937, Kidwai emerged as the most important figure in the state party organization, with a large personal following among the district leaders in the state. He also had a sizeable following among the legislators and was given the most prominent position in the state Cabinet after the Chief Minister (Pandit Pant). Kidwai performed a remarkable feat in Indian politics and in Uttar Pradesh politics in particular. In this state, with its long tradition of communal politics, Rafi Ahmad Kidwai was the only prominent Muslim political leader who rose to a position of power and influence in the state Congress and government by his own efforts and because of the attraction of his personality. Kidwai's followers in the Uttar Pradesh Congress were, inevitably, all Hindus (since there were few other Muslims in the Congress) and were all among the most secular-minded Congressmen in the state. Secular-minded is probably the only term that would apply to all of Kidwai's followers, for they were drawn from different castes and creeds and they reflected every conceivable political opinion from extreme conservatism to ardent socialism.

The secularism of Kidwai and his followers made them less concerned with the matters of language, culture, and region that were so dear to Tandon and those close to him. Acharya Narendra Dev and his band of followers, strangely enough, were closer to Tandon than to Kidwai. Narendra Dev, like Tandon, was a devotee of Hindi and was associated with prominent Hindi cultural organizations in Uttar Pradesh. Although Kidwai personally tended to be economically "progressive," the Socialists generally found Tandon a man more to their liking and, as will be shown later, the followers of Tandon and of Narendra Dev joined together to oust Kidwai and his men from their positions of power in state Congress politics.

The major difference between Kidwai and Narendra Dev personally, however, was one of political style. Narendra Dev, the man of ideology, had little sympathy—although there was never any personal enmity—for a man like Kidwai who could openly say, "It may be my vision is narrow. I rely more on the number of heads than on ideological discourses." [8] The differences between these two men, despite a certain common ground, are well expressed by a Congressman who knew and loved them both:

It was a painful thing to me that Rafi Ahmad Kidwai and Acharya Narendra Dev couldn't pull on. Kidwai's criticism of Narendra Dev was that the latter was too much of an idealist and perhaps Narendra Dev felt that Kidwai had no principles, that he was just a politician. However, one thing Acharya Narendra Dev used to tell me that, whenever there was a question of taking a progressive step, Kidwai would always agree; he [Kidwai] was very progressive in his views.[9]

The Arbiter: Pandit Pant

Of all the prominent political leaders in Uttar Pradesh before Independence, Pandit Pant had the least political power in the conventional sense. He was not a symbol of regional aspirations, nor did he represent any ideology. He had no group following whatsoever. Indeed, his lack of skill or, rather, his lack of interest in "politics" was such that he had no power even in his home district of Almora and had always to contest elections from some other district where local Congressmen had more respect for his talents. Pandit Pant was a parliamentary leader, rather than an organizational leader; he was esteemed by all Congressmen in Uttar Pradesh as a man of intelligence and integrity, but he had no group of his own. Yet, it was Pandit Pant who became the state's first chief minister and the dominating personality in state politics for the next 20 years, from 1937 until the late 1950s.

The selection of Pandit Pant as the first chief minister of Uttar Pradesh was partly the logical result of a process of elimination. Pandit Nehru was too deeply involved in national affairs to take the responsibility himself. Narendra Dev was eliminated automatically as a candidate for the chief ministership since the Congress Socialists refused to join the 1937 Cabinet. Kidwai's talents were in party organization, rather than parliamentary leadership; moreover, his selection might have precipitated internal political conflict within the state Congress party.

The only choice, therefore, was between Purushottamdas Tandon and Pandit Pant. In terms of seniority in the Congress, Tandon should have been the choice. Tandon was not only an older Congressman, but he had led the movements within Uttar Pradesh while Pant had been in the central Parliament. The choice of Pant over Tandon involved two fundamental decisions. It involved, first, a conscious acceptance by the Congress leadership of the responsibilities of office: seniority in the movement and agita-

[8] Letter from Rafi Ahmad Kidwai to Jawaharlal Nehru, April 20, 1936, in Jawaharlal Nehru, *A Bunch of Old Letters* (2d ed., Bombay: Asia Publishing House, 1960), p. 181.
[9] Interview in Meerut on December 20, 1962.

tional ability were passed over in favor of parliamentary and administrative talents. Second, the choice of Pant reflected the need for a noncontroversial chief minister, a man who had no group following and was aloof from group intrigues. Pandit Pant held no strong views likely to antagonize anyone inside or outside of the Congress; moreover, he was personally conciliatory in temperament. In short, Pant had all the qualities necessary to run the government efficiently and, simultaneously, to keep the party together. Pant performed these functions admirably from 1937 until 1955, when he was called to the central Cabinet to perform similar functions in government and party for the country as a whole.

The First Phase of Conflict

Pandit Pant's task was not an easy one. His management of the state government in the period between 1937 and 1939 firmly established his reputation as one of the great leaders in the country. However, Pant was sitting on a powder keg in his own state which, as has been mentioned above, exploded after Independence in a struggle which nearly split the Congress apart in the country. In this struggle, all the main contenders—Tandon, Kidwai, and Narendra Dev—lost something; only Nehru and Pant won unqualified victories.

In the pre-Independence period, conflict among political leaders in Uttar Pradesh was partly submerged because of the overriding importance of unity in the struggle for independence. Some preliminary skirmishes occurred, but no clear battle lines were drawn. After Independence, however, a long period of struggle began between Kidwai and his followers, on the one hand, and the followers of Tandon and Narendra Dev, on the other. The struggle reflected the differences of principle and of temperament sketched above among these political leaders. It was also a struggle for political power in state and national politics.

Two events in Uttar Pradesh are of crucial importance in the early post-Independence period for an understanding of later political alignments. One was the departure of Kidwai to the central government (actually just before Independence) and the other was the departure of Narendra Dev and some of the Socialists from the Congress. Since Pant had no group of followers of his own, Kidwai from the beginning had acted as Pant's political manager. However, Pant soon became embarrassed by Kidwai's power and had him removed to the center in 1946. Although this move freed him from Kidwai, it also left Pant temporarily without followers. Pant's problems were solved in 1948 when Narendra Dev left the Congress and most of the Congress Socialists decided not to go with him. As Pandit Pant had become "followerless," the Congress Socialists who remained in the Congress had become "leaderless." Since Kidwai's followers in Uttar

Pradesh remained loyal to Kidwai, the natural alliance was between Pant and the leaderless Socialists in the Congress. In the party organization, the leaderless Socialists turned to Purushottamdas Tandon, who was elected President of the Uttar Pradesh Congress Committee (UPCC) in April, 1948. Thus, for the first time, a single group emerged in the Uttar Pradesh Congress in control both of the state government and the Congress organization.

Pant's position was improved further in the later stages of the struggle, when Tandon made his bid for national leadership. Although Tandon was elected national Congress president in 1950 in the contest against Acharya Kripalani, he was forced to resign the following year and he soon retired from active politics. Kidwai, who organized Kripalani's campaign, lost the struggle for votes against Tandon, but was ultimately responsible for Tandon's resignation.[10] In the meantime, however, Kidwai's influence in Uttar Pradesh politics was gone. During the struggle, the majority of his followers in the state legislature and in the districts had resigned from the Congress and gone into opposition. Narendra Dev had committed political suicide by leaving the Congress in 1948.

Only Pandit Pant emerged from the affray with enhanced power and increased prestige. Pant was willing to cooperate with Tandon to oust Kidwai and his followers from power in party affairs. However, when Tandon made his bid for national leadership and when this bid became a direct challenge to Pandit Nehru, Pant withdrew from the battle and adopted the role of mediator. When the dust of the battle had settled, Pandit Pant stood undamaged, in fact with his prestige reinforced and his reputation for impartiality and noninvolvement in group intrigues intact. Pant now towered over all other Congressmen in the state, for he was now the last of the leaders of the first rank who remained in a position of prominence in Uttar Pradesh Congress affairs.

A number of conclusions about the impact of conflicts in the pre-Independence years and in the years immediately after Independence upon the future patterns of Congress politics in Uttar Pradesh emerge from this summary. First, the conflict between Tandon and Nehru and the support which Tandon received in Uttar Pradesh reflected the strength of regional identification in the state. The eventual victory of Nehru in the struggle was a warning to Congressmen from Uttar Pradesh that cultural and linguistic nationalism must be kept within bounds. In effect, Hindu revivalism

[10] Kidwai, angry because of Tandon's refusal to include him or any of his supporters on the Working Committee of the Indian National Congress, resigned from the Congress in August, 1951. Kidwai's resignation forced Nehru to act. Nehru then resigned from the Congress Working Committee. At this point, Tandon resigned as Congress president, Nehru replaced him as president, and Kidwai rejoined the Congress. Weiner, *Party Politics*, pp. 75-79.

became prohibited in the Congress party in Uttar Pradesh and the cause of Hindi and of Hindu culture was left to the communal parties, particularly to the Jan Sangh. Second, the departure of Narendra Dev from the Congress brought an end to ideology as a factor in Uttar Pradesh Congress politics. Extremes of both right and left were removed from the Congress and a moderate consensus emerged, more or less faithful to the principles for which Nehru stood—a moderate approach to questions of language and culture and a gradual, non-dogmatic approach toward "socialist" ideals. With literally nothing left to fight about, politics in the Uttar Pradesh Congress more and more revolved solely around personalistic group or factional politics. Rafi Ahmad Kidwai, the virtuoso politician, established the pattern of factional politics in this state. Those who sought to defeat him had necessarily to imitate him. It is to this new pattern of politics that the analysis must now turn.

CONTEMPORARY FACTIONAL CONFLICT IN THE UTTAR PRADESH CONGRESS

The new men of power

Since Pandit Pant would not participate in party politics himself, he had to have a party manager both to defeat Kidwai and to replace Kidwai. For this task, he chose Chandra Bhan Gupta, one of the lesser known "soldiers" of the Congress and a man of a new generation in Congress politics. Chandra Bhan Gupta was born in a Bania family of Aligarh district in 1903. He received an M.A. and an LL.B. degree from Lucknow University and joined the Bar in 1925. He participated in all the Congress movements in the 1930s and 1940s and spent eight and a half years in jail. His association with Pandit Pant went back to 1926 when, as a young lawyer, he assisted Pant in the defense of the revolutionaries tried in the famous Kakori Conspiracy Case.[11] Gupta was one of the many Congress Socialists who decided to remain within the Congress. Like Kidwai, Gupta has devoted his entire life to politics and only to politics; he has never married.

Under the wing of Pandit Pant, he soon built up a very powerful political organization. Towards the end of 1946, after the departure of Kidwai for the center, Gupta was taken into the Uttar Pradesh government as Pant's Chief Parliamentary Secretary in charge of Licenses and Permits—a position of obvious importance for the distribution of patrongae. In the same year, Gupta was elected treasurer of the Provincial Congress Committee. Thus, in a very short time, Gupta was placed in control of an overwhelming proportion of both party and government patronage, which he

[11] Shyam Sunder and Savitri Shyam, *Political Life of Pandit Govind Ballabh Pant,* Vol. I: *1887-1945* (Lucknow: Shailanil, 1960), p. 82.

used as Pant's party manager to build simultaneously a following for Pant and an opposition to Kidwai. Gupta was instrumental in forging the alliance between the Congress Socialists and the followers of Tandon which effectively isolated Kidwai and his followers in the Uttar Pradesh Congress organization.

Another new man of power to come to prominence in this period of struggle was Mohan Lal Gautam, a Brahman, also from Aligarh district and of the same generation—he was born in 1905—as C. B. Gupta. Gautam also was a member of the Congress Socialist Party, but his closest ties were with Tandon. He had worked closely with Tandon in the peasant movement in Uttar Pradesh in the early 1930s. As Gupta was Pant's party manager, Gautam was Tandon's political organizer. When Tandon was elected president of the Indian National Congress, Gautam became his general secretary. Gautam had played an important role in the defeat of Kidwai's followers in Uttar Pradesh and had a reputation for ruthlessness in party political matters. In fact, it has been suggested that the appointment of Gautam as general secretary of the Indian National Congress, even more than the election of Tandon, precipitated the final crisis at the national level.[12] The rise of Gautam to the position of general secretary, where he could preside over the distribution of party tickets for the 1952 General Elections, was too much for the followers of Kidwai and Kripalani to bear.

When Tandon resigned the presidency, Gautam also had to leave his position. The return of Gautam to state politics marked the beginning of a new struggle for power in the Uttar Pradesh Congress. Although Gautam had been exiled permanently from Delhi, Pandit Pant had room for him in Lucknow. It is just possible that Pant did not care to trust anybody, even his own creations, with too much political power and that he brought Gautam into his Cabinet in 1952 to counterbalance the influence of Gupta. Whatever Pant's intention, this was the effect. Gautam was given the politically important position of Minister for Local Self-Government and it is said that he immediately began to form a separate group within the Gupta group by building support in the municipal and district boards through the patronage of his ministry. Within two years, Gupta and Gautam had become bitter personal enemies and the struggle which began between these two men in 1952 has not yet run its full course. It has brought disruption and division in the government and in the party, in Lucknow and in every district in the state.[13]

[12] See Pran Nath Chopra, *Rafi Ahmad Kidwai: His Life and Work* (Agra: Shiva Lal Agarwala and Co. [Pvt.], Ltd., 1960), p. 146.

[13] The foregoing analysis has excluded other important political leaders who rose to prominence in state politics during this period, for example, Kamlapati Tripathi. He has been the titular leader of the anti-Gupta group in recent years. Gupta and Gautam were selected to represent "the new men of power" partly because they have been the most skilled practitioners in the new style of Uttar Pradesh politics, but also because

The art of political management: Pandit
Pant and Dr. Sampurnanand

A great gap was created in Uttar Pradesh politics when Pandit Pant left for the central government in 1955. Two important elements of stability which Pant gave to Uttar Pradesh politics went with him when he left. For one thing, Pant was the last of the prominent leaders of the nationalist movement in Uttar Pradesh, a man who occupied a position of unchallengeable authority and esteem because of his seniority in the movement and his sacrifices on its behalf, because of his integrity, and because of a certain touch of charisma drawn partly from his own personality and partly from his association with the great leaders of the nationalist movement in the country. Second, Pandit Pant was one of the most astute political managers Indian politics has produced. Although he rarely participated directly in political controversies, he knew how to make men work for him and he knew how to make enemies work together under him. Indeed, it was part of his political strategy to permit those under him to fight amongst themselves, a certain way of assuring that they would not fight him.

The transition involved in the transfer of Pant to the central government and the selection of a new chief minister for Uttar Pradesh was an easy one. The decision was made largely on the basis of seniority. There were some in the Congress who feebly attempted to nominate Tandon, but Tandon was clearly out of the running by then. The decision was made by Nehru and Pant. The choice was between Hafiz Mohammed Ibrahim, a "Nationalist" Muslim, and Dr. Sampurnanand. Ibrahim was the senior man in age, but Sampurnanand was the senior man in Congress politics. Neither man had any important group following, so that no conflict arose over the final selection of Sampurnanand.

Sampurnanand had some of the qualities which made Pandit Pant so successful a chief minister. He occupied a position of esteem in the Congress and in the society as a whole both for his political sacrifices in the nationalist movement and for his nonpolitical activities as a teacher and scholar in the Kashi Vidyapith of Banaras. Sampurnanand was one of the many Congressmen in Uttar Pradesh who managed to combine "socialism" with Hindu revivalism and cultural nationalism. A well-known socialist thinker, he was esteemed even more for his traditional learning in Sanskrit. He has been devoted to the spread of Hindi and was President of the All India Hindi Sahitya Sammelan in 1940, a cultural organization which, significantly enough, has always been led by politicians. (Tandon and Narendra Dev both were prominent leaders of this society.)

---

their great enmity for each other has been of considerable importance in political developments in the state.

Like Pant, Sampurnanand had been more or less aloof from group intrigues and was involved in no controversies. He had been identified both with Tandon and Narendra Dev against Kidwai, but he was considered essentially "nonpolitical" and impartial in outlook and in his relations with others. However, unlike Pandit Pant, Sampurnanand had no astuteness in party political matters; he kew little about the art of political management which was the secret of Pandit Pant's success.

Pant had successfully played off the new men of power—Gupta and Gautam—against each other and had thereby maintained complete freedom for himself. Sampurnanand, on the other hand, lost his political freedom and his ability to maneuver as soon as he took office. He made the mistake of depending upon only one political manager—first Gupta, then Gautam—to keep the party organization under control. In the end, his reputation for impartiality was lost and he became identified as a leader of a particular faction rather than a leader of the whole party.

Sampurnanand relied first upon Gupta, who had a decisive influence in the selection of the new ministers. Gupta's most important decision was to exclude from the government his arch-foe, Mohan Lal Gautam. The exclusion of Gautam was the first act in the new drama of Uttar Pradesh Congress affairs, an act which split the state Congress apart in factional struggle eventually leading to the downfall of the Sampurnanand Government. The new Sampurnanand ministry was composed almost completely of the old group of Congress Socialists who had remained in the Congress. Gautam himself had been a charter member of the CSP in Uttar Pradesh, but he had been expelled in 1947 for reasons which are still somewhat clouded. Gautam has described his exclusion from the first Sampurnanand ministry in a way which indicates both the relations between him and Gupta and the stakes involved: "When Sampurnanand came into power, the old CSPers finally got their opportunity to work together and run the whole affair, but I was kept out. . . . I was kept out because C. B. Gupta wanted to be the Chief Minister after Sampurnanand and I would have been his only rival. I have never worked as C. B.'s junior; it has always been the other way around and C. B. wanted to keep me out."[14]

Within two years, however, the tables were turned. In the 1957 election, C. B. Gupta and many of his supporters in the government were defeated. Constitutionally, Gupta could not be taken into the government unless he held a seat in either the Assembly or the Legislative Council. With Gupta's entry into the Cabinet barred for the time being, Sampurnanand was left without a party manager in the government. He now turned to Gautam, who was taken into the Cabinet as Minister for Cooperation. The inclusion of Gautam in the ministry was a direct affront to C. B. Gupta,

14 Interview in Lucknow on November 21, 1961.

who then began a systematic warfare against the Sampurnanand government. Gupta's position, despite his defeat and his exclusion from the government, was still very strong. He still controlled the party organization and finances and had loyal allies within the government as well: nine ministers in the Uttar Pradesh government owed allegiance to Gupta and maintained a second front for him in the government and the legislature.

For a time, efforts at compromise between the two groups were made. By the middle of 1958, however, open conflicts began to occur. Sampurnanand treated the conflicts as a challenge to him and his government and placed his prestige into the battle against Gupta. Events began to move rapidly now and more and more Congressmen in the legislature and in the party organization were forced to take sides and join either the "dissident" Gupta group or the "ministerialist" Sampurnanand group. In July, 1959, Gupta demonstrated his power in the Congress Legislature Party of the Legislative Council (upper house) of the state government. In an election for chairman of the Council, the nominee of Sampurnanand was defeated by a nominee of Gupta. In November, the nine Ministers in the Sampurnanand government who owed allegiance to Gupta resigned their posts. Not long afterwards another prominent Cabinet member, Charan Singh, also resigned, for reasons of his own, and joined the Gupta camp. In March, 1959, when an opposition motion of no-confidence in the government was being considered in the Uttar Pradesh Assembly, ninety-eight dissident Congress members of the Legislative Assembly (MLAs) submitted a memorandum to the government, which was released to the press, declaring that, although they would not vote against the government, they had no confidence in it.

The final showdown, however, was put off for another year. The biannual elections of the Provincial Congress Committee (PCC) were scheduled for 1960, so that both sides spent the remainder of 1959 and the major part of 1960 enrolling party members and organizing support in the districts for the election of delegates to the PCC. When the time for elections came in October, 1960, Gupta had a clear majority of the delegates behind him and he decided to contest the election for president of the PCC. Sampurnanand made a prestige issue of the matter and declared that, if the government's candidate for president were defeated, he would resign his position as Chief Minister. The elections were held despite Sampurnanand's threat; Gupta won not only the presidency, but every important office in the PCC Executive Committee for his followers. Sampurnanand and his government resigned a month later and C. B. Gupta was elected leader of the party in the legislature and thus became the state's third chief minister.

Sampurnanand made the mistake of permitting himself to be dominated by one factional leader: first Gupta, then Gautam. What was worse, in terms of political strategy, was his later adoption of one group as his own. Gupta never objected to Sampurnanand as Chief Minister; his targets were those who controlled the Chief Minister to the exclusion of himself. Sampurnanand placed his own personal prestige into the struggle on the side of one of the contending groups, with the result that his own prestige fell and he became identified as a factional leader, rather than the leader of the Congress and of the people of the state.

Party versus Government

Sampurnanand's fall can be traced to his personal failures as a political manager, but his fall and the rise of Gupta to the chief ministership were symbols of a struggle that dominated Congress politics throughout India in the last decade. In the context of all-India politics, Uttar Pradesh was the fourth state in the Indian Union where a Provincial Congress president became chief minister.[15]

Conflicts between the organizational and the governmental wings of parties of extra-parliamentary origin are common in democratic countries. In Uttar Pradesh, the formal debate between the opposing groups was carried on in terms of the respective roles of party and government. While Gupta was out of the government, his followers in the party demanded the right of consultation by government with the party organization on policy matters. Simultaneously, the nine Ministers in the Sampurnanand government who owed allegiance to Gupta demanded freedom of action in organizatioanl matters—in effect, the right to remain in the government while working in the party organization against the government.

Although the debate was phrased in a language of principle, there were no real policy differences between the opposing groups. To give the debate a substantive policy content, the leaders of the "dissident" group in the party raised an issue relating to the retirement age of government officials— the "dissident" group favored a retirement age of 55, the government favored a retirement age of 58. The issue was of no importance in itself; it merely served as a convenient handle for the followers of Gupta in the party organization to criticize the ministry since the ministry's position was contrary to the national policy.

Both the question of freedom of action for members of government in matters relating to party organization and the policy issue were referred to the national party leadership. On these and other similar issues, the High Command (the national leadership of the Congress) has generally avoided

---

[15] A summary and analysis of the development of conflict between the organizational and governmental wings of the state Congress parties appears in Marcus F. Franda, "The Organizational Development of India's Congress Party," *Pacific Affairs*, XXXV (Fall, 1962), 248-260.

"constitutional" niceties and has acted pragmatically in an effort to maintain political stability at all costs. Thus, on the first question of "freedom of action," the High Command gave a decision so vaguely worded that each side could interpret it to its own advantage. The national leadership did not want to take the risk of precipitating a crisis by giving a clear verdict for either group. On the retirement age issue, which required a clear answer, the High Command supported Sampurnanand, with the obvious desire to maintain governmental stability.

By far the most important issues related to the resignation of Sampurnanand and the election of Gupta as Chief Minister. Sampurnanand had placed his personal prestige and that of the government into the struggle by threatening to resign if Gupta was elected president of the PCC. On November 12, 1960, Sampurnanand submitted his resignation to the Congress Legislature Party. The supporters of the government still retained a majority in the Congress Legislature Party and they succeeded in passing a resolution requesting Sampurnanand to continue in office. At this point, the question was referred to Pandit Nehru, who advised Sampurnanand to resign. Nehru and the High Command evidently felt that Sampurnanand had made a mistake in threatening to resign over a party matter,[16] but that he should now carry out his promise.

After the question of Sampurnanand's resignation was settled, the issue to be decided was whether or not the Congress Legislature Party should have the right to elect the new Chief Minister by a free vote. The High Command again refused to decide the formal issue. The national leadership decided against the right of the Congress Legislature Party, not because it wished to establish the ascendancy of the party organization, but because it felt that the selection of Gupta as Chief Minister would better guarantee political stability in Uttar Pradesh. The pragmatic approach of the High Command to this issue is clear in the following summary of the decision, contained in the *Report of the General Secretaries* of the Indian National Congress for 1960:

The election of a new Leader posed a difficult problem. The Central Parliamentary Board was anxious to ensure orderly succession to Dr. Sampurnanand. It also desired that the new Leader should have as far as possible the full support of the Party so that he could be instrumental in strengthening unity in the Congress Assembly Party as also in the Congress organisation. A suggestion was put forward that Shri C. B. Gupta who has recently been elected the President of the PCC . . . should succeed Dr. Sampurnanand. It was, however, necessary that he

---

[16] The Central Parliamentary Board passed a resolution on October 18, 1960, regretting "that circumstances should have arisen which induced him [Sampurnanand] to offer his resignation." Cited in *Report of the General Secretaries, January, 1960 to December, 1960* (New Delhi: All India Congress Committee, 1960), p. 46.

should do so in an atmosphere of general approval. . . . The reaction to the suggestion was not one of unanimous approval in the Congress Assembly Party. A section of Congress MLAs felt that the discretion of the Party should not be fettered by any suggestion from any high quarter. It was, however, necessary in the special conditions of Uttar Pradesh that succession to Dr. Sampurnanand should be smooth and orderly to the maximum extent possible.[17]

To ensure a "smooth and orderly" succession, frantic last-minute efforts by the national leadership were necessary. Pandit Pant and Lal Bahadur Shastri, two men noted for their powers of persuasion, flew to Lucknow from Delhi and, after considerable private negotiation, succeeded in prevailing upon the leaders of the Sampurnanand group not to press their right to elect the new leader and to accept Gupta as the new Chief Minister.[18]

Although the national leadership clearly avoided making a decision on the roles to be assigned to the organizational and governmental wings of the party, its intervention in favor of the unanimous selection of Gupta as Chief Minister involved a recognition of the fact that political stability could not be assured without the cooperation of the state party leadership. The victory of the party organization over the government, in Uttar Pradesh as in other states, marked a fundamental change in the character of the political leadership governing the Indian states. In Uttar Pradesh, an historical period ended when Pandit Pant left for the center. Pant was the last of the prominent leaders of the nationalist movement from Uttar Pradesh to take an active part in politics at the state level. Sampurnanand, though not of the first rank of political leaders in Uttar Pradesh, had some of the personal prestige associated with more prominent leaders. The new political leadership is singularly different. People like Gupta and Gautam have little stature in the society other than what they achieve through the party organization. For these men, politics is a vocation; they do not bring status and prestige to office, but rather seek status and prestige through office.

One important consequence of this twofold change in political leadership —the change in generations and the change brought about by the rise of party men to government office—has been an increase in the frequency and in the intensity of internal factional quarrels in the Congress party in the states. Largely for this reason, the national leadership of the Congress took the bold step in 1963 of attempting a wholesale reorganization of political leadership in the states. In Uttar Pradesh, the most significant change was the replacement of Gupta by a new Chief Minister and the forced return of Gupta to the party organization. It is useful to examine the events leading up to this change in Uttar Pradesh politics in the context of the whole range of center-state relations within the Congress organization.

[17] *Ibid.*, pp. 47-48.
[18] *Leader*, November 30, December 1, 2, 1960.

Center-state relations

The evidence from Uttar Pradesh indicates that there are two important characteristics of center-state relations in the Congress organization. In the first place, the relationship between the central and national party leadership in the past has been largely informal rather than structured; it has been based upon the influence which people like Pandit Nehru, Pandit Pant, and Lal Bahadur Shastri have wielded in Uttar Pradesh politics because of their close connections with the state Congress and their reputations for impartiality. Second, the major role which the High Command plays in Uttar Pradesh Congress politics is one of mediation; the end of mediation is always to maintain the unity of the party and the stability of the state government and to prevent one group from liquidating another. Direct dictation from the national leadership to the state leadership occurs occasionally. The national leadership may insist upon the resignation of a PCC president or a chief minister who fails to maintain party unity and whose actions prejudice governmental stability. However, the High Command finds it difficult to impose new leadership upon the state Congress or upon the state government.

Although Pandit Pant was taken into the central Cabinet in 1955, one of his major tasks until his death remained that of maintaining a measure of stability in the Uttar Pradesh Congress. Thus, during the selection of candidates to contest the 1957 elections, Pant occupied a pivotal position on the state Parliamentary Board and saw to it that neither faction could liquidate the other through an imbalance in the ticket selections.[19] He also exercised all his powers of persuasion to postpone a showdown between the followers of Gupta and the followers of Sampurnanand. For example, Gupta had planned to show his control over the party organization in the 1958 PCC elections, but was persuaded by Pant not to force a contest at that time. Later in the year, Lal Bahadur Shastri (at that time a senior minister in the central government from Uttar Pradesh) performed a similar function at a requisitioned meeting of the PCC.[20] The last-minute flight of Pandit Pant to Lucknow in 1960 to ensure the unanimous election of Gupta as Chief Minister has already been mentioned.

During the prime ministership of Nehru, when all efforts at mediation failed, the last resort of the national leadership was a "suggestion" or a directive from Pandit Nehru personally. Thus, when Pandit Pant came to

[19] In the 1962 selection of candidates, which took place after Pandit Pant's death, state faction leaders deadlocked on a large proportion of the seats and left the decision to the Central Parliamentary Board. In this case, a structured relationship between the state and central party organizations replaced the informal one which existed while Pant was alive.

[20] *Times of India,* October 20, 1958.

Lucknow to supervise the transfer of leadership from Sampurnanand to Gupta, he arrived armed with a letter from Pandit Nehru to Dr. Sampurnanand and to C. B. Gupta expressing Nehru's wish that Gupta be elected leader of the party.[21] At times, however, even Nehru's wishes were not instantly accepted by state party leaders. After the selection of Gupta as Chief Minister, a new PCC president had to be elected to replace Gupta, according to the Congress constitution. In January, 1961, Pandit Nehru expressed his clear wish that Ajit Prasad Jain, a man sent from the center and unaffiliated to either group in the state Congress, be appointed the new PCC president.[22] Jain, as an old follower of Kidwai, was acceptable to the Sampurnanand group, but not to Gupta. In this case, there was considerable delay and much negotiation between the rival groups until finally Nehru addressed a personal letter to Gupta in March, suggesting the name of A. P. Jain.[23] Despite this second "suggestion" of the Prime Minister, Jain was not accepted by the Gupta group until May. Nehru's wishes again prevailed, but not without considerable delay.

In all of their activities in state Congress politics, the national leaders have been concerned primarily with maintaining party unity and government stability. Sufficient evidence of the High Command's role in this respect has been given. It should be stressed, however, that the High Command has been unwilling to achieve unity and stability at the expense of one faction and in favor of another. Since neither ideological nor policy issues are involved in state factional disputes, the central leaders have had no interest in the victory or defeat of local groups. A constant dilemma, therefore, is that the unity and stability which the High Command seeks can never be achieved for long. As long as opposing factions are tolerated in the state Congress, as they must be, conflict will continue. The greatest danger to the Congress organization in the future lies in the passing, not simply of Nehru, but of all the peacemakers at the center. After Pant's death in 1961, the entire burden of peacemaking in the Uttar Pradesh Congress fell upon Lal Bahadur Shastri and upon Nehru. The prospects for continued stability in the state Congress rest upon the continued existence of impartial arbiters at the center who command respect in state Congress politics.

Despite the important role of the central leadership in solving state factional disputes, the power of the High Command over state politics should not be overly stressed. The 1963 change of chief ministers in Uttar Pradesh illustrates both the extent and the limits of the power of the High Command in state Congress politics. In July, 1963, the Chief Minister of Madras publicly announced a suggestion, which was quickly approved by the

[21] *Leader*, December 1, 1960.
[22] *Statesman*, January 24, 1961.
[23] *Statesman*, March 8, 1961.

Prime Minister, that senior ministers in both the central and state governments all over India should resign from government to devote more time to party work and to strengthening and unifying the Congress organization. The "Kamraj Plan" (named for the Madras Chief Minister) was designed to check the growth of unrestrained factional conflict which had been going on in the Congress party at the center and in many of the states (particularly in Uttar Pradesh, Madhya Pradesh, Andhra, and Orissa) since the 1962 General Elections. In Uttar Pradesh, C. B. Gupta's resignation from the chief ministership was accepted and a new Chief Minister and a new Cabinet were selected.

The acceptance of Gupta's resignation had been preceded by months of intense factional struggle, reminiscent of the events leading up to the resignation of Dr. Sampurnanand. Differences between Gupta and A. P. Jain, the PCC President, had been growing bitter. Rifts occurred in the government also, leading to the resignation of ten ministers, deputy ministers, and parliamentary secretaries. On one occasion, Gupta found himself and his followers in a minority on the PCC Executive Committee.

Although the national leadership insisted upon Gupta's resignation, this time the High Command gave the Congress Legislature Party freedom to elect the new leader. A contest was held between a nominee of Gupta and a nominee of the opposing group. Gupta's candidate, Mrs. Sucheta Kripalani, was successful and became the state's fourth chief minister in September, 1963.

Until the end of 1963, under the Kamraj Plan, the national leadership had done no more in Uttar Pradesh politics than fill its traditional role of ensuring party unity and governmental stability. After the election of Mrs. Kripalani, as after the election of Gupta, talks were held in Delhi with the new Chief Minister to express the High Command's wish that the new Chief Minister would carry out this double role and would form a Cabinet representative of both major groups in the state party. Both Gupta and Mrs. Kripalani showed considerable independence of the national leadership after taking office. Gupta did not admit factional opponents into his Cabinet until after the 1962 election. Mrs. Kripalani formed a more representative Cabinet shortly after her election, but differences over individual appointments between her and the national leadership occurred.

The question for the future is whether the national leadership intends to play a more positive role in state Congress politics. Until 1963, the High Command had played largely a negative role in the sense that it would not tolerate in office, either as PCC president or as chief minister, a Congressman who could not maintain unity and stability. If the national leadership were to interfere more actively in state Congress politics in selecting PCC presidents and government ministers, it would have to face considerable resistance. Whatever role the national leadership adopts, the continuance of factional conflict in state Congress politics is a certainty.

Mrs. Kripalani, the wife of the Acharya, has no roots in state Congress politics. She joined the Uttar Pradesh government for the first time in 1960. It is likely that Gupta nominated her for this very reason, in the expectation that she would be dependent upon him as a party manager. Her selection as the Chief Minister and the manner of her selection have, at least temporarily, reversed the relationship between party and government in Uttar Pradesh politics. Unlike Gupta, she is a non-party person and, also unlike Gupta, she was elected in an open contest in the Congress Legislature Party, Clearly, the respective roles of party and government in Uttar Pradesh Congress politics remain undefined, either by decree or by precedent.

CONGRESS FACTIONS AND DISTRICT POLITICS

Some of the leaders and some of the issues involved in the internal politics of the Congress party in Uttar Pradesh have been examined in the previous sections. In this section, the characteristics of factional conflict in the Uttar Pradesh Congress—the causes of conflict, the social composition of Congress factions, and the ties that bind leaders and followers—will be discussed.

Conflict and alliance

The first and most obvious characteristic of contemporary factional politics in the Uttar Pradesh Congress is the predominantly personal nature of factional groups. Although the language of conflict is often phrased in terms of important principles and although a policy issue may sometimes be seized upon as a pretext for factional struggle, factions and factional conflict are organized completely around personalities and around personal enmities among party leaders. A second characteristic of factional conflict in the Uttar Pradesh Congress is the shifting character of political coalitions. Alliances develop and splits and defections occur wholly because of the mutual convenience and temporarily shared power-political interests of group leaders. At times, the Congress appears to be split into two camps, as during the struggle between the party organization and the Sampurnanand government; actually, neither side in this struggle was ever monolithic. Gupta acquired his decisive position in party affairs as a result of gradual accretions of supporters, only some of whom owed him personal allegiance; the rest joined Gupta for reasons of their own. The pro-Government forces were similarly composed of a number of faction leaders, among whom Mohan Lal Gautam was only one.

What are called "groups" in Uttar Pradesh politics, for example the

Gupta group or the former Sampurnanand group, are actually very loose coalitions of local, district faction leaders, tied together at the state level partly by personal bonds of friendship, partly by caste loyalties, and most of all by political interest. The membership of these groups is constantly changing so that often it appears that there are no persistent conflicts and no permanent alliances, that all is perpetually in flux. In fact, lying at the core of factional conflict and constituting a boundary line for group conflict and for shifting alliances are lasting personal enmities between prominent leaders. It is personal politics with a vengeance.

The inner core of a faction, which is usually very small, is bound together by a relationship which is in many ways similar to the *guru*[24]-disciple relationship in education and religion—a relationship which is cemented by the warmest personal ties of affection and loyalty between master and disciple, leader and follower. It is the closeness of the ties among the members of the inner circle which often makes for the most intense hatred of those outside the faction. The faction leader is literally a potentate for a small circle of followers, for whom he holds a nightly *darbar* and from whom he expects unswerving and unquestioning loyalty. Men who are used to such esteem as part of their daily lives are quick to take offense when those outside the circle do not offer them sufficient respect. Trivial misunderstandings between faction leaders can lead to a lifelong enmity. As a result, an atmosphere of bitterness pervades contemporary politics in the Uttar Pradesh Congress.

To make sense out of changing factional alignments, it is essential not only to identify the participating factions, but to isolate the lasting enmities between certain faction leaders. Within the boundaries of such personal enmities, there is considerable fluidity. The enmity between C. B. Gupta and Mohan Lal Gautam was one important boundary line for Uttar Pradesh Congress factional conflicts. Since 1955, Gupta and Gautam have never formed an alliance for any reason. However, the allies of these two protagonists freely form coalitions with either side for temporary political advantage.

Alliances among faction leaders from the districts can be lasting or temporary. Like the faction itself, each group or coalition of factions has a relatively solid inner core. On the other hand, there are some faction leaders who will not form permanent political alliances with any group, but retain complete independence and switch alliances at their convenience.

The composition of factions and groups

The most important man in any faction, of course, is the leader. Moreover, there can be only one leader in a faction. Wherever there is more

[24] Spiritual teacher.

than one leader, at least for the purposes of this study, there is something broader than a faction—a group or a coalition of factions. Faction leaders differ widely in personal temperament, but an ideal type can be constructed, in many ways similar to the Japanese leader described by Scalapino and Masumi.[25] The ideal Indian faction leader has seniority, education, integrity; he has an understanding of people's personal problems and struggles; he is personally conciliatory in temperament (as long as he is shown proper respect) and is able to solve disputes. Like the Japanese leader, the Indian faction leader is politically adept; as Indians say, he has "tact" and knows the art of political manipulation. Most important, he is selfless and generous and provides money and jobs to his followers.

A faction in the Uttar Pradesh Congress might be described as a clique with a larger, fluctuating membership.[26] The inner circle of the faction remains with the leader through thick and thin, for the members of the clique are attracted to the leader by the character of his personality. The larger, fluctuating membership remains with the leader only so long as he can provide material benefits or the likelihood of material benefits in a not too distant future. These men represent the "floating vote" of internal Congress politics.

Both the members of the inner circle and the outer circle of followers generally come from diverse social and economic origins. This is true equally of the inhabitants of an *ashram*[27] and the members of a faction. It is not to say that there are no differences in the composition of factional groups. The most important social category in Uttar Pradesh politics, as elsewhere in India, is caste. Personal enmities between faction leaders occur more frequently and are more intense when the opposing leaders come from different castes. The inner core of a faction also is likely to be somewhat more socially homogeneous than the outer circle.

Table 3 shows the differences (and similarities) in caste and community composition of faction leaders in the Gupta and Sampurnanand (later called Gautam-Tripathi) groups at various times between 1958 and 1963. The predominance of Banias in the Gupta group and of Brahmans in the Sampurnanand (or Gautam-Tripathi) group are outstanding features of

[25] "The ideal Japanese leader is one possessing seniority, the personality and skill required to bring divergent elements together, and access to funds. He should be a man capable in effecting compromises, achieving a consensus—in these respects a man adept at political tactics and strategy." Robert A. Scalapino and Junnosuke Masumi, *Parties and Politics in Contemporary Japan* (Berkeley: University of California Press, 1962), p. 18.
[26] The relationship between cliques and factions is described in the context of politics in a Mysore village by Alan Beals, "Leadership in a Mysore Village," in Richard L. Park and Irene Tinker, eds., *Leadership and Political Institutions in India* (Princeton: Princeton University Press, 1959), pp. 433-437.
[27] A place of work and worship for master and disciples.

the table. Equally important is the broad spread among caste and community groups represented at all times on both sides. Social diversity dictates coalitions among caste and community groups as a political necessity. Politics works in the same direction by dividing the allegiances of various caste groups.

TABLE 3

CASTE AND COMMUNITY COMPOSITION OF GROUPS
IN THE UTTAR PRADESH CONGRESS

Caste and Community	1958 Gupta[a]	1960 Gupta[b]	1960 Sampurn-anand[c]	1963 Gautam-Tripathi[d]
Brahman	1	3	7	5
Kayastha	1	1	0	0
Rajput	0	2	4	0
Jat	0	1	1	1
Bania	5	4	1	1
Scheduled Castes	0	0	2	1
Muslim	2	1	3	0
Unknown	0	1	1	1
Total	9	13	19	9

[a] Includes the ministers who resigned from the Sampurnanand government in October, 1958.

[b] Includes the members of the Gupta group elected to the Executive Committee of the PCC in 1960.

[c] Includes the ministers of the Sampurnanand government who refused to join the Gupta government, but does not include Sampurnanand (a Kayastha) himself.

[d] Includes the ministers who resigned from the Gupta government in 1963.

There is more division among castes other than Brahmans and Banias. Since the prominent leaders of the Gupta group are Banias and the leaders of the Gautam-Tripathi group are Brahmans, the other caste groups and the Muslims tend to have weaker loyalties to either side. Political differences also divide Banias and Brahmans, so that there usually have been some Brahmans in the Gupta group and some Banias in the Gautam-Tripathi group.

The importance of district politics

The political differences which divide faction and group leaders are not differences over ideology or policy. For the most part, differences arise over political influence and patronage in a faction leader's home district. Control over the District Congress Committee (DCC) or over an important Congress-controlled district institution, such as the District Board or a municipal board, is a stepping-stone to power in state politics. Under the new system of politics that has been described in the preceding pages, the state party organization, the Pradesh Congress Committee, has great influence over the state government. The delegates to the PCC are elected from the districts. Any district Congressman who can control the votes of the delegates to the PCC from his district is a man of potential power and influence in state politics. Conversely, any man who wants power in state politics must have support in the districts.

The rise of party men from the districts to positions in the government and the extent to which groups at the state level are collections of district faction leaders is clear from the composition of the last Sampurnanand government and the first Gupta government. Among the 19 ministers of the Sampurnanand government who resigned with Dr. Sampurnanand and refused to join the first Gupta government were men representing 17 districts. Only two districts were represented by more than one minister. For 14 of the ministers, detailed biographies are available. Of the 14, 8 occupied positions on the District Congress Committee or on the District Board or on a municipal board in their home districts before joining the ministry. Three of these 8 ministers were ex-presidents of their DCCs; 1 had been secretary of his DCC and president of his District Board; 3 others had occupied important positions on their district boards, 1 as president, another as vice-president, and a third as chairman of the Education Committee; the eighth had been a member of his Municipal Board.

The proportion of influential district leaders in the first Gupta government was much greater, as should be expected. The 22 members of Gupta's first government came from 16 districts. Biographies are available for 17 ministers, of whom 12 held important positions in their districts. Nine ministers had been members or officers of their DCCs—5 were ex-presidents; all the remaining 3 had been at one time presidents of their respective district boards.

It should be noted in passing that there are no significant regional differences in the composition of the two governments. In the two governments together, ministers from 27 districts were represented. In both cases, the regional distribution was very broad—including all the important regions in the state. Six districts were represented by ministers in both governments. In fact, an important way of defeating a factional rival in a particular district is to appoint one of his opponents from his home district as a minister; the minister may then use the patronage of his ministry to build a rival faction in the district.

The most important aspect of district factional politics that must be noted is the fact that local factional systems are largely autonomous. That is, factional conflicts in the district arise out of social and political differences in the local environment. For the most part, district faction leaders bargain with leaders of groups at the state level for positions of power and patronage. However, group leaders at the state level can influence the course of factional politics in a district, as has been mentioned, by giving positions of power in the party and in the government to local faction leaders.

This integration of separate factional systems is facilitated by the institutional structure of the Congress party organizations. A detailed description of the structure of the Congress organization is given in the Appendix. Here, it is necessary to note only that the most important point of contact between the state and district party organizations comes in the selection of candidates to contest the general elections to the state Assembly and to Parliament and to contest important local elections, such as the chairmanship of district and municipal boards. The procedure followed is that the DCCs make recommendations to the state Parliamentary Board, which may accept the recommendations of the local committees, choose from a number of names when more than one candidate is recommended, or may even select a candidate not recommended by the DCC. Thus it is of some importance for district faction leaders to be associated with group leaders in the state party organization. The situation is very much like what would exist if the British system of party organization were imposed upon American politics.

It follows from this description of the internal politics of the Congress organization in Uttar Pradesh that state Congress politics cannot be understood without a knowledge of political behavior in the districts. The rest of this study will be concerned with the patterns of politics and with the struggle for power in five district Congress organizations. In each district, the analysis will center around the causes, the character, and the consequences of Congress factionalism for the functioning of the Congress organization at the grass roots level. The analyses will be organized around three aspects of Congress organization—the motivations and aspirations of faction leaders; the ability of the Congress to operate local institutions of self-government and cooperation; and the capacity of the Congress to win elections. A special chapter will be devoted to the relationships between the local Congress and the local administration. In all of the district case studies, the interrelationships between district and state politics will be shown.

A major concern of the case studies will be to relate the problems of Congress organization and the character of local factionalism to the social and economic environments in which the Congress must operate. Districts have been selected for case studies to present as sharply as possible some of the problems which exist in the environment of the Congress party in Uttar Pradesh, to illustrate the diversity of that environment, and to discover the effect of different environments upon the ability of the Congress to function successfully. Although much of the analysis that follows is concerned with factions, the Congress will be studied as a political organization in all its aspects, so that factionalism may be seen in the context of the total political activity of the local Congress organizations.

The districts selected (see fig. 4) provide a cross section of the economic

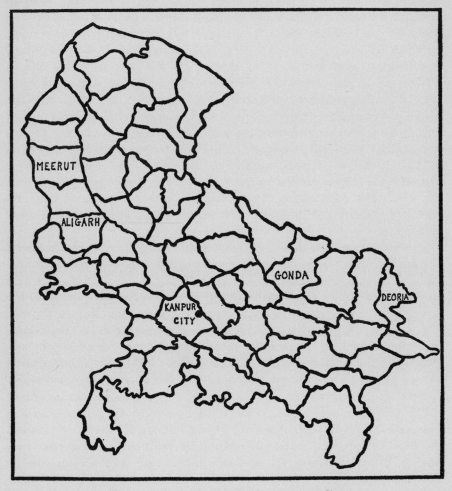

Fig. 4. Districts selected for case studies.

and social environments in Uttar Pradesh.[28] In Gonda, the functioning of the Congress is analyzed in an environment traditionally dominated by the owners and managers of large landed estates. In Aligarh, the Congress oper-

[28] The socio-economic environment of each district selected is discussed in the introductions to the case studies. The following table summarizes some of the available

ates in a setting of Hindu-Muslim tension. Politics in Deoria district center around the problems of people involved in the sugar industry. Meerut provides a contrast to Gonda, for Meerut is a district where peasant proprietor castes dominate economic and political life. Finally, the working of the Congress organization will be studied in Kanpur, the great industrial city of Uttar Pradesh.

statistics on area and population for the four rural districts (Gonda, Aligarh, Meerut, and Deoria) analyzed.

Characteristic[a]	Gonda	Aligarh	Meerut	Deoria
Area				
Square miles	2,829	1,941	2,322	2,087
Rank[b]	7	27	17	24
Population				
Persons	2,073,237	1,765,275	2,712,960	2,375,075
Rank	9	11	1	7
Rural Density (1951)				
No. of persons per square mile	635	672	802	982
Rank[c]	18	15	9	1
Urban population				
Percent	4.9	16.2	20.6	2.4
Rank	38	16	11	45
Literacy				
Percent	11.7	19.8	22.4	14.1
Rank	50	18	11	39
Scheduled Castes (1951)				
Percent	7.7	16.6	13.5	13.6
Rank[c]	50	28	40	39

Sources: *Census of India, 1961, Paper No. 1 of 1962: Final Population Totals; Census of India, 1951, Paper No. 1 of 1957* and Vol. II: *Uttar Pradesh,* by Rajeshwari Prasad, Pt. I-A—*Report* (Allahabad: Superintendent, Printing and Stationery, 1953).

[a] Figures from 1961 census unless otherwise stated.
[b] Out of 54 districts.
[c] Out of 51 districts.

IV.

Gonda: Party Rebellion

THE ENVIRONMENT

Gonda, with an area of 2,829 square miles and a population just over 2,000,000, is one of the largest districts in Uttar Pradesh, ranking eighth in area and ninth in population. Its large area gives the district a density precisely on the median for the state as a whole—733 persons per square mile. The district is overwhelmingly rural, containing a town population of less than 5 percent of the total.[1] Only two towns in the district are of considerable size: the largest is Gonda, with a population close to 45,000, followed by Balrampur, with a population of over 30,000.[2]

In terms of agriculture, industry, communications, health, and education, Gonda is one of the most backward districts in the state. There are eight fairly large sugar mills in the district, most of them old and decrepit and, like the other sugar mills in eastern Uttar Pradesh, economically inefficient in comparison with the newer mills in western Uttar Pradesh and in south India. Aside from the sugar industry, there is no other industry of any importance in the district. New agricultural methods are being introduced in Gonda, as elsewhere in Uttar Pradesh under community development, but progress has been slow. Rice, corn, wheat, and sugar cane are the principal crops of the district. Roads are poor, rutted, and unpaved in many parts of the district and bazaars difficult to reach for a large proportion of the agricultural population. Male literacy is 12.3 percent, the seventh lowest in the state.[3]

Geographically, the district is divided neatly into two portions by the Rapti River, which flows west to east across the northern half of the dis-

[1] *Census of India, 1961, Paper No. 1 of 1962, Final Population Totals*, pp. 350-351.
[2] *Ibid.*, pp. 238-239.
[3] *Ibid.*, p. 351.

trict. Between the Rapti River and the Nepal border, the soil and climate are typical of the *tarai* regions of India. Below the Rapti River, the southern portion of the district merges into the eastern Gangetic plain.

The ethnic diversity of the population is as marked in Gonda as elsewhere in Uttar Pradesh. Numerically, Brahmans, Muslims, Koris, Ahirs, Kurmis, and Rajputs, in that order, are the best represented communities in the district.[4] The better-educated and more politically active communities are Brahmans and Rajputs in the rural areas and, in the towns, the usual urban castes of Banias, Khatris, and Kayasthas.

The aspect of the socio-economic environment of the district which is most relevant to this case study is the pattern of land tenure. Gonda district, like the rest of Oudh before *zamindari* abolition, was a land of great estates; over two-thirds of the nearly 3,000 villages of the district were owned outright by or paid their land revenues to 24 *talukdars*. Of the 24 *talukdars*, the most numerous and the most prominent were Rajputs; before *zamindari* abolition, there were 16 Rajput, 3 Brahman, 3 Sikh, and 2 Muslim *talukdars* in the district.[5]

The *talukdars* of Oudh never have formed a cohesive political group. A number of attempts have been made, before and after Independence, to exploit politically and collectively the enormous influence of these great landed proprietors, but with little success.[6] Many of the *talukdars* have been active in politics in their own districts, sometimes as independents, other times associated with various political parties. In post-Independence politics, all the political parties have tried to use the influence of the *talukdars* by offering them party tickets to contest the general elections.

The case sudy which follows is not intended to be an analysis of the role of the *talukdars* in politics. The focus of this study is upon the Congress organization. The *talukdari* system was a special kind of rural environment in which the Congress had to operate before Independence and for four years after Independence. In 1951, the *talukdari* system was abolished; but, even today, the rural environment in Gonda district and in Oudh as a whole is affected profoundly by the influence of the old *talukdars* and their descendants. What is presented here is a case study of how the Congress developed and how it maintains itself in this kind of rural environment.

[4] *Census of India, 1921*, Vol. XVI: *United Provinces of Agra and Oudh,* by E. H. H. Edye, Pt. I (Allahabad: Government Press, 1923), table XIII.

[5] *District Gazetteers of the United Provinces of Agra and Oudh,* Vol. XLIV: *Gonda,* by H. R. Nevill (Naini Tal: Government Press, 1905), pp. 76-77.

[6] P. D. Reeves gives an acount of attempts and failures to organize the landlords of Uttar Pradesh for political action in the period between 1920 and 1937 in "Landlord Associations in U. P. and Their Role in Landlord Politics, 1920-1937," n.d. (Mimeographed.)

THE GONDA CONGRESS: THE RULE
OF THE RAJA OF MANKAPUR

The development of factional conflict

On November 17, 1955, the President of the Uttar Pradesh Congress Committee (UPCC) announced in Gonda: "I have expelled Mr. Baldeo Singh, President of the Gonda District Congress Committee from the primary membership of the Congress for an indefinite period and I will not fail to take similar drastic action against anybody, whoever he may be, if I find him playing a disruptionist role in the Congress." [7] The announcement was made from the house of Mr. Ishwar Saran, the Congress candidate in a bye-election being held in the district. Baldeo Singh was expelled because he had turned "rebel," after being refused the Congress ticket for the bye-election, and was contesting the election as an independent against the official Congress candidate. Baldeo Singh, with the help of most of the prominent Congressmen of the district, defeated the official Congress candidate. True to his threat "to take similar drastic action" against "disruptionists" in the Congress, the UPCC President announced in Lucknow on January 24, 1956, that the UPCC Council had expelled twenty-four Congressmen of Gonda district for working against the Congress candidate. Among the Congressmen expelled were two MLAs, the Chairman of the District Board of Gonda, and two officers and fifteen regular members of the DCC.[8] On the following day, the Congress President dissolved the entire DCC and appointed an *ad hoc* Congress committee in its place.[9]

With these weighty words and drastic actions, the President of the Uttar Pradesh Congress destroyed an active and powerful district Congress organization. In this chapter, the reasons for the breakup of the Gonda Congress and the consequences for the later development of the Congress organization in the district will be described. The conflict over the Congress ticket in this bye-election was not really between Ishwar Saran and Baldeo Singh, but between Ishwar Saran and Raghvendra Pratap Singh, the informal leader of the Gonda Congress at the time and the *talukdar* of one of the largest estates in the district from 1942 until 1951. To understand the reasons for this conflict, it is necessary to go back to an earlier period in the history of the Gonda Congress.

The first Congress Committee in Gonda district was established in 1908 by Babu Bindeshwari Prasad, a Kayastha from Lucknow. Bindeshwari Prasad came to Gonda town in the same year, after receiving his law degree

[7] *National Herald*, November 18, 1955.
[8] *National Herald*, January 24, 1956.
[9] *National Herald*, January 25, 1956.

from Allahabad University, to practice with his brother-in-law before joining the High Court at Allahabad. However, Bindeshwari Prasad did so well in Gonda that he decided to remain there. Bindeshwari Prasad became president of the Gonda Congress Committee in 1908 and remained president until 1934. In the late twenties, Bindeshwari Prasad was elected chairman of the District Board, a position which he occupied until 1935.[10]

The Congress organization in Gonda district did not prosper under the guidance of Babu Bindeshwari Prasad. Bindeshwari Prasad belonged to an older generation of Congressmen who had joined the Congress organization before Gandhi's arrival; he did not believe in jail-going and did not go to jail in any of the movements. In 1934, Ishwar Saran, a contractor, also a Kayastha of Gonda town, became president of the District Congress Committee. Ishwar Saran had come into prominence under the patronage of Bindeshwari Prasad, but he belonged to the younger, jail-going generation of Congressmen. Shortly after Ishwar Saran became president of the DCC, personal differences developed between him and Bindeshwari Prasad, with the result that the latter left the Congress. Ishwar Saran tried to manage the Congress as a family concern; he remained president of the DCC himself until 1938, when his brother was elected president.

Factional conflict within the Gonda Congress developed during the regime of Ishwar Saran. Up till this time, the Gonda Congress had been run largely by people from Gonda town. The situation changed in 1930, when Raghvendra Pratap Singh, a Rajput and the younger brother of the Raja of Mankapur, joined the Congress. The Mankapur raj was a fairly large estate of Gonda district, collecting revenue from about 200 villages in Mankapur and Nawabganj parganas of Utraula tahsil. Raghvendra Pratap was studying in England in 1930; he returned from England to participate in Gandhi's Dandi march, which opened the Salt Satyagraha of 1930-1931. He was jailed in this movement, again in 1932, and again in 1941. When Raghvendra Pratap returned to Gonda and joined the Congress organization, he found that "Kayasthas and vakils (lawyers)" of Gonda town "controlled the Congress and the District Board."[11] The position on the District Board was changed in 1935 when Raghvendra Pratap's elder brother became chairman. Raghvendra Pratap himself was not so successful immediately in wresting control of the district Congress from the "Kayasthas and vakils." In 1936, Raghvendra Pratap set up one of his men to contest the election for president of the DCC against Ishwar Saran, but his man was defeated. In 1938, Raghvendra Pratap again set up a candidate against the brother of Ishwar Saran and again was defeated.

During the struggle for control over the Gonda Congress, a lasting per-

[10] Interview in Gonda on August 15, 1962.
[11] Interview in Mankapur on August 19, 1962.

sonal enmity developed between Ishwar Saran and Raghvendra Pratap. After the 1938 DCC election, there was no occasion for conflict between the two men until after the war, since most Congressmen were in jail in this period. Raghvendra Pratap himself was jailed in 1941, but was released soon afterwards in connection with a dispute with his younger brother over the inheritance of the estate. The circumstances of his release from prison in 1942 led to personal recrimination by Ishwar Saran against him. At the Bombay session of the All India Congress Committee (AICC) in 1946, both Ishwar Saran and Raghvendra Pratap were delegates; Ishwar Saran objected at the meeting to the seating of Raghvendra Pratap, arguing that the latter had obtained release from prison in 1942 by apologizing to the authorities. The following year, Ishwar Saran again came into conflict with Raghvendra Pratap, now the Raja of Mankapur, by leading a delegation of *kisans* (peasants) of Gonda district to Lucknow, where a complaint was lodged with the UPCC and the Uttar Pradesh government that the Mankapur estate, among others, was extracting *begar* (forced labor) from its tenants and was ejecting large numbers of tenants from their lands.[12]

Despite Ishwar Saran's attempts to discredit and remove his rival in the Gonda Congress, the Raja succeeded in taking control of the District Congress Committee in the early postwar period. Ishwar Saran himself resigned from the Congress in 1948 along with the Socialists who left the Congress in that year. From 1948 until 1955, the Gonda Congress remained largely a private preserve of the Raja of Mankapur. With his main rival in the Gonda Congress gone, the Raja was able to gain control not only of the district Congress, but of the District Board, the District Cooperative Development Federation, and the Cane Unions. The Raja thus controlled both the district Congress and local government and cooperative institutions.

The state leadership of the Congress party had no reason to be unhappy with the Gonda Congress under the leadership of the Raja. In the 1952 election, nine Congressmen were returned to the state Assembly out of eleven seats in the district. Relations between C. B. Gupta, the state party manager, and the Raja were excellent. Then, in 1953, Ishwar Saran, tired of his sojourn in the political wilderness, rejoined the Congress and succeeded in gaining the support of Mohan Lal Gautam, C. B. Gupta's bitter rival in the state party organization.[13] Ishwar Saran returned to prominence in the political affairs of Gonda town in the same year, when he was elected chairman of the Municipal Board.

The opportunity for a direct challenge to his old rival in the Gonda Congress did not come to Ishwar Saran again until 1955, when an Assembly

---

[12] *Leader*, August 16, 1947.
[13] A description of Congress groups at the state level is given in chap. iii.

seat in the district fell vacant and a bye-election was scheduled for the end of the year. The candidate of the Raja's group was the manager of the Mankapur estate and the president of the DCC, Baldeo Singh. Ishwar Saran was supported at the state level by Mohan Lal Gautam. Baldeo Singh's name was accepted unanimously by the state Parliamentary Board (controlled at this time by C. B. Gupta) and sent to the Central Parliamentary Board. Mohan Lal Gautam worked tirelessly on behalf of Ishwar Saran and succeeded in persuading the members of the Central Parliamentary Board that Ishwar Saran should be given the ticket. The Central Board overruled the state Board and Ishwar Saran was declared the official Congress candidate in the bye-election.

The impact of the selection of Ishwar Saran upon the Gonda Congress organization has been shown. The question is, why did a relatively minor dispute over a party ticket lead to the destruction of an entire district Congress organization? Within the local Congress, we have traced the development of conflict between Ishwar Saran and Raghvendra Pratap, which resulted in bitter personal enmity between the two men. Raghvendra Pratap was not prepared to have his control over the district Congress questioned through the interference of party leaders from Lucknow and Delhi. Raghvendra Pratap felt that party leaders from outside were bent upon "lowering his prestige . . . . Gautam was really behind it all. They [outside party leaders] put up Ishwar Saran and they wanted to make him the leader. Ishwar Saran was of Socialist views and was encouraged to rejoin the Congress. My party was the controlling factor, and was in a majority in the district at the time." [14] To the Raja, the selection of Ishwar Saran was a personal affront and an attempt to "lower his prestige." Ishwar Saran's "Socialist views" were less important than the personal enmity between the two men. When outside political leaders attempted to impose Ishwar Saran upon him, the Raja "felt harassed and politically run down in his district."[15]

The personal enmity between the two men was such that they simply could not tolerate each other and work together in the same organization. The second question, then, is why did Mohan Lal Gautam give his support to Ishwar Saran? What could Gautam hope to gain by interfering in local rivalries? A participant in Gonda Congress politics at the time gives the answer: "Ishwar Saran was supported by Mohan Lal Gautam for the Congress ticket in the bye-election. . . . There were two parties in the province. C. B. Gupta and Sampurnanand wanted Baldeo Singh to have the ticket. . . . C. B. Gupta was helping the Raja because, on Ishwar Saran's resignation [in 1948], there was no other party except the Raja. So, he helped the Raja for four or five years. Then, because C. B. Gupta was helping the

[14] Interview with Raghvendra Pratap Singh in Lucknow on April 25, 1962.
[15] *Ibid.*

Raja, so Mohan Lal Gautam helped Ishwar Saran."[16] Mohan Lal Gautam
was attempting to set up, through Ishwar Saran, a group loyal to him in the
district, which would provide delegate votes for him in the PCC elections
in his battle for control of the state party organization.

Ironically enough, the PCC, which took such drastic action against the
Raja and his followers, was controlled by the Gupta group. The PCC really
had no other choice; there had been flagrant indiscipline in the actions of
leading Congressmen of the district against the official Congress candidate.
Despite the expulsion of the Raja from the Congress, Mohan Lal Gautam
gained no immediate advantage in Gonda politics against the Gupta group.
Ishwar Saran was defeated in his election and the officers of the new *ad hoc*
Congress Committee were selected by C. B. Gupta. Both sides lost in the
conflict and the strength of the Congress organization in the district suffered
most of all; in the 1957 election, the Raja and his followers contested the
elections in several constituencies in the district as independents and defeated the Congress in four. In the district as a whole, the Congress lost
eight seats out of thirteen; whereas, in 1952, the Congress had lost only
two seats out of eleven.

This brief history of the Gonda Congress reveals a number of aspects of
party organization and factional conflict in Uttar Pradesh, which will be
illustrated again in other districts. First, the primacy of factional interest
over party loyalty is apparent. The Raja and his followers felt that their
position of dominance was being threatened by the selection of an old
rival for the Congress ticket and by the intervention of outside leaders;
rather than submit to such a threat, the Raja chose to work against and defeat the official Congress candidate, even if it meant expulsion of his group
from the Congress. Second is the importance of personal prestige and personal enmity in factional conflict. The Raja, a rural-based Rajput, and Ishwar Saran, a Kayastha from the town, were natural opponents from the
start and fast became bitter personal enemies. The Raja could not tolerate
the selection of Ishwar Saran as the Congress candidate because it seemed
to be an attempt to lower his prestige. The Raja was, thus, reacting to a
threat both to his political dominance and to his personal status. Finally, this
history reveals something about the relationship between local and state
party leaders—that the relationship is an informal one between local factional leaders and state factional leaders, brought together by mutual interest. Ishwar Saran and Mohan Lal Gautam had nothing in common except
that Gautam could offer Ishwar Saran an Assembly ticket in return for the
latter's support in factional conflict at the state level.

[16] Interview in Lucknow on October 18, 1962.

The Raja of Mankapur

The history of the Gonda Congress raises two general questions about the role of large, landed interests in party politics. First, there is the question why a man like the Raja of Mankapur chose to join the Congress, which was, even during the nationalist movement, openly working toward the "emancipation" of the tenants from the *zamindars* and *talukdars* and toward the abolition of *zamindari*. The second question is how the Raja was able to operate so successfully in Congress politics after *zamindari* abolition; that is, what were the sources of the Raja's strength in local politics?

The first question, essentially, asks what incentives the Raja of Mankapur had for participation in the nationalist movement and in the Congress organization. One cannot discount purely nationalist motivations for Raghvendra Pratap's decision to leave England and join Gandhi's Civil Disobedience movement. When Raghvendra Pratap first joined the Congress, he was a young man and had no direct responsibility for the estate, which was then in the hands of his elder brother. It is said that Raghvendra Pratap joined the Congress against the express wishes of his family. Moreover, Raghvendra Pratap's participation in the movement nearly cost him the inheritance of the estate; for, his elder brother died in 1941 when Raghvendra Pratap was in jail. Had Raghvendra Pratap not secured his release from jail at that time, the estate would have gone to his younger brother.

Patriotism was certainly a factor in Raghvendra Pratap's decision, but other motives were also present. For one thing, it was considered a great sacrifice by others for a man of wealth, with a secure position in society, to take the risks to his personal security and fortune involved in joining the Congress and participating in the movements. Older Congressmen in Gonda have remarked that they were very much impressed when Raghvendra Pratap joined the Congress, that a person of his wealth and status would take the step. Thus, the act of joining the Congress gave to Raghvendra Pratap the esteem of Congressmen and of public opinion in general, at a time when the *talukdars* and *zamindars* were considered enemies of the nationalist cause and friends of the British. Renunciation is one of the highest virtues in Indian society; Raghvendra Pratap received esteem in proportion to his sacrifice for his participation in the movement.

However, Raghvendra Pratap's participation in the movement was not all sacrifice. Even before Independence, the material rewards of party politics were great. Most of the local government and cooperative institutions, which are now the instruments for implementing the national plan, were in existence before Independence. Control of these local institutions always has been the major prize in district politics. In a sense, Raghvendra Pratap succeeded, for a time, in enlarging his *zamindari* to include the whole district. Through the local government and cooperative institutions which came under the control of the Raja's faction, Raghvendra Pratap could distribute more loans and jobs than were ever available through the Mankapur estate; his return was not the land revenue, but the political loyalty of his beneficiaries, which made of him something more than a large *zamindar*— in the words of one local politician, Raghvendra Pratap became "the uncrowned king of Gonda district."

Finally, there was genuine economic advantage for a large *talukdar* in the Congress. The terms of the Zamindari Abolition Act were not harsh in the first place and could be made more advantageous for a *zamindar* who had influence with the state Congress leadership and with the local administrative staff. After *zamindari* abolition, the Raja of Mankapur was left with 2,000 acres of land still in his private possession—a large estate by any standard and huge in a country where four acres is an average landholding.

Few *zamindars* in Uttar Pradesh were left with this much land after *zamindari* abolition. Still fewer put their resources to such advantageous use —politically and economically—as did the Raja of Mankapur. There were many larger estates in Uttar Pradesh than Mankapur, but there are few in Uttar Pradesh today so well-maintained and so prosperous as Mankapur. Most of the large ex-*zamindars* in Uttar Pradesh today live in decaying mansions and constantly are forced to sell off their lands to maintain what little they have left. The Raja of Mankapur was as wise economically as he was successful politically. Today, the Mankapur estate is a small-sized agro-industrial complex, including 2,000 acres of land, a livestock farm, a 350,000-rupee cold storage, a tube well parts distributing agency, a petrol tank, and a mango canning factory.

The Raja of Mankapur could afford to break with the Congress organization because he had a political and economic base in his old *zamindari* area, from which it would have been difficult to dislodge him. When the Raja was in Mankapur, there was a steady stream of visitors to his veranda, mostly villagers and ex-tenants from the surrounding area, coming to him for favors, loans, support in local disputes. No less than fourteen village panchayat presidents were personal employees of the Raja. Baldeo Singh, the manager of the Mankapur estate, is also president of the Mankapur Community Development Block, which includes over a hundred villages. The Raja himself was president of the Mankapur Cooperative Cane Growers' Union, which determines the quota of cane to be collected from each cultivator served by the Union, takes it from him for delivery to the factory, pays him, and gives him loans when he needs them.

Another source of strength for the Raja was an alliance with a nearby estate, owned by the Raja of Gonda. The Gonda Raja is not now active in local politics, but the manager of the estate, Ragho Ram Pande, a Brahman, had been a loyal ally of Raghvendra Pratap for many years. Ragho Ram Pande was the Secretary of the DCC in 1955 and was expelled from the Congress at the same time as Raghvendra Pratap. The Gonda estate at one time included almost the whole of Gonda district; at the time of *zamindari* abolition, it was the second largest estate in the district. Ragho Ram Pande, the manager of the estate, has a network of influence in the area of the old Gonda estate which complemented that of the Raja of Mankapur. Ragho Ram Pande himself has been the president of Jhanjhari Community Development Block, chairman of the Gonda Cane Union, and a member of the Board of Directors of the District Cooperative Development Federation. Ragho Ram Pande added ethnic strength to the alliance as well. The followers of Raghvendra Pratap were mostly Rajputs, those of Ragho Ram Pande Brahmans. Brahmans are the most numerous caste in the district and in every subdivision of the district but one. Brahmans and Rajputs are also the two most influential and the largest proprietary castes in the district.

The Raja of Mankapur, through his personal resources and through a strong alliance with another large estate, thus had a formidable political and economic base in the district. In the remainder of this chapter, we will be concerned with the resources which the local Congress can bring to bear against such a political opponent.

The Gonda Congress after the split

The Raja of Mankapur had so effectively dominated the Gonda Congress during his period of control that, when he and his followers were expelled, there was no single Congressman in the district with a large enough following even to attempt to take control of the DCC. Ishwar Saran had long ago lost his group following inside the Congress organization and, as we saw, gained no advantage from the Raja's expulsion. After the Raja's expulsion, the Gonda Congress became essentially a coalition of leaders without followers, none of whom was sufficiently strong to dominate the organization.

For president of the first *ad hoc* Congress Committee, appointed in 1956, the state party leadership selected Lal Bihari Tandon, a Khatri and a lawyer of Gonda town. Tandon is one of the oldest Congressmen of Gonda district —a man with little group following and one who had generally avoided factional controversies. The general secretary was Sant Baks Singh, a younger Congressman, a Rajput, and a lawyer from Balrampur town. Another secretary and later president of the DCC was Balbhadra Prasad Shukla, originally a small tenant-farmer from rural Balrampur, a Brahman, and a full-time Congress worker. An alliance largely of middle-class professional people from the towns and middle-class farmers was put together with men such as these. The only Congressmen with greater wealth and more status were Syed Ali Jarrar Jafery, a Muslim and the manager of the Balrampur estate, and Devendra Pratap Singh, the brother of the Raja of Mankapur, himself the owner of 1,000 acres of land formerly part of the Mankapur estate. Each of these men had some factional following in his local area, based upon personal influence or control of some local government, cooperative, social service, or educational institution. None had a base as large or as secure as that of the Raja of Mankapur. Yet, by careful coordination amongst themselves and with the state Congress leadership, the local Congress was able eventually to defeat the Raja's party in the fight for control of local institutions and in the General Elections of 1962. The methods and resources which the Congress used to defeat the Raja will be described below.

THE FIGHT FOR CONTROL OF LOCAL INSTITUTIONS

The Raja's faction, expelled from the dominant Congress party in the district, operated as a locally autonomous opposition party in the 1957 elections. After the expulsion of the Raja's faction, the Congress had to face a situation in which the Raja and his followers controlled most local government and cooperative institutions and, after the 1957 elections, occupied a position of electoral dominance in a large territorial segment of the district. In 1959, the Raja and his followers formally joined the Swatantra party, formed on an all-India basis in the same year. The development of the Raja's faction into a locally powerful opposition political party offers an opportunity to test Key's hypothesis that increased interparty competition leads to decreased intraparty factionalism.[17]

A direct test of the Key hypothesis is complicated by the fact that district politics in Uttar Pradesh is integrated into and, in some respects, inseparable from state politics. Some factional politics is bound to continue in every district as long as factional politics continues to dominate the internal affairs of the Congress party at the state level and as long as there are state party leaders eager to form loyal local factions. However, since five district Congress organizations will be examined, all operating within the same framework of state-level factional politics but with different degrees of interparty competition, it will be possible to control the effects of factionalism at the state level upon the internal cohesion of the local Congress organizations. As each district is discussed, it will be necessary to describe the extent and effects of external influences upon local factional conflicts.

[17] V. O. Key, Jr., *Politics, Parties, and Pressure Groups* (3d ed.; New York: Thomas Y. Crowell Co., 1952), p. 351.

Factional alliance: The District Board Presidency

Political dominance of a district rests less upon the number of members of a party or a faction elected to the state Legislative Assembly than upon control of the local government and cooperative institutions within the district itself. It is the local government and cooperative institutions in the district which distribute most of the patronage available. Under the new scheme of "democratic decentralization" currently being implemented in Uttar Pradesh,[18] the President of the District Board has become one of the most powerful men in each district. In most districts in Uttar Pradesh, where interparty competition is less keen than in Gonda, the selection of the District Board president has been a major cause of factional conflict. In Gonda, where the fight for the District Board presidency was an interparty struggle, the contest served to unite, if only temporarily, all factions within the local Congress.

There were two major reasons for factional unity within the Congress during this election, which was held in November, 1961. One was, clearly, that the District Board president controls the greatest amount of patronage available in the district;[19] to lose control of the District Board means the loss of political dominance in the district. Second, little could be gained by opposing or "sabotaging" the election of the Congress candidate. Until virtually the last minute, the Swatantra party had a clear majority on the Board,[20] and therefore the bargaining power of individual Congress leaders was small, since the Swatantra already had the majority. How the Congress succeeded in overcoming the Swatantra majority on the Board is an interesting case study in factional alliance. The study also will throw some light upon the role of government in keeping the Congress in power.

The new scheme of "democratic decentralization" has been carried out in stages and has been carefully designed, in each stage, to ensure that the Congress will be in control of the district board in every district in Uttar Pradesh. When the first election of presidents of the boards took place under the new legislation,[21] the boards were composed partly of elected,

[18] See chap. ix.

[19] The most important source of patronage for the District Board President is the power to appoint and transfer village primary school teachers. Eventually, every *gaon sabha* in Uttar Pradesh will have a primary school. Even now, the District Board President in a district such as Gonda has control over upward of 1,000 jobs from this source alone.

[20] Election of the president of the District Board is "indirect," that is, by the members of the Board and not by the general electorate.

[21] In 1958, the old District Boards were merged with the District Planning Committees in each district and placed under the chairmanship of the district magistrates. In June, 1961, elections were held in most districts in Uttar Pradesh for presidents of the

partly of nonelected members. Of the nonelected members, some became members by virtue of holding some other position in local government or educational institutions, others were direct nominees of the state government. To overcome the Swatantra majority on the Board required careful coordination between local Congress leaders and the state Congress party and government leadership, as well as among local factional leaders themselves.

By agreement among local Congress leaders, Sant Baks Singh was the Congress candidate. Until the District Board election, Sant Baks Singh had been a member of the Gautam-Tripathi group, defeated in state politics by C. B. Gupta. However, Gupta reportedly agreed to support Sant Baks Singh in the District Board election and the latter's candidacy was approved by the state Parliamentary Board.

The support of the state Congress leadership was essential in the election of Sant Baks Singh. Under the rules for membership of the district boards, all MPs, MLAs, and members of the Legislative Council (MLCs) of the district automatically become members. Where an MP represents a constituency which includes portions of two districts, the MP is entitled to choose which board he wishes to join; also, where an MP, MLA, or MLC is a resident of one district but elected from another district, he can choose the board he wishes to join. Through the influence of the state Congress leadership, three MPs and one MLA who had previously been members of district boards in neighboring districts, were persuaded to opt for membership of the Gonda Board instead. Thus, the Congress hoped to add four votes to its side in one blow.

Local Congressmen found other equally ingenious ways of adding new, voting members to the Gonda Board. For example, it was discovered that a number of important local Congressmen occupied two or more institutional positions, each of which entitled them to mempership on the Board. Thus, it was found that one Congressman occupied the positions of managing director of the District Cooperative Bank and vice-president of the District Cooperative Development Federation: either position entitled him to membership of the District Board. It was decided that this Congressman should resign from the vice-presidency of the DCDF and that another Congressman should be elected in his place, thus adding another Congress vote to the District Board. Another Congressman had a triple right to membership of the Board, as a government nominee, as the district convener of the Bharat Sewak Samaj,[22] and as an MLC. This Congressman resigned from the first two positions, another Congressman was nominated by the govern-

---

District Boards, who then took over charge from the district magistrates. In Gonda, as a result of litigation, the elections were not held until November, 1961.

[22] A nongovernmental social service organization.

ment to the Board in his place, and still another Congressman was elected as convener of the Bharat Sewak Samaj. A third Congressman held a dual right to membership of the Board in his capacities as a government nominee and as the chairman of the Municipal Board, Balrampur; he resigned the first position and was replaced by a new Government nominee. In such ways, local Congressmen hoped to add nine or ten additional votes for their candidate. Not all of the attempts were successful; many were frustrated through writ petitions filed in the courts by the Swatantra party candidate and through other ways. The number of successes and failures, however, is less important than the high degree of cooperation among local Congressmen which such maneuvering involved. In the end, the local Congress, through these and other similar maneuvers, succeeded in adding two or three additional Congress votes to the District Board. The addition, small as it was, proved decisive; the Congress candidate defeated his Swatantra opponent on November 3, 1961, by 36 votes to 35.

In most districts in Uttar Pradesh, the position of District Board president and other offices in local government and cooperative institutions are a major source of factional conflict within the local Congress and simultaneously instruments of patronage for state party leaders who wish to build loyal groups in the districts. The selection of the Congress candidate for the Board presidency is generally hotly contested within the local Congress and in the state Parliamentary Board, which makes the final decision, sometimes ignoring the wishes of the dominant local faction. In Gonda, where the Swatantra threat was serious, the selection of Sant Baks Singh as the Congress candidate caused no friction either at the local or the state level. The same threat of loss of control of the District Board also made it possible for local and state Congress leaders to collaborate in some rather delicate maneuvering. The Congress operated, during this struggle, with a degree of cohesion that did not exist before the election and distintegrated immediately after success was achieved.

Factional Conflict: The District Cooperative Development Federation

Both before and after the District Board election, there were factional conflicts for control of some of the other local institutions in the district. The case of the District Cooperative Development Federation (DCDF) is an example. The DCDF is the apex institution in the district for most of the local cooperative societies engaged in production, marketing, and distribution. The DCDF distributes fertilizers, builds and operates brick-kilns, distributes iron and cement, and sometimes has a hand in the distribution of consumers' goods as well. The DCDF is, thus, clearly an important agency for the distribution of goods, services, and patronage; for this reason, it is a prize for contending factions.

Like the District Board, the structure of the DCDF is designed to ensure that this important source of patronage does not fall into the hands of opposition political parties. The chairman of the DCDF is the District Magistrate, who normally does not attend the meetings, but who can exercise powers of decision and voting when necessary or when government wishes him to do so. The Assistant Registrar of Cooperative Societies for the district is also a member of the Board of Directors of the DCDF. In addition to the two government officers, there are two direct government nominees on the Board, which includes eleven members in all. The vice-chairman and the six remaining members are elected by the Annual General Meeting of the Federation. The two district officers generally try to keep aloof from open factional and party struggles, but are often forced to support the Congress on serious matters and decisive votes. Normally, however, the affairs of the DCDF are handled by the Honorary Secretary, the effective executive head of the organization and one of the two Government nominees; the Honorary Secretary also maintains the records of the Federation.

The position of Honorary Secretary of the DCDF is an instrument of patronage in the hands of the Minister of Cooperation in the state government, who can appoint to this position someone in the district who, in turn, will support the Minister by building a group loyal to the latter in the district. Thus, in 1959 when Mohan Lal Gautam was Minister of Cooperation, he appointed his old friend Ishwar Saran to this office. When Gupta became chief minister in 1960 and Gautam went out of the ministry, the new Minister of Cooperation disposed of Gautam's political appointees in the districts and substituted his own. A minister cannot simply replace at will a government appointee whose term has not expired, however. In order to replace a government nominee, there must be some evidence of malfeasance. Thus, local factional leaders opposed to Ishwar Saran presented various charges against him for corruption and embezzlement to the Minister, who then had grounds for ousting Ishwar Saran and making a new appointment.

The Congressman who replaced Ishwar Saran as Honorary Secretary remained in office only until the next change in the Ministry of Cooperation occurred. After the 1962 election, a new minister was placed in charge of Cooperation. In the district, local Congressmen followed the same practice that had been used with Ishwar Saran; charges of misappropriation and misuse of funds were sent to the Minister of Cooperation, who then removed the new Honorary Secretary and replaced him with another factional leader. A former official of the DCDF described this second change-over as follows: "A, B, C, and D were all against E [the Honarary Secretary] because he was . . . misappropriating and misusing the funds of the DCDF. On that ground, he [the Honorary Secretary] was removed. A representation to the Minister was sent by some public man. [On behalf of these people?] Yes, on behalf of these people, led by D and he too was once Honorary Secretary and he too misappropriated funds." [23]

Factional struggle over the position of Honorary Secretary was both open and bitter, involving serious criminal charges against the persons involved. Since the position of Honorary Secretary is appointive, unlike the position of chairman of the District Board, factional struggle can go on without the possibility of a loss of the position to the opposition. Where there is no compulsion for unity posed by interparty competition, factional conflict within the Congress, which always exists below even the most placid-looking surface, explodes.

The cohesion of the local Congress clearly is not aided by the participation of party and government leaders from Lucknow. However, outside leaders do not generate factional antagonisms; the antagonisms exist at the local level and are simply helped along by outside participation. The interference of outside leaders in local rivalries makes it impossible for a single faction to gain and maintain control of the local Congress organization and Congress-controlled institutions of patronage in the district. Government thus contributes to the continuance of factional politics in the district in two ways—directly, by participation in local, internal Congress politics, and, indirectly, by framing and manipulating rules and regulations to ensure that opposition political parties cannot threaten the dominance of the Congress over local institutions.

THE 1962 GENERAL ELECTIONS: CONGRESS AGAINST SWATANTRA

The center of Swatantra influence in Gonda lies in the south-central portion of the district below the Rapti River. In electoral terms, Swatantra strength in the district is concentrated within the Gonda parliamentary constituency, which includes five Assembly constituencies—Mankapur, Gonda East, Gonda West, Gonda North, and Mahadeva. In 1957, the Raja's party contested the parliamentary seat and four of the Assembly seats. The Raja's candidates were successful in three of the four constituencies contested—Mankapur, Gonda East, and Mahadeva; the fourth Assembly seat and the parliamentary seat were lost by very narrow majorities. The Congress won only one Assembly seat and the parliamentary seat; the fifth Assembly seat went to a Jan Sangh candidate. In 1962, Swatantra won the

[23] Interview in Balrampur on August 23, 1962.

[24] The Swatantra victory in the parliamentary contest was not made official until August, 1964. The Swatantra candidate polled 82,478 votes against 80,902 for the Congress. However, the Congress candidate asked for and was granted a recount in which he emerged the victor by 80,937 votes to 80,439 votes for Swatantra. The recount has

parliamentary seat [24] and two of the five Assembly seats; the Congress was successful in three constituencies and the Jan Sangh in none. The vote for the Congress and for Swatantra in the 1957 and 1962 elections is given in table 4. As the table shows, the Congress vote increased in four of the five Assembly constituencies and declined in one Assembly constituency and in the parliamentary constituency. On the whole, the Congress improved

TABLE 4

VOTE FOR CONGRESS AND SWATANTRA IN ONE PARLIAMENTARY
AND FIVE ASSEMBLY CONSTITUENCIES OF GONDA
DISTRICT, 1957 AND 1962 ELECTIONS

Constituency	Congress		Swatantra	
	1957	1962	1957	1962
		Percent		
Gonda (Parliament)	45.4	40.8	44.8	41.5
Assembly				
Mankapur	32.8	41.2	67.3	56.1
Gonda East	36.9	32.8	38.1	31.1
Gonda West	33.3	40.1	...	31.9
Gonda North	20.2	25.6	28.9	29.1
Mahadeva	36.2	44.0	36.7	34.2

its electoral position against the Swatantra party significantly. In this section, the success of the Congress in these constituencies will be related to its ability to control factional conflict, to choose candidates suitable for their constituencies, and to win electoral support.

Factional conflict may affect the success of the Congress election campaign in three ways. Factional competition in the distribution of tickets may lead to the selection of candidates unsuitable for their constituencies; that is, factional loyalty may be a more important consideration in the selection of a particular candidate than his strength in the constituency. A second problem is that of coordination between the parliamentary candidate and his five supporting Assembly candidates. To maximize the possibility of success for all candidates, the ideal would be to select candidates from a single faction for the five Assembly constituencies and for the parliamentary constituency. Otherwise, there is the possibility that some of the "base" Assembly candidates will fail to support the parliamentary can-

---

since been overturned by an Election Tribunal. It has been established that there was tampering with the ballot papers between the first and second counts, by which nearly 2,000 ballot papers cast for the Swatantra candidate were illegally invalidated by double-stamping. The judgment of the Election Tribunal has been reported in the *Citizen*, August 29, 1964.

didate and vice versa. Finally, there is the direct threat of open rebellion or of internal sabotage within each constituency by rejected candidates or opposing local factions.

Congress factions and the selection of candidates

The distribution of Congress tickets for the general elections is a wholly internal party matter. Since there is no outside threat to impose unity upon Congressmen, the selection of Congress candidates is always an occasion for open factional conflict. When the local Congress is organized on a multifactional basis, as in Gonda, there can be no question of local party bosses agreeing amongst themselves and presenting a united slate of candidates to the state Parliamentary Board for approval. In Gonda in 1961-1962, there were no local Congressmen powerful enough to negotiate with the state party leaders for the distribution of tickets in the district as a whole or in any segment of it; in a multifactional situation, it is every man for himself.[25] When there is no local party boss to appease, the decisions on the distribution of tickets are made by the state party leaders, who can bargain freely among themselves.

In the bargaining process, the reports of district observers[26] are ignored and the merits of competing candidates unconsidered. Those who have no factional ties with state party leaders have little chance. In 1961-1962, the state party leaders adopted the following procedure: compromise was sought in distributing tickets to the most important followers of the two groups in each district; in this way, unanimous decisions were reached in a large number of cases. In constituencies where the competing applicants were considered unimportant to either group or where rival applicants were unaffiliated, the rival candidates were "bracketed" together and the decisions were left to the Central Parliamentary Board (CPB).

In Mankapur, Gonda East, and Gonda North Assembly constituencies, the state party leaders reached unanimous decisions. For Mankapur, there was no conflict; of the five constituencies, Mankapur (the constituency of the Raja himself) was the least desired, since it was the constituency most likely to be lost to Swatantra. For the Mankapur constituency, the state Congress selected Devendra Nath Misra, the personal secretary of Mohan Lal Gautam. The CPB accepted the choice of the state Board in this constituency.

For Gonda North and Gonda East, the state leaders agreed on two members of the dominant Gupta group—Ram Lal Gupta and Ram Samujh

[25] Cf. multifactionalism in Florida in V. O. Key, Jr., *Southern Politics in State and Nation* (New York: Alfred A. Knopf, 1949), chap. v.
[26] On this point and the candidate selection process in general, see the Appendix.

Misra. In district politics, these two men were relatively new and together formed a local faction. However, both these decisions were overturned by the CPB. Ram Lal Gupta is a lawyer of Gonda town; for Gonda North (a rural constituency), the CPB replaced Ram Lal with a man who had rural roots in the constituency, a landowner and a mahant of a temple. In Gonda East (semi-urban, semi-rural) constituency, the CPB replaced Ram Samujh with Ishwar Saran, one of the oldest Congressmen of the district, with greater influence in the town. Both the mahant and Ishwar Saran owed allegiance to the Gautam-Tripathi group in state politics.

In Gonda West, reserved for Scheduled Castes, two candidates were bracketed—Ganga Prasad (Gautam-Tripathi group) and Din Dayal Karun (Gupta group). The CPB here gave a decision in favor of Ganga Prasad, the incumbent MLA. Finally, in Mahadev, two new men, both unaffiliated, were bracketed. The CPB gave the ticket to Vishnu Pratap Singh who, as the son of the *talukdar* of the largest estate in the constituency, had much stronger local ties than his rival.

Thus, in the end, the Gautam-Tripathi group came out with a clean sweep in the Assembly constituencies; that is, not a single nominee of the Gupta group received a ticket in these five constituencies. However, strangely enough, for the parliamentary constituency, the state Congress had made no recommendation. For this constituency, the CPB selected Ram Ratan Gupta, a prominent industrialist of Kanpur and a close associate of C. B. Gupta.

The selection of Ram Ratan Gupta to contest the Gonda parliamentary constituency indicates, for one thing, that there are central party leaders with a sense of humor. Ram Ratan Gupta has, for long, sought entry into the halls of Parliament. Though an important factional leader of Kanpur City, he would have no chance of success from Kanpur's parliamentary constituency, which has a large proportion of industrial laborers. A militant opponent of Congress socialism, Ram Ratan remains in the Congress because it suits his purposes in Kanpur politics and because of his friendship with the former Chief Minister, C. B. Gupta. However, it also suits Ram Ratan's purposes to support other political parties occasionally. In Kanpur City, Ram Ratan founded a newspaper to support him and oppose his rivals in local factional conflicts; often, opposing his rivals meant supporting local Communists. It is also said that Ram Ratan controls the Swatantra party organization in rural Kanpur through his brother, Ram Gopal Gupta.[27]

What was most ironical in the CPB's selection of Ram Ratan to contest in the stronghold of the Raja of Mankapur was the fact that Ram Ratan had a personal association with the Raja and even had helped finance the Raja's

[27] *Citizen*, February 10, 1962.

election campaign in 1957; in return, the Raja supported for Parliament from Gonda in 1957 Shyam Behari Vaish of Kanpur, a nominee of Ram Ratan. Now, to gain his cherished goal of entry into Parliament, Ram Ratan had to fight in a constituency where previously he had worked with the opposition. Moreover, he had to fight in a constituency where all but one of his "base" Assembly candidates owed allegiance to an opposite factional group in the state Congress.

The irony of the selection surely did not escape the attention of those who made the decision. Yet, the decision was by no means wholly irrational. The parliamentary contest in Gonda had been difficult for the Congress in 1957 and promised to be even more difficult in 1962. No Gonda Congressman had sufficient local influence or the requisite financial resources to compete against the influence and resources of the Raja of Mankapur in the latter's home territory. In 1957 also, the Congress candidate was an outsider with a large purse (the candidate was the Raja of Kasmanda, a former *talukdar* of Sitapur district). The size of Ram Ratan Gupta's purse certainly was a factor in the Congress decision.

The candidates and the campaign

Despite the open factional conflict over the distribution of tickets for the five Assembly constituencies, the candidates finally selected probably were the best choices the Congress could have made to maximize its chances of success in each constituency. The responsibility for the tactically rational selections, however, was wholly that of the central party leaders. In two constituencies, the state Parliamentary Board, because of factional conflict, was unable to make a decision and left the choice to the center. In two out of the three cases in which the state Board reached unanimous decisions, the CPB overruled the decisions and replaced the candidates selected with candidates better suited to maximize the Congress vote in their respective constituencies.

However, the decision of the CPB for the parliamentary ticket created a problem of coordination between the Assembly and parliamentary candidates, who belonged to opposite factional groups. The solution to the problem rested with Ram Ratan Gupta. Ram Ratan brought with him to Gonda not only his purse, but an army of Congress workers and laborers from his mills and a fleet of jeeps. In addition to his own huge resources, Ram Ratan could count on the support of local Congressmen who owed allegiance to the Gupta group. Ram Lal Gupta and Ram Samujh Misra, the two rejected Gupta-group candidates for the Assembly constituencies, immediately came under the patronage of Ram Ratan. Still, a parliamentary candidate, no matter how great his resources, cannot hope to win in a constituency covering over a thousand scattered villages without the support of "base" candidates in the Assembly constituencies. Thus, alliance and coordination with his factional rivals in the Assembly constituencies was essential. It was Ram Ratan's money which solved the problem; Ram Ratan decided to finance the election campaigns of all five Congress Assembly candidates and to provide them with jeeps, banners, and posters[28] in return for their guarantees of support to him in his contest.

Factional alliances of this sort are not easily achieved. Under different conditions of factional and interparty competition, open rebellion or internal sabotage is the usual outcome. However, alliances are arranged more readily in a multifactional situation than under any other conditions of factional competition; multifactional competition is the most fluid of all factional situations. Still, it is doubtful that factional alliance could have been achieved between the Assembly candidates and the parliamentary candidate were it not for the fact that Ram Ratan had material benefits to offer in return for the support of the Congress Assembly candidates.

The alliance between Ram Ratan and the Congress Assembly candidates also prevented any possibility of open rebellion or significant internal sabotage. Ram Lal Gupta and Ram Samujh Misra, under other conditions, might have resigned from the Congress and contested as independents or they might have worked secretly in opposition to the official Congress candidates; however, since they had come under the patronage of Ram Ratan, they were bound not to upset the alliance between Ram Ratan and their local factional opponents.

Finally, the conditions of interparty competition made alliance essential for all. Division in the Congress ranks would have benefited none but Swatantra. Thus, both the special character of factionalism in the Gonda Congress and the threat of a strong and united opposition party made possible a temporary cohesion within the Congress organization, an alliance based upon mutual interests for a specific purpose.

The election

Internal cohesion is a necessary, but not sufficient condition for the electoral success of a political party. The Congress was able to improve its electoral position against the Swatantra party for three additional reasons. First, thanks to Ram Ratan Gupta, the Congress had material resources equal, if not superior, to those of Swatantra. Second, the Congress benefited by opposition party fragmentation. Third, the Congress was able to mobilize much greater diversity of support from the electorate than Swatantra.

The importance of money in elections needs little comment. The workers, jeeps, petrol, banners, and posters to cover over 1,000 villages and small towns in a parliamentary constituency or even the more than 250 vil-

[28] *Ibid.*

lages of an average Assembly constituency require large sums of money. Neither Congress nor Swatantra lacked the material resources for this campaign.

Even more important than money in the success of the Congress was the fragmentation of opposition forces. In Gonda district as a whole, there are two strong opposition parties—Swatantra and the Jan Sangh. Both parties are conservative on economic issues, but are divided by their attitudes to traditional Hindu society. The Jan Sangh is an openly Hindu, communal party with rigid ideology and firm discipline; the Jan Sangh party leaders consider Swatantra a party of opportunists, composed merely of right-wing Congressmen. Nonetheless, negotiations between the two parties were carried on; they broke down less because of ideological differences than because of failure to reach agreement on the distribtuion of constituencies; negotiations failed because the two parties could not agree on the distribution of tickets for three of the thirteen Assembly constituencies. The failure of the negotiations hurt Swatantra more than the Jan Sangh; Swatantra won only two Assembly constituencies in the district and the Jan Sangh four.

Had the Jan Sangh-Swatantra negotiations succeeded, the Congress literally would have been wiped out in Gonda district. In only one constituency (Mahadev) in the entire district could the Congress have succeeded against a Jan Sangh-Swatantra alliance. A comparison of the vote for the Congress and the combined vote for the Jan Sangh and Swatantra in the five constituencies being considered here is given in table 5. In the parlia-

TABLE 5

COMPARISON OF CONGRESS VOTE AND COMBINED VOTE OF THE JAN SANGH AND SWATANTRA IN FIVE CONSTITUENCIES OF GONDA DISTRICT, 1962 ELECTIONS

Constituency	Congress	Jan Sangh-Swatantra
Mankapur	21,918	29,849[a]
Gonda East	12,893	23,267
Gonda North	8,925	19,897
Gonda West	11,462	13,824
Mahadev	17,039	15,186
Total	72,287	102,023

[a] Opposition vote in Mankapur is for Swatantra only; there was no Jan Sangh candidate in this constituency.

mentary contest, there was no Jan Sangh candidate. The Jan Sangh Assembly votes were split by the Congress and Swatantra in the parliamentary constituency. Had there been a Jan Sangh–Swatantra alliance, the parliamentary seat also would have gone to Swatantra.

No single opposition party can match the diversity of support which the Congress can muster over a broad area. In Gonda, Swatantra influence was confined to the rural areas, especially areas formerly under the direct control of the Mankapur and Gonda estates. The importance of the traditional influence of the former landed proprietors for Swatantra successes in these elections is best illustrated in the Mankapur constituency, the constituency of the Raja of Mankapur. In the 1962 election, the constituency contained over 350 villages, of which 149 were formerly part of the Mankapur estate. A comparison of the ten polling stations in the constituency in which the Raja polled highest with the ten in which his main rival (a Brahman on a Congress ticket) polled highest reveals the following pattern. The Raja polled from 78.5 percent to 91.7 percent of the vote in his ten best polling stations, which contained 38 villages. Of the 38 villages, 33 were formerly owned by the Raja, the previous status of 2 villages was unknown, and only 3 were clearly not part of the Raja's former estate. The Raja's Congress opponent polled from 68.5 percent to 80.2 percent of the vote in his ten best polling stations, which contained 37 villages. None of the 37 villages were previously part of the Raja's estate. Many of the villages in which the Congress candidate achieved his highest successes contained large numbers of Brahmans and Chamars, whereas the caste composition of the villages in which the Raja achieved his highest successes showed no evident patterns.[29] In other words, two different factors were important in the election in Mankapur—caste voting and the traditional influence of the Raja, which cut across caste allegiances. The traditional influence of the Raja was decisive in determining voting patterns in areas which were formerly directly under his control, but his prestige could be neutralized by other factors in areas where he was known only by reputation or by his political activities.

In contrast, the Congress succeeded in defeating Swatantra in three very different constituencies. In Mahadev, the Congress succeeded in a wholly rural constituency because its candidate came from the family of the former owners of the largest estate in the constituency. In Gonda West, the Congress retained its traditional strength in a constituency reserved for Scheduled Castes. In Gonda East (divided between Gonda town and its surrounding rural areas), the Congress candidate acquired a strong enough lead in the town to overcome the rural strength of the Swatantra candi-

[29] The information on the previous status of the villages examined was derived from the records of the Mankapur estate. Data on the caste composition of the villages was drawn from the *Census of India, 1891, District Census Statistics, N.-W. Provinces and Oudh, Fyzabad Division* (Allahabad: Government Press, 1896). On the use of the 1891 census, see notes to table 9, p. 158.

date. Thus, the Congress was able to combine urban and rural support, as well as support from proprietary and nonproprietary, elite and nonelite castes to achieve its victories in these three constituencies.

CONCLUSION

The Congress party in Gonda district today is by no means a vital and dynamic organization. Congress organization in the district probably never will regain the position of dominance which it occupied under the regime of the Raja of Mankapur. Yet, this case study reveals that the local Congress organization can sustain great setbacks and continue to survive and, in fact, recover lost ground. The district Congress organization is not limited by local resources. When interparty competition is keen, the local Congress can count upon the support of government and state party leaders; when there are difficult constituencies to contest, there are wealthy candidates from outside who can be brought in to supply material resources. The Congress is aided also by opposition fragmentation and by the fact that no single opposition party can compete against the resources of the Congress and the diversity of electoral support which the Congress can mobilize.

Participation of outside party leaders in local affairs is not wholly beneficial to the district Congress. It was outside intervention which caused the breakup of the Gonda Congress in the first place. Outside intervention also favors the continuance of factional conflict and makes it impossible for a single local group to achieve a position of dominance in the district Congress.

However, outside intervention does not cause factional conflict. Factional antagonisms are generated locally. Moreover, local leaders are not merely manipulated by outside party leaders; local leaders themselves seek the support of state party leaders in local conflicts.

The Gonda Congress has gone through three stages of factional development. In the pre-Independence period, the Congress was organized on a bifactional basis; two factions competed for control of the district Congress. After Independence, until 1955, a single faction controlled the Gonda Congress. From 1955 until the present, the district Congress has been organized on a multifactional basis.

In many respects, multifactionalism is more stable than bifactionalism or unifactionalism. A unifactional situation would be most stable if the local Congress were isolated from outside intervention. However, with local factions integrated into a statewide political group network, multifactionalism permits fluidity, bargaining, and temporary alliances of mutual convenience.

The Gonda Congress represents an example of a weak, local Congress organization which has regained some of its lost political strength through factional alliance. The next case study is of a strong Congress organization which destroyed its position of electoral dominance in factional conflict.

V.

Aligarh: Organizational Self-Destruction

THE ENVIRONMENT

Gonda and Aligarh have little in common. The differences between the two districts partly reflect differences between the western and eastern districts of Uttar Pradesh. Aligarh district lies in the fertile northern Doab (between the Ganges and the Jumna rivers) of the western Gangetic plain. The district borders on the Punjab and shares some demographic and cultural features with that state. Jats form the third largest caste in the district and are as enterprising cultivators as their counterparts in the Punjab. In fact, all castes cultivate in Aligarh district and the general standard of agriculture is high. Irrigation facilities are widespread and well-utilized. The district has been selected as one of eight districts in India to come under the "Intensive Agricultural District Programme" for increasing agricultural production through the introduction of a "package plan" of improved agricultural practices. The major crops in the district are *bajra* (a millet), wheat, barley, and gram.

The district is of average size for the state, just under 2,000 square miles. However, Aligarh has a fairly large population—1,765,275 according to the 1961 census—and thus has a high density of 909 persons per square mile. The district has a large urban population, over 16 percent of the total,[1] with two towns of considerable size. Aligarh town is the largest in the district, with a population of 185,000; Hathras comes next with a population over 64,000.[2] Both towns have some industry. Aligarh is famous all over India for its brass and iron locks; Hathras has two textile mills. Road and rail communications are good in most parts of the district. Male literacy is close to 20 percent.[3]

[1] *Census of India, 1961, Paper No. 1 of 1962, Final Population Totals*, pp. 348-349.
[2] *Ibid.*, pp. 276, 302.
[3] *Ibid.*, p. 349.

The pattern of land relationships was much different in Aligarh from the *talukdari* system which prevailed in Gonda. There were a number of large *zamindars* in Aligarh district before *zamindari* abolition, but they did not dominate the economic life of the district in the same way as did the great *talukdars* of Gonda. There was only one *zamindar* in Aligarh district paying a land revenue of Rs. 35,000 or over,[4] compared to seven in Gonda district.[5] Many of the large estates in Aligarh were owned by Muslims, but Rajputs, Jats, and Brahmans also were prominent as landed proprietors. The main proprietary castes in the district now are Brahmans, Rajputs, and Jats, in that order. Numerically, the largest castes in the district are Chamars, Brahmans, Rajputs, and Jats.[6] Muslims account for approximately 12 percent of the total population of the district.[7]

Aligarh has been of special importance in Indian politics, particularly during the nationalist period, because of the important influence of Aligarh Muslim University. The University has for long been an important center of Muslim culture and Muslim politics in India and was closely associated with the Muslim League and the demand for Pakistan. The existence of this University in a Hindu-majority district has been a source of tension between members of the two communities, particularly in Aligarh town, where Muslims form 35 percent of the population. Hindu-Muslim riots have been common in Aligarh both before and since Independence. In October, 1961, just before the 1962 General Elections, one of the most serious riots in Uttar Pradesh since Independence originated in Aligarh town and spread to other parts of the state.

This chapter is a case study of the functioning of the Congress in a situation of communal tension. For obvious reasons, relations between the local Congress and the University have not been close. The leadership of the Congress party in Aligarh, as in other districts, is based upon the elite proprietary castes in the rural areas of the district. Conflicts within the Congress have nothing to do with Hindu-Muslim tensions. However, the riot of 1961 had an important effect upon the functioning of the local Congress organization in the 1962 General Elections, an effect for which the Congress was not prepared. Before discussing the development of communal tension and its impact upon the Congress organization, it will be necessary

[4] *Final Settlement Report of the Aligarh District*, by S. Ahmad Ali (Allahabad: Superintendent, Printing and Stationery, United Provinces, 1943), p. 27.
[5] *Final Settlement Report of Gonda District*, by Jai Krit Singh (Allahabad: Superintendent, Printing and Stationery, United Provinces, 1944), p. 18.
[6] *Census of India, 1931*, Vol. XVIII: *United Provinces of Agra and Oudh*, by A. C. Turner, Pt. II (Allahabad: Sdperintendent, Printing and Stationery, 1933), table XVII.
[7] *Census of India, 1951*, Vol. II: *Uttar Pradesh*, by Rajeshwari Prasad, Pt. II-C (Allahabad: Superintendent, Printing and Stationery, Uttar Pradesh, 1953), table D-II.

to describe the condition of the Congress party organization on the eve of the 1961 riot and the General Elections of 1962.

THE ALIGARH CONGRESS: BIFACTIONAL CLEAVAGE

Sometime in 1941, two prominent Congressmen from Aligarh district were sitting in Agra Jail talking to Acharya Narendra Dev, the famous Socialist leader. At one point, the conversation took an unfriendly turn when one of the Congressmen, Mohan Lal Gautam, spoke harshly to the other Congressman, Thakur Malkhan Singh; in reply, Thakur Malkhan Singh, the elder of the two men, slapped Gautam across the face.[8] If the history of factional conflict in the Aligarh Congress is any indication, neither of the two men ever forgot the insults exchanged in the Agra Jail. Factional conflict in the Aligarh Congress since Independence has been open, bitter, and violent. Thakur Malkhan Singh, in 1962, charged Gautam with the responsibility for the murder of six people of the former's faction in the period between 1953 and 1960.[9] In 1958, two students of Ahen Inter-College, in Hathras tahsil, were seriously injured in a police firing; the police had opened fire on a crowd of students who had mobbed Mohan Lal Gautam, then the Minister for Cooperation and Agriculture in the Uttar Pradesh government, during his visit to the College.[10] Gautam described the Ahen incident as "an organized attempt of my political rivals in the Congress to murder me."[11]

Compared to Aligarh, factional conflicts in the Gonda Congress are mild. In fact, factional conflict in Aligarh has, at times, reached an intensity unmatched elsewhere in Uttar Pradesh. The organizing principle of factional conflict in Aligarh, as in Gonda, has been personal enmity between political opponents. Status considerations played a role in intensifying factional antagonisms in Aligarh as in Gonda. However, factional conflict has been much more intense in Aligarh than in Gonda for three reasons—the absence of strong opposition political parties, the presence of two powerful state Congress leaders in the same district, and the bifactional structure of political competition.

Thakur Malkhan Singh[12] was a much older Congressman than Gautam. He was born in 1889 in a Kirar Rajput family of small tenant farmers in a village in Aligarh district. He attended the Government High School at

[8] Interview in Aligarh on December 27, 1961.
[9] *Ibid.*
[10] *Hindustan Standard*, May 8, 1958.
[11] *Times of India*, May 9, 1958.
[12] Thakur Malkhan Singh died on January 24, 1962.

Aligarh and, afterwards, took his B.Sc. degree from American Christian College at Allahabad in 1916. Most of Malkhan Singh's nonpolitical activities were in the field of education; he taught in, managed, and founded a number of high schools and colleges in Aligarh and elsewhere. He was active in politics and incurred the displeasure of the authorities for his assistance to revolutionary students even before the first Congress movement in 1921. Malkhan Singh was imprisoned in all of the major Congress movements. In 1929, he took an LL.B. degree from Agra and set up practice in Aligarh for a short time.[13] His wide-ranging political and nonpolitical activities and his seniority in the nationalist movement established Malkhan Singh's reputation as one of the most prominent Congressmen of Aligarh district and brought to him a significant following from among the younger Congressmen of the district. After the war, Malkhan Singh was elected president of the Aligarh DCC.

Malkhan Singh had been a member of the Congress Socialist Party and was one of the thirteen MLAs who resigned their seats in the Uttar Pradesh Assembly in 1948 to contest elections against the Congress. Malkhan Singh was the only prominent Congressman of the district to resign from the Congress at this time; his most important followers in Aligarh remained in the Congress and in control of the DCC. A leader without followers, Malkhan Singh fared badly, for a time, after his resignation in 1948; he lost the bye-election in 1948 and lost again in the General Elections of 1952 as a Socialist candidate. However, in 1955, Malkhan Singh again re-entered the legislature, after defeating the Congress candidate in a bye-election from Aligarh town on a PSP ticket.

When Malkhan Singh entered the legislature in 1955, Mohan Lal Gautam was out of power in the state government and C. B. Gupta was the most influential Congressman in the State party and in the Government. Shortly after his return to the legislature, both his old followers in the Aligarh Congress and C. B. Gupta requested Malkhan Singh to rejoin the Congress.[14] Malkhan Singh's followers in the Congress had been having some difficulty in keeping the faction together in the prolonged absence of their leader and dissensions had begun to affect the cohesion of the group. C. B. Gupta was looking for allies everywhere, since he was himself engaged in battle with Mohan Lal Gautam for control of the state party organization. Thakur Malkhan Singh's opposition to Gautam was well-known; he could be counted upon to keep Gautam and Gautam's men from gaining power in Aligarh district by exploiting differences in the Aligarh Congress. On February 16, 1955, Malkhan Singh announced in Lucknow that he had re-

[13] Interview with Thakur Malkhan Singh in Aligarh on December 27, 1961.
[14] *Ibid.*

joined the Congress because the Congress had now declared that its goal was a "socialistic pattern of society." [15] In April, Malkhan Singh was elected President of the Aligarh DCC unanimously; an additional measure of his old followers' loyalty to him was evidenced in this election, Malkhan Singh being authorized at that time to nominate the office-bearers and the Executive Committee of the DCC.[16] Two of Gautam's men in the district were appointed by Malkhan Singh to the Executive Committee of twenty members, but Gautam himself was excluded.[17]

Gautam returned to power in the Uttar Pradesh government in 1957, but both the state party organization and the Aligarh DCC remained in the hands of his rivals. The first major contest between Gautam and his opponents in the Aligarh Congress occurred in 1957 on the question of selection of Congress candidates to contest the elections for Chairmen of thirteen Town Area Committees in the district. Although Gautam was one of the most powerful ministers in the state Government at the time, he was not able to secure a single ticket for a member of his group in his home district.[18]

The Town Area Committee Chairmen elections of 1957 in the district created much bitterness between rival factions in the Congress. In March, 1958, one Moolchand, the Congress Chairman of the Jalali Town Area Committee, was attacked one evening by twelve people and murdered. After the murder, it was reported in the press that relations between Moolchand and the local police had been "strained"; Moolchand had been prosecuted on criminal charges by the local police, but was acquitted by the High Court. Before his death, it was reported, the local police were attempting to implicate Moolchand in some other criminal charges. Moolchand, supported by Malkhan Singh, had appealed to the Home Minister, Kamlapati Tripathi, for protection, without success. It was reported that Moolchand's murder was the second murder which had been committed in the district "as a result of group rivalry and strained relations with the police." [19]

In May, a meeting of the Aligarh DCC, under the presidentship of Malkhan Singh, passed a resolution expressing concern over the murder of Moolchand; the resolution directly implicated Mohan Lal Gautam in the murder of Moolchand and blamed the district officers and the Home Minister for failing to provide police protection to the victim. The Committee also noted that several murders of this sort had taken place before "and that

[15] *Hindustan Times*, February 17, 1955.
[16] *Hindustan Times*, April 24, 1955.
[17] *National Herald*, April 29, 1955.
[18] Interview with Thakur Malkhan Singh in Aligarh on December 27, 1961.
[19] *National Herald*, March 21, 1958.

the district officers had failed to maintain law and order and protect leading citizens." [20]

In May and June of 1958, new acts of violence occurred in Aligarh as a direct result of factional rivalries. The DCC resolution implicating Gautam directly and the Home Minister and the district officers indirectly in the murder of Moolchand was passed on May 2. On May 8, the Ahen police firing occurred. The Ahen incident arose directly out of a contest between Gautam and Malkhan Singh for control over the College Executive Committee. On May 9, the Uttar Pradesh Congress President was forced to take note of the serious conditions prevailing in Aligarh Congress affairs; the President remarked in Lucknow "that the faction fights in the Aligarh District Congress Committee had outstripped all bounds of decency and civilised political conduct." [21]

The Congress President's harsh comments on Aligarh Congress affairs had no immediate effect. On May 19, the house of Sahib Singh, a prominent member of the Malkhan Singh faction, was robbed in the absence of its owner; Sahib Singh reported to the police "his suspicion that the miscreants broke into his house with the intention of murdering him on account of group politics in the district Congress." [22] In June, a clash between rival groups in the Harduaganj Town Area occurred in which three persons suffered serious injuries.[23]

The accusations and acts of violence which took place in these months became grounds for civil and criminal litigation between the rival Congress factions. The Ahen dispute was taken into civil court towards the end of May.[24] Early in June, Gautam announced his intention to file a defamation suit against the President, officers, and members of the Executive Committee of the Aligarh DCC for their implications in the resolution of May 2 that Gautam had been responsible for the murders in the district.[25] Throughout May and June, thirty-five arrests were made in connection with the Ahen incident; among those arrested, but later released, were two Congress MLAs of Malkhan Singh's faction, the Chairman of the Aligarh District Board (also of the same faction), as well as the Manager and the Principal of the Ahen College.[26] On the intervention of the President of the Indian National Congress, the Aligarh DCC withdrew its resolution of May 2,[27] after which Gautam gave up his plan to file suit for defamation.

[20] *National Herald*, May 8, 1958.
[21] *Times of India*, May 10, 1958.
[22] *Express*, May 22, 1958.
[23] *National Herald*, June 14, 1958.
[24] *Express*, May 30, 1958.
[25] *Hindustan Times*, June 4, 1958.
[26] *Express*, June 14, 1958.
[27] *National Herald*, June 17, 1958.

However, factional rivalry, tension, and litigation on other matters continued.

The acts of violence and the open charges and accusations made by Congressmen in Aligarh against each other have been emphasized here to illustrate the extremities to which factional conflict can be carried. Congressmen in Aligarh could afford to fight each other with no restraints because the Congress organization in Aligarh was in such a dominant position in the district that there were no external incentives for internal unity. In the 1952 General Elections, the Aligarh Congress won all ten of the Assembly seats in the district and both of the parliamentary seats; in 1957, the Congress lost only one Assembly seat to an independent. The Congress also controlled almost every local government and cooperative institution of importance in the district.

A second factor in the intensity of factional conflict in Aligarh was the fact that two important leaders were contesting for power in the same district. Gautam has held power at the state level and, at times, in national politics throughout most of his active political career; he has been a powerful state party organizer as well as a prominent minister in the state government. Malkhan Singh, though a less important figure in state politics than Gautam—partly because of Malkhan Singh's self-exile from the Congress in the period between 1948 and 1955—was, before and after his period of resignation from the Congress, a member of the PCC executive committee and a member of the AICC. In 1961, he was brought into the Gupta government as a deputy minister. Both Malkhan Singh and Gautam were men of power and influence, men who had participated in all the Congress movements and had acquired status in the Congress for their activities during the nationalist period. Most important, both men were fighting for bigger stakes than merely control of a local party organization. Malkhan Singh rejoined the Congress and threatened Gautam's position in Aligarh district at just the time when Gautam had received a setback in state politics, when C. B. Gupta had caused Gautam's exclusion from the ministry in the new Sampurnanand government.[28] Gautam could not hope to challenge Gupta in state politics without a firm base in his home district; Gautam was fighting for his political life.

A third element intensifying factional conflict was the influence of status considerations. Aligarh was too small a place to accommodate two leaders of the stature of Malkhan Singh and Gautam. There could be no question of one man accepting an inferior position in the district with respect to the other. In an interview shortly before his death, Malkhan Singh made a point of stating that he had been a prominent figure in the nationalist move-

[28] See chap. iii, p. 46.

ment when "Gautam was a boy of eight or ten doing . . . work in the Congress office." [29]

Finally, there is the character of factional competition in the Aligarh Congress. Malkhan Singh and Gautam formed two poles in district politics, with the result that conflict in the Aligarh Congress naturally became bifactional. In a politics of personal prestige, bifactional conflict, unlike multifactionalism, has little fluidity and leaves little room for bargaining and compromise. Alliances of mutual convenience are out of the question when the conditions of interparty competition provide no incentive for unity. In the absence of an outside threat, bifactional conflict follows the ideal-typical form of factional struggle—whatever one faction does, the other faction opposes; when one faction says "black," the other says "white."

Wherever the two factions have opposed each other in local affairs, they have fought with every means at their disposal. Since most local institutions were completely dominated by the Congress, the fight for control of these institutions in Aligarh became solely a factional fight. While Congressmen were fighting each other, a powerful threat to the electoral position of the Congress in the district developed as a direct consequence of the Hindu-Muslim riot of 1961. Preoccupied with their own internal struggles, Congressmen were unable to see what was happening in their environment; the result was a complete debacle in the General Elections of 1962. In the remainder of this chapter, the factional struggles of the Congress for control of local institutions and the consequences of the struggles for the cohesion of the Congress organization in the 1962 elections will be described.

THE FIGHT FOR CONTROL OF LOCAL INSTITUTIONS

In a politics of status, bifactional competition does not permit bargaining, compromise, or accommodation; opposing factions seek each other's liquidation by every possible means. Another important feature of bifactional conflict in Aligarh is its pervasiveness. Neither faction will permit the other to retain a sphere of influence; each faction seeks the other out wherever the other faction has strength. The result is that factional conflict inevitably enters into every local institution of importance—public and private. The manner of functioning of any local institution becomes less important than who controls it. If one faction controls an institution and the other faction cannot gain control, the "out" faction prefers that the institution should not function at all. Neither party interest nor the interests of the institutions involved, much less the public interest, provide any boundaries for this kind of factional conflict. Two examples of bifactional conflict within local institutions in Aligarh district will illustrate these propositions.

[29] Interview with Thakur Malkhan Singh in Aligarh on December 27, 1961.

The Hasain Cooperative Society

Hasain is an area within the Sikandra Rao Assembly constituency. The entire constituency has been a center of conflict between the Malkhan Singh and Gautam factions in the Aligarh Congress. Factional struggle here has had some caste overtones and has partly reflected tension between Brahmans and Rajputs, the two most influential castes in the area. From 1952 until 1957, Nek Ram Sharma, a Brahman and a follower of Gautam in this period, was the MLA from the Sikandra Rao constituency. The most prominent Rajput politician in this constituency has been Kushal Pal Singh, a member of the Malkhan Singh faction and, at various times, an officer of the District Congress Committee, president of the Hasain Block Development Committee, and a member of the Executive Committee of the District Board. Nek Ram Sharma and Kushal Pal Singh opposed each other in local affairs.

After the 1957 election, conflict between the members of the two factions developed for control of the Hasain Cooperative Society, a "large size" society, serving thirty-six villages in the area. The followers of Nek Ram Sharma and Gautam controlled the affairs of the Society until March, 1957, when Kushal Pal Singh was elected president of the Society and a new Board of Directors of members of his faction was installed. One of the first acts of the new Board of Directors was to accuse the outgoing directors of misuse of the funds of the Society for their own personal advantage. It was found that one of the outgoing directors was in default of payment to the Society of a debt of Rs. 5,000 in his and his relatives' names. The new Board made representations to the administrative staff of the Cooperative Department in the district for action to be taken for the recovery of this debt. The defense of the alleged defaulters was a countercharge against the new President for embezzlement of the funds of the Society by taking compulsory subscriptions, from recipients of loans, to a social organization.[30]

In June, 1957, Mohan Lal Gautam became Minister for Cooperation. In July, an enquiry was set up into the affairs of the Hasain Society by the officers of the Cooperative Department. No action was taken against the alleged defaulters; however, in August, the new Board of Directors of the Society was removed and the affairs of the Society put under administrative rule. Eighteen months after the suspension of the Board of Directors, a criminal prosecution was instituted against Kushal Pal Singh by the state of Uttar Pradesh for the alleged embezzlement. The suspension of the Board and the criminal prosecution of its President was carried out for an

---

[30] The major source for the material in this section is the complete file of the cases described, filed under Suit No. 24 of 1960 in the court of the Civil Judge, Aligarh.

alleged embezzlement of Rs. 32.50.[31] After seven months of enquiry and hearings in the Court of a Special Magistrate in Aligarh, the prosecution case was declared by the Court false and concocted and Kushal Pal Singh was acquitted. The Court also ordered the prosecution of three officers of the Cooperative Department for their part in framing the false charges.

Kushal Pal Singh himself filed a civil suit for damages against the officers of the Cooperative Department and against Mohan Lal Gautam as well. Kushal Pal Singh charged that it was actually Gautam who, as Minister for Cooperation, had instigated the false prosecution against him for political reasons. The Civil Court took a different view of the matter from the court which had tried Kushal Pal Singh. The Civil Court cleared all the defendants of the charge of implicating Kushal Pal Singh in a false case and found instead that the officers of the Cooperative Department had reasonable grounds for prosecuting him.

The dispute between the two factions was pursued in this way for three years, with neither side gaining any satisfaction. Throughout this period and afterwards, the Hasain Cooperative Society remained without a Board of Directors. There is no question that the source of the dispute and the reasons for the litigation were wholly political and based upon factional antagonisms between the groups involved. More than an "embezzlement" of a paltry sum was involved in this dispute. The entire dispute was part of the bitter struggle for political influence and personal prestige in district and state politics.

The Municipal Board Presidency

The power of state ministers over local, elected officials and local institutions is an important instrument in district factional struggles. The strength of a faction in local politics depends upon its ties with state political leaders. While Mohan Lal Gautam was in power, the dominant faction in Aligarh district had to contend not only against local factional rivals, but against the power of the state government. In 1960, when Gautam left the ministry and C. B. Gupta became chief minister, the tables were turned and the power of the state government was directed against the followers of Gautam in Aligarh district. The case of the Aligarh Municipal Board Presidency is an example.

Malkhan Singh's faction has dominated in Aligarh district politics in the rural areas; but, in the town, Gautam's faction has been stronger. In 1957, the Malkhan Singh and Gautam factions nominated different candidates to contest the presidency of the Aligarh Municipal Board. The state Parliamentary Board was deadlocked in choosing between the two candidates

[31] Approximately $6.50.

and the decision was left to Dr. Sampurnanand, the Chief Minister, who selected Babu Lal Sharma, the candidate of the Gautam faction. The candidate of Malkhan Singh's faction broke party discipline and contested against the official Congress candidate, but lost in a very close contest; he was expelled from the Congress for six years as a disciplinary measure.

Nothing could be done by the Malkhan Singh faction to oust Babu Lal Sharma until the change in the state government took place in 1960. Shortly after the Gupta group took control of the state party organization and the government, the expulsion of Malkhan Singh's candidate was rescinded and action was instituted to remove Babu Lal Sharma from office. In July, 1961, an order of the state government was issued suspending Babu Lal Sharma from his position as president of the Aligarh Municipal Board on the grounds of "gross misconduct and abuse of powers." [32] As in the case of the Hasain Cooperative Society, the dispute was taken to court. At the Allahabad High Court, Babu Lal Sharma succeeded in having the suspension order against him revoked for lack of specification of the charges against him. Within less than two weeks after the revocation of the suspension order, the state government again issued an order suspending Babu Lal Sharma, this time giving more particulars. In a writ petition filed by Babu Lal Sharma to have the second order revoked, Babu Lal's lawyer argued that the state government was suspending his client "to humiliate him because he belonged to the opposite group in the State Congress" and claimed that the suspension was a "case of political vendetta." [33]

While litigation against Babu Lal Sharma was pursued, the Aligarh Municipal Board remained without an elected president. After Babu Lal's suspension, another Gautam supporter was elected president; but, he too was removed by the state government for technical reasons relating to the conduct of the election.

With Gautam out of power in the state government and his supporters removed from office in the Aligarh Municipality, the two props of Gautam's power in Aligarh affairs were gone. The control of Malkhan Singh's faction over district politics seemed more secure than ever.

The District Board Presidency

Just as the absence of interparty competition permits unrestrained intraparty factionalism, the removal of a factional threat permits further intraparty splintering. The pressure upon the dominant faction in the Aligarh Congress from the Gautam faction was very much lessened by the withdrawal of Gautam from state office and by the rise to power in the

[32] *National Herald*, November 8, 1961.
[33] *Statesman*, November 23, 1961.

state government of the Gupta group. The Malkhan Singh faction lost its incentive for unity and soon split in two. The immediate cause of the split was the contest for the District Board presidency in 1961.

Faced with strong interparty competition in the contest for the presidency of the District Board in Gonda, the Gonda Congress was able to unite to defeat its opponent. In Aligarh, the Malkhan Singh and Gautam factions maintained internal unity as long as they were threats to each other. In the contest for the presidency of the Aligarh District Board, the Malkhan Singh faction faced no threat either from opposition parties or from the Gautam faction.

Three men have been prominent leaders of the Malkhan Singh faction— Malkhan Singh himself, Nawab Singh, and Sri Niwas. Sri Niwas has little personal following in the district outside of his own constituency and has not been prominent in factional disputes; he is personally an accommodating man and places party interest above factional interest. Malkhan Singh and Nawab Singh both had separate personal followings. A prominent protégé and supporter of Malkhan Singh, as has been seen, was Kushal Pal Singh. Nawab Singh has had similarly close ties with a previous District Board President, Sahib Singh.

Nawab Singh wanted Sahib Singh to be given the Congress ticket for the District Board and received the support of Malkhan Singh for his candidate. However, Sri Niwas felt that Sahib Singh, an uneducated man, was not a suitable person to place in charge of the district administration. In place of Sahib Singh, Sri Niwas suggested the name of Kushal Pal Singh. It is said that Malkhan Singh then changed his views and secretly supported Kushal Pal Singh. When the state Parliamentary Board adopted Kushal Pal Singh as the Congress candidate, the unity of the Malkhan Singh faction ended.

Nawab Singh and Sahib Singh now formed a separate faction. In the District Board election, Sahib Singh allegedly supported a Swatantra party candidate against Kushal Pal Singh, but the Congress candidate won by an overwhelming majority. Nawab Singh and Sahib Singh then reportedly planned to sabotage the 1962 election campaigns of all Congressmen who had opposed them in district affairs. Since neither man was a candidate for election himself, both were free to sabotage others without fear of reprisal.

THE 1962 GENERAL ELECTIONS: COMMUNAL CONFLICT

While Aligarh Congressmen were planning to sabotage each other's election campaigns, the political environment of the Congress was changing rapidly. The split in the Malkhan Singh faction occurred in the summer of 1961. The Hindu-Muslim riot broke out in October—four months before the General Elections of 1962. The two events were wholly unrelated. Yet, the split in the dominant faction in the Aligarh Congress and the riot of October, 1961, were the two most important factors in the defeat of the Congress in the 1962 elections in the district.

As a direct result of the October riot, the Congress party in Aligarh district was, for the first time, faced with a serious challenge to its position of electoral dominance in the district. As a result of its own internal conflicts, the Congress organization in the district failed to meet the challenge. Before the General Elections of 1962, the Congress held nine out of ten Assembly seats and both the parliamentary seats. After the election, the Congress held only three Assembly seats and neither of the parliamentary seats.

The defeat of the Congress was caused by an alliance, made possible by the October riot, of conservative Muslim leaders from Aligarh Muslim University, rural Chamars, and rebel Congressmen. The formation of the alliance and the reasons for the failure of the Congress in the 1962 elections will be described below. Since the October riot and the activities of Aligarh Muslim University teachers in the election played a decisive role in the campaign, it will be necessary to describe briefly the history of Aligarh Muslim University and its political role in national and local politics.

The University and the Muslims

"Communists" and "Communalists."—Aligarh Muslim University has been not merely an educational institution; it has also been a "movement." Founded as the Muhammadan Anglo-Oriental College in 1877 by Sir Syed Ahmad Khan, the school was established to rectify the educational "backwardness" of the Muslim community in India with respect to the new forms of education that had developed under British rule. The college became a university under the Aligarh Muslim University Act of 1920.[34]

The University has always been in a somewhat anomalous position. Though situated in the Muslim minority province of Uttar Pradesh, it became the intellectual center of the Muslim League and was described by Jinnah as the "arsenal" of the League. By the end of the nationalist period, the University was thoroughly dominated in terms of administrative staff, faculty, and students by members and supporters of the Muslim League.

After Independence and partition, the University had to adjust to the secular policies of the new Government of India. No purge of the University staff was necessary, since the most prominent Muslim Leaguers at the University migrated to Pakistan. However, many of the staff members who remained at the University were certainly orthodox and some were revivalists, if not communalists. The conservative elements in the University retreated into the background after Independence and partition, par-

[34] Aligarh Muslim University, *Prospectus for the Session, 1961-62*, p. 1.

ticularly when Dr. Zakir Husain became the vice-chancellor in 1947. Dr. Zakir Husain attempted to change the character and the image of Aligarh Muslim University by bringing into the University and placing in key positions liberal-minded, nonorthodox Muslim administrators and teachers. Under Dr. Zakir Husain's tenure, a few Communists also became prominent in University affairs.

Dr. Zakir Husain was succeeded by Colonel B. H. Zaidi, who tried to continue the policies of his predecessor. However, during Colonel Zaidi's vice-chancellorship, the conservative elements in the University began to rebel against the policy of liberalization. The University staff split into two camps—loosely called "Communists" and "communalists"—which opposed each other not only on new policies for liberalizing the social and cultural atmosphere of the University,[35] but on appointments and promotions in the administration and in the various faculty departments. The division in the University became sharper and more bitter towards the end of Colonel Zaidi's tenure. Early in 1961, the conflict between progressives and conservatives in the University came to a head in the elections to the Academic Council and later to the Executive Council, the governing body of the University. The conservatives administered a sharp defeat to the progressives in both these elections.

The Hindu-Muslim Riot of 1961.—The University councils elections were the beginnings of a chain reaction. In Aligarh town and particularly in the three Hindu colleges of the town, where RSS [36] influence is strong, the councils elections in the University became a pretext for a propaganda campaign, in which the University was described as a "citadel of Pakistani agents." [37] Relations between the University and the town have always been, at best, nonexistent and, at worst, ridden with tension. A Muslim-majority university in a Hindu-majority town would, in itself, be sufficient cause for tension. The association of the University with the demand for Pakistan has made it a target for Hindu communalists since partition. Added to the traditional political reasons for hostility between the town and the University has been an increasing feeling of resentment and jealousy in recent years on the part of both teachers and students in the three degree colleges of Aligarh town against the superior environment, facilities, and salaries offered by the university.

Against this background, it is possible to understand how a minor scuffle among some students of the University over the Student Union elections of October, 1961, led to a Hindu-Muslim riot which engulfed the whole

[35] For example, a major issue between the two groups has been the question of the participation of women in University cultural activities.

[36] The RSS (Rashtriya Swayamsevak Sangh) is a militant Hindu, semi-secret society.

[37] Letter of Ansar Harvani, M.P. to the *Pioneer*, October 13, 1961.

town and spread to other districts in western Uttar Pradesh. The Student
Union elections of 1961 were fought wholly on communal lines. Shortly
before the elections of October 1, the leaders of the Hindu students[38] of the
University arranged among themselves to withdraw all the Hindu candidates but one for twelve posts on the Student Union Executive Committee.
No corresponding action was taken by the Muslim candidates; however,
communal feeling in the election was such that, despite the strategy of the
Hindu candidates, not a single Hindu student was elected to any of the
posts. The 1961 election was the first University student election in ten
years in which no Hindu was successful.

In the aftermath of the election, a scuffle occurred in one of the University hostels between rival student groups of the two communities, in
which the Hindu students were aided by a group of their coreligionists
from the Hindu colleges of the town. Although no one was seriously injured in the scuffle, a rumor was spread throughout the town that a Hindu
student had been killed in the University. On October 3, large mobs from
the town, composed mostly of students from the Hindu colleges, burned
some shops in the University market areas and attacked some University
employees; rioting, during which fourteen Muslims were killed, spread
throughout the town. Nearly 600 people were arrested as a result of the
rioting and curfew was enforced in the town for two weeks.

Though the local Congress organization had nothing to do with the riots
and murders that took place, the Hindu-Muslim riot of October, 1961,
coming just before the General Elections of 1962, was an important factor
in the defeat of the Congress in the 1962 elections in Aligarh district. After
the riot, the Muslim conservatives in the University, who laid the blame for
the rioting upon inadequate police action, joined hands with two other opposition forces in the district to defeat the Congress. The Congress leaders,
preoccupied with their own internal conflicts and unaware of the strength
of the opposition forces gathering against them, helped to defeat themselves.

The University, the Muslims, and the Congress.—Aligarh Muslim University now—as always—provides the major source of Muslim political
leadership in the district. Before 1947, as has been seen, the University was
the intellectual headquarters of the All-India Muslim League. The relationship between Aligarh Muslim political leaders and the local Congress, as
well as the attitudes of Muslim political leaders in Aligarh towards the Congress, reflect both the traditional estrangement between the Congress and
the Muslims and the current ideological conflicts among Muslims in the
University. There is no Muslim in Aligarh district who has held or now

[38] It is estimated that approximately 35 percent of the students in the University are
Hindu.

holds any significant position of power or influence in the Aligarh Congress. However, after Independence, until the elections of 1962, both the progressives and the conservatives in the University who took any part in local politics gave their support to the local Congress organization.

The Congress, for its part, has reserved one constituency in the district for a Muslim candidate in every general election. In 1952, the Aligarh City Assembly constituency was given to a Muslim. In 1957 and 1962, Congress Muslim candidates contested from the Aligarh parliamentary constituency. The change from an Assembly to a parliamentary constituency for the Congress Muslim candidate is a reflection of the unimportant role of Muslims in the Aligarh Congress. It is more of an honor to sit in the legislature at Delhi than at Lucknow, but the fight for power in district and state politics revolves around the distribution of Assembly tickets, not parliamentary tickets.

The Congress ticket in Aligarh is always given to Muslims who have a reputation as "Nationalists" and for whom politics is not a vocation. For example, in 1957, the Congress candidate for Parliament from the Aligarh constituency was Jamal Khwaja. Jamal Khwaja was only thirty-one in 1957 and had no record in politics; however, his father was the leading "Nationalist" Muslim of Aligarh. Jamal Khwaja was a lecturer in Philosophy at the University from 1953 until his election to Parliament. He was recommended again by the local Congress for the parliamentary ticket in 1962, but he declined the offer and returned to teaching.

To replace Jamal Khwaja, the Congress selected Jarrar Haider to contest the 1962 election. Jarrar Haider had a deeper interest in political affairs than Jamal Khwaja and had joined the Congress in 1937 when he was a student of the University. A prominent lawyer of Aligarh and legal adviser to the University, Jarrar Haider's participation in politics declined as his practice increased. However, he remained active in University affairs and became identified strongly with the "progressives" in University politics. He was surprised when some local Congressmen approached him to request him to contest for Parliament in 1962.[39]

The faith of the progressives, like Jarrar Haider, in the Congress was not shaken by the Aligarh riots of 1961. For the most part, the progressives and the Communists in the University identified intellectually with the national leadership of the Congress and with the party's socialist ideology. Their participation in local politics is limited to supporting Congress candidates who hold progressive views and opposing both Hindu and Muslim candidates who adopt a communal outlook.

However, the so-called "communalists" or conservatives in the University became extremely embittered towards the Congress after the 1961 riot

[39] Interview with Jarrar Haider in Aligarh on September 17, 1962.

and felt that the Congress and the government had not done enough to protect Muslim lives and property. One Muslim of the conservative group in the University, who opposed the Congress in the 1962 elections, expressed the views of the entire group in this way:

I continued to be a member of the Congress till now; but, I found that the Congress was not playing fair game to the minorities and the downtrodden classes. [Before the Aligarh riot, there were] the Jabalpur riots; . . . justice was not done there and there was a report by some MPs which indicated this. Subhadra Joshi [a Congress MP] said that policemen took part in incendiarism and looting. Then, these riots spread and the Government did nothing to stop it. If the Government wanted to stop it, there would be no riots.[40]

This kind of feeling of bitterness towards the Congress and the government, which developed after the Jabalpur and Aligarh riots, led the most influential conservative Muslim leaders associated with the University to oppose the Congress actively in the 1962 elections.

The Muslim conservative leaders realized that they could not challenge the Congress by themselves. Muslim influence is concentrated in the town; and, even in the town, an open appeal to Muslims might lead only to a polarization of Hindu and Muslim voting, in which the Hindu majority would make itself felt. Alliance with other communities and with other opposition forces was essential.

The Muslim conservative leadership of the University provided only one link in the triple alliance against the Congress. The most that the Muslim conservative leaders could offer was a heavy Muslim vote against the Congress from the city. In the rural areas, the Muslim vote is proportionately much smaller than in the city, scattered in isolated pockets, and thus not so easily influenced by the Muslim University leaders. The central core of the alliance against the Congress came from the Chamars, who compose the bulk of the low-caste landless laborers in the rural areas and form the largest caste in the district. The alliance between urban Muslims and rural Chamars was forged by their respective leaders within the University.

The Republican Party

Muslims and Chamars have little in common but a deep resentment among some members of both communities against the economic and political dominance of elite Hindu castes in contemporary India. During the nationalist period, an occasional visionary Muslim or Scheduled Caste politician dreamed of the possibilities of a political alliance between Muslims and Scheduled Castes. However, when the demand for a separate state became the exclusive goal of the Muslim League, whatever possibility there

[40] Interview in Aligarh on September 14, 1962.

was of such a political alliance before Independence became out of the question. In 1943, the famous Scheduled Caste leader, Dr. Ambedkar, condemned both Gandhi and Jinnah "for the mess they have made of Indian politics."[41]

The development of the political consciousness and the political effectiveness of the Scheduled Castes as a group has been hindered by the continued educational backwardness of most low castes and by the diversity of and the mutual differences among the thousands of low-caste groups which come under the constitutional definition of Scheduled Castes. The center of Scheduled Caste political activity has been in and around Bombay City and has only recently spread to other parts of the country. In Uttar Pradesh, the Chamars are the best educated and the most politically conscious group among the Scheduled Castes. The Republican Party, which is the political vehicle of the militant Scheduled Caste movement, is dominated in Uttar Pradesh by the Chamars. Chamars are invariably close to the very bottom in the status and economic hierarchies of rural Uttar Pradesh. Throughout the state, they are employed in the rural areas primarily as agricultural laborers and, in the urban areas, in inferior menial occupations —as leather workers, factory hands, coolies, or rickshaw drivers.

Aligarh district has the heaviest concentration of Chamars in Uttar Pradesh; Chamars constitute close to 22 percent of the population of the district and are numerically dominant in all but two of the six tahsils of the district. The Chamars have not only numbers in Aligarh district, but a dynamic and popular leader in the person of B. P. Maurya. B. P. Maurya was the master strategist in the alliance of Muslims, Chamars, and rebel Congressmen, which succeeded in defeating the Congress organization in Aligarh in the 1962 elections.

Maurya comes from the town of Khair in Aligarh district. He took a B.Sc. and an LL.M. degree from Aligarh Muslim University and joined the Faculty of Law in the University as a Lecturer in 1960. Before joining the Law faculty, Maurya had worked for the advancement of his community of Chamars. In 1957, Maurya and one of his followers contested two Assembly constituencies in the district unsuccessfully. Maurya has led the movement in Aligarh, begun earlier in Bombay, for the conversion of the Scheduled Castes to Buddhism.[42] As a result of his work among the Chamars and his education, Maurya has become the hero of his community. In May, 1961, a criminal case was registered against him for allegedly assaulting a policeman who had tried to arrest a rickshaw driver for a traffic violation.[43]

[41] From the preface by B. R. Ambedkar to *Ranade, Gandhi, & Jinnah* (Bombay: Thacker and Co., Ltd., 1943).

[42] The conversion to Buddhism by some Scheduled Castes represents a protest against the inequalities of Hindu society.

[43] *National Herald*, October 29, 1961.

During the Hindu-Muslim riot of 1961, Maurya acquired some popularity among Muslims for his criticisms of the Hindu community and for carrying out relief work among Muslims. In the University, he has been sponsored by the Dean of the Faculty of Law, a leading member of the Muslim conservative group in University politics.

The Scheduled Caste vote has been a mainstay of the Congress in Uttar Pradesh since independence. Until the 1962 election, the Republican Party and its predecessor, the Scheduled Caste Federation, achieved no successes in Uttar Pradesh politics. For the most part, the Scheduled Castes in Uttar Pradesh have accepted the patronage of the Congress government [44] and have given their votes to the Congress party in return. The Scheduled Caste leaders who have been given Congress tickets in the reserved constituencies are non-militant and have no power in the local or state Congress organizations. The numerous organizations in Uttar Pradesh for the advancement of the Scheduled Castes and "depressed classes" have been content to serve as agencies for the distribution of Congress patronage.

The Republican party leaders feel that Scheduled Caste members who join the Congress betray the aspirations of the low castes. The Republicans are militant opponents of the Congress which, they claim, is dominated by the elite Hindu castes. To oppose the Congress, Republicans are willing to seek alliances with any party or individual whose principles are not opposed to their own.

In 1962, the Republicans were able to cover all ten Assembly constituencies and both parliamentary constituencies in Aligarh district either with candidates of the Republican Party or with candidates with whom the Republicans had alliances. The center of Republican influence in the district was in the Aligarh parliamentary constituency and its five component Assembly constituencies. The Republican candidate for Parliament from Aligarh constituency was B. P. Maurya himself; Republicans also contested directly three of the Assembly constituencies and had alliances in the remaining two. In the Aligarh town constituency, the Republican candidate was Dr. Abdul Bashir Khan, a leading Muslim conservative and the proctor of the University for a time; as proctor, Dr. Abdul Bashir was responsible for student discipline during the events which led up to the October riot.

In 1957, the Congress won the Aligarh parliamentary constituency and four of the five Assembly constituencies; in 1962, the Congress lost every seat. The Republicans won the parliamentary seat, the Aligarh City Assembly seat, and one seat reserved for Scheduled Castes. Two seats went to

---

[44] Under the Constitution of India and various acts of legislation, members of Scheduled Castes are entitled to certain privileges and special concessions, such as reservation of seats in the legislatures, posts in the administrative services, scholarships in colleges and universities, and so on.

Republican-supported Congress rebels; the fifth constituency went to a Swatantra party candidate. The alliance between B. P. Maurya and the Muslim conservative leaders from the University was decisive in determining the election outcome in the parliamentary contest; Maurya could not have won without the overwhelming support he received from the Muslim voters of Aligarh town. The rout of the Congress in the other constituencies was partly due to the loss of much of its previous support from the Chamars and partly to the important role of Congress rebels and of internal sabotage in the campaign.

The Congress: Rebellion and sabotage

Congress rebels.—According to the official figures of the state Congress office, Aligarh district ranked first among all the districts in Uttar Pradesh in terms of the number of Congressmen who contested against the official Congress candidates in the 1962 elections. Altogether, nine Congressmen contested against the official Congress candidates in seven constituencies in the district. In four constituencies, the Congress rebels were elected. One of the four rebels was Dr. Abdul Bashir Khan, who contested on the Republican Party ticket from Aligarh town; the other three ran as independents with Republican support. None of the defeated Congress rebels had Republican support.

The pacts between Republicans and rebel Congressmen were essential to both. The alliance of Muslims and Chamars was important only in the town; outside of Aligarh town, Muslims are unimportant both in numbers and influence. For example, in Iglas constituency, which falls within the Aligarh parliamentary constituency, Jats are the dominant community in numbers and economic power. After Jats, in number, come the Chamars. In Iglas, Maurya had a pact with Sheodan Singh, a Jat and a Congress rebel. Sheodan Singh had been associated with the dominant faction in the Aligarh Congress for some time after Independence and he had contested on the Congress ticket from Iglas in 1952, 1957, and in a bye-election in 1959. Sheodan Singh had had a long rivalry with the Raja of the Mursan estate, also a Jat and the largest *zamindar* in the district. In 1952, Sheodan Singh defeated the Raja; however, in 1957, the Raja defeated Sheodan Singh and another Jat candidate. Sheodan Singh filed an election petition against the Raja for corrupt practices and succeeded in having the election declared void and the Raja debarred from contesting in any election for four years. After the election result was overturned by the court, a bye-election was held in which the Raja's wife contested against Sheodan Singh and another Jat candidate. This time, both Sheodan Singh and the Rani were defeated and the third Jat candidate was successful.

Sheodan Singh had fallen out with the dominant faction in the Aligarh

Congress before the 1957 election and had received the Congress ticket in that year only through the intervention of one of the state Congress leaders. In 1962, Sheodan Singh did not apply for the ticket. However, when the Congress selected the Rani of Mursan for the Congress ticket from Iglas, Sheodan Singh's anger was aroused and he decided to contest again against the Rani, this time as an independent.

In the 1962 election from Iglas, there were eleven candidates altogether—ten of them Jats and one a Brahman. Jat votes were so divided that, had it not been for the pact between Sheodan Singh and Maurya, the Brahman candidate would have succeeded on the basis of undivided Brahman support. However, Sheodan Singh was elected with some Jat and a majority of Chamar votes, while the Brahman came in second and the Rani third. In the vote for Parliament from Iglas, however, Jat votes were less divided. Maurya polled almost exactly the same number of votes from Iglas as did Sheodan Singh, but polled 3,000 votes less than the Jat candidate for Parliament in this segment of the constituency. Maurya's pact with Sheodan Singh was less helpful to the former than his alliance with the Muslim conservatives in Aligarh town. Sheodan Singh could not gain for himself, much less transfer to Maurya, an undivided Jat vote in the same way as Dr. Abdul Bashir could both gain and transfer to Maurya an undivided Muslim vote in the town. On the other hand, there is no doubt that Republican support was decisive in the victory of Sheodan Singh in Iglas.

Sabotage.—Powerful as the alliance against the Congress was in Aligarh district, a united Congress might have been able to resist the opposition forces against it and might have prevented a total failure in the 1962 elections. Had even the dominant faction in the local Congress been united, the election results might have been different. However, in the 1962 elections in Aligarh district, the Congress campaign was affected not only by the rivalry between the Gautam and Malkhan Singh factions, but by a split within the Malkhan Singh faction as well. As has been seen, the dominant faction split over the selection of the Congress candidate for president of the District Board. In this split, Nawab Singh and Sahib Singh were on one side, Malkhan Singh and Sri Niwas on the other. Malkhan Singh's death on the eve of the election made rapprochement impossible. It was reported that Sahib Singh was personally responsible for most of the sabotage in the 1962 Congress campaign in Aligarh; in his work, he was allegedly aided by Nawab Singh who, on the death of Malkhan Singh, became the leader of the dominant faction and as general secretary of the DCC was responsible for the coordination of the Congress campaign.

The importance of cooperation between the Assembly and parliamentary candidates has been illustrated in the Gonda study. A major problem in the Congress campaign in Aligarh was the absence of such cooperation. Jarrar

Haider, the Congress candidate for parliament, was imposed upon the local Congress organization by the Central Parliamentary Board. A "Nationalist" Muslim, a highly educated and a cultured man, concerned with ideological issues and with the progress of socialism and secularism in the country, Jarrar Haider is the kind of Congressman that the central party leaders would like to have in Parliament. Jarrar Haider had some support from local Congressmen of the Gautam faction, but he was not a member of either faction in the local Congress. The dominant faction had nominated a member of the faction for the ticket and resented the imposition of Jarrar Haider by the central party leaders.

In the campaign, neither group worked for Jarrar Haider. The result was that Jarrar Haider trailed behind every Congress Assembly candidate but one and placed third or fourth in every constituency (table 6). In fact, Jarrar Haider was not really in the running for Parliament.

TABLE 6

VOTE FOR CONGRESS ASSEMBLY CANDIDATES AND THE PARLIAMENTARY CANDIDATE
IN FIVE CONSTITUENCIES IN ALIGARH DISTRICT, 1962 ELECTION

| Constituency | Assembly | | Parliament | |
	Votes	Position	Votes	Position
Aligarh	16,164	2nd	7,260	3rd
Koil	6,365	3rd	3,919	3rd
Iglas	7,264	3rd	6,976	4th
Khair	14,766	2nd	9,941	3rd
Tappal	8,737	3rd	8,995	4th
Total	53,296		37,091	

Communal feeling was strongest in the parliamentary election; the contest was primarily between Maurya and Shiv Kumar Shastri, an independent candidate supported by the Arya Samaj, the Jan Sangh, and also reportedly by the Sahib Singh–Nawab Singh Congress faction. A Gorakshat (cow-protection) Front was established during the campaign, led by the Jan Sangh and the Arya Samaj; as one parliamentary candidate put it, the contest was between "meat-eaters" (Maurya and his Muslim allies) and those "interested in the safety of the cow."[45]

Sabotage was not restricted to the parliamentary contest. In all the constituencies, it was generally reported that Nawab Singh and Sahib Singh's followers worked against candidates of the Gautam faction and Gautam's followers worked against candidates of the other faction. Sometimes the sabotage took the form of actual canvassing by Congressmen against Con-

[45] Interview in Aligarh on September 25, 1962.

gressmen; in some constituencies, opposition candidates were set up and financed by one faction against the candidate of another or rebel Congressmen were supported. Most of the sabotage occurred in the five Assembly constituencies composing the Aligarh parliamentary constituency. In these five constituencies, two Assembly candidates—Mohan Lal Gautam himself in Khair and Anant Ram Verma in the town—belonged to the Gautam faction and two to the dominant faction; the fifth candidate was unaffiliated, but was opposed by the dominant faction. As one Congressman remarked, "The Congress organization in all the five constituencies was actually working at cross purposes and the main obstacle that the Congress candidates had to contend with were not the opposition parties, but their personal opponents inside the Congress party itself."[46]

Election epilogue

As a result of its own internal conflicts, the Congress party in Aligarh district was unable—indeed, it did not try—to cope with the problems which arose in its environment. The debacle of the Congress in the 1962 election was a direct consequence of the Hindu-Muslim riot of October, 1961. The tension that grew up between Hindus and Muslims during the riot continued into the elections. The alliance between Muslims and Chamars to oppose the Congress created a counteralliance among right-wing, Hindu communal elements. Communal slogans and verbal attacks on various communities were the dominant features of the campaign in Aligarh. The Congress was caught in the middle of this communal situation; though the Muslim-Chamar alliance was established to oppose the Congress, Hindus did not gather around the Congress in the same way as Muslims and Chamars did around the Republican Party.

Communal feelings were exploited primarily in the parliamentary election and in the Assembly election for Aligarh town. In the other Assembly contests, local rivalries took precedence. In the town, Muslims and Chamars supported the Republican candidates for Assembly and Parliament overwhelmingly. In the Hindu localities, the vote went to the Congress in the Assembly contest and to the Arya Samaj candidate in the parliamentary contest. Thus, the Congress candidate for Parliament lost both Muslim votes because of the Muslim-Chamar pact and Hindu votes because of the counteralliance of conservative Hindu parties and independents.[47]

[46] Interview in Aligarh on September 17, 1962.

[47] The election results in the ten polling stations in Aligarh town in which each major candidate for both Assembly and Parliament polled his highest votes in 1962 reveal the following patterns. In the Assembly contest, the successful Republican candidate (Dr. Abdul Bashir Khan, a Muslim) polled between 83.7 and 95.4 percent of the total vote in his ten best polling stations, which covered 26 *mohallas* (neighborhoods) in the town. The median percentage of Muslims resident in these *mohallas*, according to the

The 1962 election in Aligarh illustrates the necessity for opposition forces to combine the votes of different castes and communities to challenge the Congress in a broad area. What was true for Gonda is true for Aligarh —no single party can match the diversity of support which the Congress can muster in a district. The Republican party alone, Muslims alone, or rebel Congressmen alone could have achieved only limited success; together, they cut away the major props of Congress support in previous elections.

It is unlikely that the opposition success against the Congress can be maintained in future elections in Aligarh. Rebel Congressmen, Muslims, and Chamars have so little in common that the maintenance of such an alliance is difficult to imagine. Many rebel Congressmen are political entrepreneurs, whose only consistent principles are their lack of allegiance to any party, group, or alliance. In addition, a feeling of mistrust exists between some members of the two communities of Chamars and Muslims. Another weakness exists in the Republican party itself, in that it has support among Chamars only. None of the other Scheduled Castes or "backward classes" supported Maurya in the 1962 election. A united Congress will have little to fear from the Republicans in future contests.

CONCLUSION

The Gonda study revealed that the local Congress organization has great resilience and can survive major setbacks. Though the Aligarh Congress has suffered a severe electoral defeat, its position in district politics is, even now, more secure than the position of the Gonda Congress. The difference is that there is still no cohesive opposition to the Congress in Aligarh and very little opposition at all to Congress control of local institutions. Political strength in a district depends more upon control of local institutions

1951 census, was 89.6 percent. The Congress candidate (Anant Ram Verma, a Hindu) polled between 62.4 and 69.5 percent of the total vote in his ten best polling stations, which covered 32 *mohallas*. The median percentage of Muslims in these *mohallas* was only 2.3 percent, but of caste Hindus 88.7 percent. In contrast, in the Aligarh town component of the Aligarh parliamentary constituency, the Congress candidate (Jarrar Haider, a Muslim) won a plurality of the votes in only 1 of the 96 polling stations. The remaining 95 polling stations were divided between the winning Republican candidate (B. P. Maurya, a Chamar) and the Arya Samaj candidate (Shiv Kumar Shastri, a Hindu). Nine out of 10 of B. P. Maurya's best polling stations (between 81.8 and 95.2 percent of the vote) were the same as the Republican Assembly candidate's best. The Congress loss of the Hindu vote in the parliamentary contest is clear from the results in the Arya Samaj candidate's ten best polling stations (between 72.9 and 85.5 percent of the vote), which covered 25 *mohallas*. Four of the Arya Samaj candidate's ten best were the same as the Congress Assembly candidate's best polling stations. The median percentage of Muslims in the 25 *mohallas* was only 0.6, whereas that of caste Hindus was 96.4.

than upon the number of legislators elected to the state Assembly from the district. The Congress ticket is itself a patronage instrument and only one instrument among many which the local Congress has at its disposal.

The future of the Congress in Aligarh district and the possibility of a recovery of its electoral strength depend largely upon the ability of Aligarh Congressmen to unite in future contests with opposition forces. The entire factional situation in the Aligarh Congress has been altered partly by the deaths of prominent leaders and partly by political changes in the balance of power in state Congress politics. Mohan Lal Gautam has been out of power in the state government since 1960, and he and his supporters in the district were defeated in the 1962 elections. Malkhan Singh died just before the 1962 election and Sahib Singh just after the election. The kind of bitter bifactional conflict which developed between the 1957 and 1962 elections is not likely to occur again.

The Aligarh Congress is now in a position, with respect to its political leadership, similar to that of the Gonda Congress after the expulsion of the Raja of Mankapur. There is no leader and no faction in Aligarh district today powerful enough to dominate alone the district Congress and district politics. The future prospect for the Aligarh Congress is similar to the present condition of the Gonda Congress—a coexistence of a number of political leaders with strictly local influence, bargaining among themselves and forming temporary alliances of mutual convenience.

VI.

Deoria: The Politics of Sugar

THE ENVIRONMENT

Deoria, lying in the northeastern corner of Uttar Pradesh, bordered on the north by Nepal and on the east by the state of Bihar, is one of the poorest districts in India. With a population of 2,375,075 in an area just over 2,000 square miles, the district has the fourth highest density in the state—1,138 persons per square mile. Only the districts of Varanasi, Lucknow, and Meerut, all of which have large urban populations, have a higher density. In Deoria, however, 97.6 percent of the population lives in the rural areas;[1] there are only three towns in the district with a population over 10,000—Deoria (28,000), Barhaj (15,000), and Padrauna (14,000).[2]

The great density of population in the district creates the twin problems of uneconomic landholdings and high unemployment. The per capita landholding in the district is less than half an acre. The sugar factories of Deoria district provide seasonal industrial employment to approximately 15,000 people. The rest of the unemployed must go to the big cities to find employment—to Kanpur, Bombay, Calcutta. No new industry was allocated to Deoria in the first two plans and none are allocated in the third plan.

Deoria's problems are heightened by the annual floods, which inundate vast areas of the district for several months of the year. The floods begin in the middle of June and continue until the end of September, fed by two major river systems—the Great Gandak and the Rapti-Ghagra systems. Major flood control projects have been on blueprints for several years, but technical reasons have delayed some projects and the lack of cooperation

[1] *Census of India, 1961, Paper No. 1 of 1962, Final Population Totals*, pp. 350-351.
[2] *Ibid.*, pp. 239, 241.

112

from the Nepal government has prevented the damming of the Great Gandak in the hills of Nepal.

Although no other rural district in Uttar Pradesh has as high a population density as Deoria, there are other eastern districts where poverty is even more extreme. Living conditions in Ghazipur, Azamgarh, and Ballia districts were described so vividly in a speech by a Congress MP in Parliament in 1962 that the Prime Minister was moved to order the appointment of an inquiry commission to examine the economic problems of the eastern districts.[3] What makes the difference between Deoria and other eastern districts of Uttar Pradesh is sugar. Sugar cane is the only cash crop in Deoria district. Peasants fortunate enough to have both land and the water to cultivate cane upon it may be able to live a somewhat better life than others. However, those who do grow cane are more dependent upon the government and upon the market economy than other peasants, since the government sets the price of sugar cane to be paid by the factories to the growers and since the peasant must buy his rice in the market. The result of this dependence upon government and the market economy is that both political and economic issues are more important to the cane growers than to other peasants. For these and other reasons, the life and much of the politics of the district revolve around sugar—around the financial ties between the millowners and the political parties, the development of trade unions in the sugar factories, and the expression of the demands of the cane growers for a higher cane price. In this chapter, the effects upon the Congress organization of the economic and political problems of the sugar industry will be examined.

THE DEORIA CONGRESS: THE ABSENCE OF POLITICAL LOYALTIES

Interparty competition has been strong in Deoria district since the first general election of 1952. It is not surprising, then, that factional conflicts have been milder here than elsewhere. There have been no political murders in Deoria district and no litigation between rival factions. There are a few politicians in Deoria who wield real power in the district Congress and in local political affairs, but no man and no single faction now dominates the local Congress. In fact, there are few real factions in the Deoria Congress. One Congressman of some influence in district politics spoke of the difficulties of building a cohesive faction. He complained that ". . . there is no loyalty, that people change groups depending on their interests of the

[3] The commission began work in January, 1963. See the *National Herald*, January 18, 1963.

moment. . . . There are just individuals who, in times of crisis, combine together. There is hardly a permanent group. Mutual interests are the paramount force in deciding who is with whom."[4]

The absence of party loyalties is the most fundamental fact of contemporary politics in Uttar Pradesh. In Gonda and Aligarh, factional loyalties
have existed and continue to exist to some extent. In both districts, factional
loyalties provide the link between the parochial units of Indian society—
family, village, caste—and the political parties. Factional loyalty in the
Uttar Pradesh Congress replaces party loyalty. Factional politics is an intermediate, perhaps a transitional, form of politics. It is something "more"
than parochial politics—a politics based upon language, caste, tribe, or religion—and something "less" than party politics in the European and American sense, involving an impersonal allegiance to a party as an institution or
as an ideology. (See F. G. Bailey's comments on the absence of allegiances
to party in Orissa politics in *Politics and Social Change: Orissa in 1959*,
p. 154.)

Most political leaders in Uttar Pradesh reject parochial politics, partly
because of principle and partly because of the rational calculation that, in a
society as diverse as that in Uttar Pradesh, there is little prospect for the development of politically effective parochial groups. But it is a long step
from the rejection of parochial loyalties to the development of party loyalties. Factions perform the function of political recruitment for political
parties in Uttar Pradesh. In the absence of a fully-developed factional system, each man follows his own interests and acts as a one-man faction.

The Deoria Congress is actually a mixture of factions and individuals,
somewhat like the Gonda Congress. There is a vacuum of political leadership within the district Congress similar to the situation in the Gonda Congress after the expulsion of the Raja of Mankapur. It was not always so.

The Deoria Congress was led during the nationalist period by one of the
numerous minor "saints" who, like Gandhi himself, combined religion and
politics. Deoria's saint was Baba Raghava Das, "the Gandhi of the eastern
districts." Baba Raghava Das was a Maharashtrian Brahman who lost his
whole family in a cholera epidemic in the early years of this century and
came to Deoria in search of peace and spiritual inspiration at the feet of a
well-known *guru* of the district. When his *guru* died, Baba Raghava Das
replaced him as the spiritual leader of the area and took charge of the
ashram which his *guru* had established. Older Congressmen and ex-Congressmen of Deoria say that it was because of Baba Raghava Das that people
of the area went to jail and made personal sacrifices during the Congress
movement.

Baba Raghava Das maintained the undivided allegiance of all Congress-

[4] Interview in Kasia on July 20, 1962.

men in Deoria district until 1948, when he left active politics to join the Sarvodaya movement.[5] After the departure of Baba Raghava Das from district politics, three distinct factional groups emerged to contest for the leadership of the Deoria Congress. A combination of ideological, regional, caste, and personal differences divided the three factions.

The chief lieutenant of Baba Raghava Das was Ram Dhari Pande, a Brahman from Padrauna tahsil in the north of the district. Ram Dhari Pande is not a saint and he could not prevent divisions in the Deoria Congress. However, he led the largest faction in the district, composed predominantly of Brahmans from Padrauna. The second largest faction was led by Genda Singh, a Bhuinhar, also from Padrauna. The third faction, much smaller than the other two, was also led by a Brahman, Sarju Prasad Misra, but was based upon the southern (Deoria-Salempur) portion of the district.

The main contest for leadership was between the two largest factions. However, the existence of a third faction gave the contest fluidity and prevented a direct confrontation between the two main factions. Sarju Prasad Misra was elected president of the DCC, with the help of the Genda Singh faction and a member of the latter faction was elected to the post of general secretary.

The differences between the two largest factions provided all the elements for the kind of intense factional struggle that has occurred in other districts. For one thing, Genda Singh's faction was affiliated with the Congress Socialist Party. For another, there was a difference in the caste composition of the leadership of the two factions, one led by Brahmans, the other by Bhuinhars. Finally, there were personal differences. Ram Dhari Pande had been Genda Singh's political leader; but, Genda Singh and other members of his faction had felt betrayed by Ram Dhari Pande. One member of the Genda Singh faction described the differences between Ram Dhari Pande and his old followers in this way:

When Ram Dhari Pande was elected to the Assembly [in 1937], he left his old friends and began friendship with the great capitalists of the district. He became a great friend of Kedar Nath Khetan who, at that time, owned three or four sugar factories, as well as shares in Bombay *suti* [textile] mills. Ram Dhari Pande became a friend of this man and left all his old friends and old habits; his attitude toward public service ended. He was engaged in fulfilling his personal ambitions and wanted to have land, money, everything. . . . The big landlords and this Kedar Nath Khetan gave him land and money.[6]

In the eyes of some of his old followers, Ram Dhari Pande had, in effect, given up his qualifications for factional leadership. Factional leaders differ in many ways; but, the ideal factional leader should have certain personal

[5] A movement for rural social regeneration based upon Gandhian ideas.
[6] Interview in Lucknow on May 17, 1962.

attributes, particularly simplicity in personal habits, a lack of material ambitions, and, most important of all, faithfulness to old friends.[7] When his followers thought that Ram Dhari Pande had lost these attributes, he lost much of his old factional following.

Two factors prevented the development of intense factional struggle in the district Congress. One was the looseness of the factional system. Neither of the two major factions could control the district Congress by itself so that the third faction acted as a balance wheel, preventing a polarization of factional conflict. The other was that the Genda Singh faction left the Congress party in 1948 and developed into an opposition political party. After the departure of the Socialists from the Deoria Congress, the Ram Dhari Pande faction remained the only really cohesive group in the local Congress and took control of the DCC.

The departure of the Genda Singh faction reduced intraparty factionalism and created interparty competition. The Socialist party contested against the Congress in the 1952 election and gained a complete victory in all four Assembly constituencies and in the parliamentary constituency from Padrauna tahsil. In the ten remaining Assembly and two parliamentary constituencies of the district, the Congress was successful. Within the district Congress, there is no weightage favoring party delegates from successful constituencies. The Ram Dhari Pande faction remained Padrauna-based and maintained control of the DCC, despite its demonstrated unpopularity with the general electorate. The leader of the faction himself was defeated in the parliamentary election in 1952 from Padrauna. The strength of a faction in the district Congress party does not depend only or primarily upon electoral support.

The strength and cohesiveness of a faction within the Congress party organization depend upon the personal characteristics of the leader and the material benefits he can distribute. Ram Dhari Pande lost his hold over a group of his followers because it was believed that he sought material advantage for himself and forgot his "old friends." But Ram Dhari Pande's new friends provided him the material benefits to keep the greater part of his faction intact. Ram Dhari Pande's two most important supporters have been the head of a family that owns four sugar mills in the district and the ex-Raja of the Padrauna estate, formerly the largest *zamindar* in the district. Another ally of Ram Dhari Pande in recent years has been Raj Bhansi Tiwary, from the southern part of the district, the managing director of the District Cooperative Bank. This combination of friends kept some cohesive-

[7] Cf. Scalapino and Masumi's description of the ideal Japanese faction leader, whose qualities include "loyalty and steadfastness to one's friends and followers," *Parties and Politics in Contemporary Japan* (Berkeley: University of California Press, 1962), pp. 18-19.

ness in the Ram Dhari Pande faction and kept the faction in control of the district Congress from 1948 until 1960.

No other Congressman in the district has been able to develop such a powerful combination of supporters and build a faction to compete with that of Ram Dhari Pande. However, over the years, Congressmen from the Deoria-Salempur side of the district have begun to feel resentment at the long rule of the Padrauna faction of Ram Dhari Pande. For over twenty years, until 1960-1961, Padrauna people had dominated both the district Congress and the District Board. Though this regional resentment did not express itself in factional organization, Ram Dhari Pande began to be concerned.

In the intraparty elections for DCC President and for President of the District Board held in 1960 and 1961, Ram Dhari Pande again gave grounds for others to say that he was unfaithful to old friends. Again, it was a search for new friends that lost him the support of the old. The Deoria-Salempur Congressmen were determined to end the dominance of Ram Dhari Pande and the Padrauna faction over district politics. In this goal they were aided by C. B. Gupta, for the Padrauna faction was allied with the Gautam-Tripathi group in state politics. Ram Dhari Pande, fearing this alliance of some Deoria Congressmen with the state party leader, sought to make friends with old enemies to ensure the success of his faction.

There was no controversy among the members of the Padrauna group over the selection of a candidate for the DCC presidency. For this post, all members of the group agreed upon the name of Raj Mangal Pande, a young and influential lawyer from the town of Kasia in Padrauna tahsil. However, the leader of the District Bank faction expected that one of his men would be sponsored by Ram Dhari Pande for the presidency of the District Board in return for the Bank faction's support for Raj Mangal Pande for DCC President. Instead, Ram Dhari Pande gave his support to an old enemy from Padrauna whose friendship he sought. The result was that the Bank faction sided with the Deoria-Salempur Congressmen and Ram Dhari Pande's candidates lost both contests.

As in the earlier contest in the Deoria Congress for control of the DCC, which took place after Independence, there was little bitterness and no violence involved in these two intraparty elections. The fluidity of the factional system made bargaining, compromise, and adjustment essential. The existence of a floating element of independent Congressmen and independent factions prevented a polarization of conflict.

But the fluidity of the factional system is only one reason for the mildness of this factional struggle in the Deoria Congress. Another reason is that the Deoria Congress is dominated by a single caste and largely by what amounts to an extended kin-group of Pande-Tiwari Brahmans. Leaving aside the two Assembly constituencies in the district reserved for Scheduled Castes, there are twelve Assembly constituencies and three parliamentary constituencies open to all in the district. In the 1962 election, ten of the Congress candidates out of fifteen were Brahmans; of the ten Brahmans, six were either Pandes or Tiwaris. On the DCC Executive Committee of twenty members, twelve are Brahmans and, of these, seven are Pandes or Tiwaris. The contest for DCC President between the Padrauna and Deoria-Salempur groups was fought by two Pandes. A non-Brahman Congressman commented on Brahman dominance of the Deoria Congress in this way: "Among Congressmen [in the district], the Brahmans have got a majority. They have got full clutches [*sic*] over the organization and they don't want any other community to come in. . . . A division is growing up in the district of Brahmans versus non-Brahmans. The Brahmans no doubt contributed much during the freedom struggle, so they had a hold on the organization, but they don't want to let anyone else get a hold." [8] In fact, Brahman dominance of the district Congress is largely coincidence. Elite proprietary castes dominate the district Congress and every other major political party in the state in every district without exception. In Deoria district, there are three major proprietary castes—Brahmans, Rajputs, and Bhuinhars. Bhuinhars are influential in a portion of Padrauna tahsil and largely support the PSP. Rajputs are important landowners in most parts of the district and support the Socialist party in some areas and the Congress in others. However, all parties and all factions are multi-caste in composition. The Congress is dominated by Brahmans because Brahmans are the most influential community in numbers and economic power and have the highest proportion of educated people of any caste in the district.

At the same time, the fact that all factions in the Deoria Congress are Brahman-led moderates factional conflict. Factional antagonisms in Gonda and Aligarh were sharpened by caste differences among prominent faction leaders. The conflicts between opposing factions in Gonda and Aligarh did not stem from caste rivalries; but differences in the cultural backgrounds of opposing leaders intensified personal enmities. It is now a well-known fact of contemporary political science that overlapping loyalties tend to mitigate political conflicts. The common Brahman background of opposing factional leaders in Deoria has the same effect.

The Deoria Congress has passed through three stages of factional development. In the nationalist period, a local "Gandhi" kept a sense of unity among Deoria Congressmen. After Independence, a multifactional system of political competition developed, with one faction dominant. The dominance of the Ram Dhari Pande faction continued until 1960-1961, when a

[8] Interview in Deoria on July 8, 1962.

loose coalition of individuals and smaller factions was formed to end that dominance. The winning coalition has no cohesiveness and has already been breaking up. In the meantime, Ram Dhari Pande has retired from active politics. Now there is no leader or faction capable of uniting or dominating the district Congress. The conclusion seems inescapable that a fluid multifactionalism is the future of every district Congress party in Uttar Pradesh—at least until interparty competition becomes keen enough to foster party loyalties among Congressmen and to give precedence to party interest above factional and individual interest.

Factional conflict and fragmented political opposition not only prevent the development of political loyalties; they also work against the effective expression of political demands. Political demands in Deoria arise largely out of the relations among the people and institutions involved in the sugar industry. In the next section, the effects of factionalism upon political organization in the sugar industry will be examined.

THE POLITICS OF SUGAR

India is the fourth largest sugar-producing country in the world.[9] Approximately half of the current production of Indian sugar comes from Uttar Pradesh.[10] In 1959, there were 69 sugar factories in Uttar Pradesh—37 of them in the western and central parts of the state and 32 factories in the 4 eastern districts of Basti, Gonda, Gorakhpur, and Deoria.[11] The largest sugar-growing and sugar-producing district in Uttar Pradesh is Deoria district, which alone contains 14 sugar factories.

The sugar industry is the second largest industry in India after textiles. The politics and the economics of the sugar industry are among the most complex problems in contemporary India. The problems of the sugar industry are most acute in Uttar Pradesh and particularly so in eastern Uttar Pradesh. The crux of the sugar problem in eastern Uttar Pradesh is that, in this part of the state where large numbers of people live on the borderline between extreme poverty and outright starvation, sugar is the only cash crop, the sugar factories provide the only means of industrial employment in the region for those pushed off the land, and the sugar industry is failing. There are two main reasons for the decline of the sugar industry in eastern Uttar Pradesh. First, the factories in eastern Uttar Pradesh are among the oldest existing sugar factories in India and cannot compete with the

[9] After the Soviet Union, Cuba, and Brazil; production figures for 1959-60 in *Indian Sugar*, X, No. 9 (December, 1960), 626-627.

[10] *Ibid.*, p. 617.

[11] Government of India, Tarriff Commission, *Report on the Cost Structure of Sugar and Fair Price Payable to the Sugar Industry* (Bombay: Government of India Press, 1959), pp. 83-85.

more modern factories, with higher crushing capacities, which have been
springing up partly in west Uttar Pradesh and in the Punjab, but even more
so in south India. The disadvantage of eastern Uttar Pradesh factories compared to the new factories is compounded by the fact that the quality of
the cane grown in eastern Uttar Pradesh—that is, the sucrose content of the
cane—is lower than in other parts of the country. A corollary to the inability of the sugar factories in eastern Uttar Pradesh to compete with the
newer factories is that the market of the eastern Uttar Pradesh factories,
which once included the whole of India and a large share of the British
market, now is confined largely to Uttar Pradesh.[12]

The politics of sugar, as it affects the eastern districts, centers around
three different groups of people involved in the sugar industry—the millowners, the millworkers, and the cane growers. The politics of sugar, in
all its ramifications, deserves separate treatment as a research project. In this
chapter, the subject will be touched upon only in outline, emphasizing the
role of the Congress and opposition parties in Deoria with respect to the
issues and institutions involved in the sugar industry in the district.

The Congress and the millowners

Opposition party leaders claim that the sugar millowners of Deoria district and elsewhere support the state and national Congress election funds,
as well as individual Congress candidates in the major sugar districts. In
return for this support, it is alleged, the Congress government rewards the
millowners by being lenient in the collection of tax arrears due from the
mills and by joining hands with the "sugar magnates" in exploiting the cane
growers. The alleged exploitation of the cane growers comes in the price
per maund [13] of cane paid to the cane growers, which is fixed by the Union
government, in consultation with the state governments, and which the opposition leaders claim is much too low. A new form of "exploitation" of
the cane growers is the decision taken by the Union government in December, 1962, to relate the cane price to the sucrose content of the cane
supplied by the growers. In the present state of sugar cane cultivation in
Uttar Pradesh, the linking of the cane price to the recovery rate amounts
to a reduction in the cane price, from the previously fixed rate of Rs. 1.62
per maund to Rs. 1.59, according to official estimates.[14]

Opposition party leaders also charge that Deoria Congressmen return
favors and services for the financial support they receive from the millowners. Mention has already been made of the close relationship between

[12] Bhagwati Prasad Khetan, Director of the Lakshmiganj factory in Deoria district,
describes the difficulties of the sugar factories in east Uttar Pradesh in *Problems of
Sugar Industry in Eastern Uttar Pradesh* (Gorakhpur, 1961).
[13] One maund equals approximately 44 pounds.
[14] *National Herald*, December 15, 1962.

Ram Dhari Pande and a prominent "sugar magnate" of the district, Kedar Nath Khetan. It is well known that the two men have had a long association. One Congressman remarked that

Khetan supported not only Ram Dhari Pande, but the Congress in general. . . . Ram Dhari Pande started going to Khetan during the Independence movement. We needed money and we didn't care from where it came; these big people saluted the British, but supported the movement. Many of these industrialists tried to cash it back [that it, their previous help]. Thus, whenever Kedar Nath Khetan needed help, Ram Dhari Pande helped him, for example, for his nomination as MLC. Kedar Nath Khetan has given many donations to the Congress.[15]

There is no doubt that the millowners support the Congress financially— and other political parties also to some extent. The extent of the millowners' "investment" in the Congress and the nature of their return on the investment is less easy to determine. One opposition party candidate in the last election claimed that every sugar factory had to pay a minimum of Rs. 16,000 for the 1962 Congress election fund and that each Congress candidate in Deoria district received Rs. 3,000 for his campaign. Whatever the actual amount of contribution, the Congress not only receives contributions from the millowners, but it expects those contributions. The Kanpur Congress has been known to levy a spindle "tax" on the textile mills. In the sugar industry, contributions to the Congress are based upon the production of each factory.[16]

One millowner in Deoria district complained that revenge was taken against him for failing to contribute to the Congress. One of his mills was in arrears of the cane cess due to the Uttar Pradesh government and was auctioned off to realize the cess. The millowner implied that it was not really the arrears in the Government cess that caused the loss of his mill, but his failure to pay the Congress cess. "The Collector [District Magistrate] . . . was prejudiced against this mill. Some Marwari people and the Collector were in one group. The Marwaris have been against us. They have their sugar factories and they owe twenty-five or thirty lakhs [of Rupees] and nothing is done, whereas we were auctioned off because of eight lakhs. The Congress wants a huge amount as *chanda* [contribution] and we can't pay, so we are subject to all kinds of harassment." [17]

Some Congressmen are on the payroll of the sugar factories. For example, one of the most prominent Congressmen in the district is the company lawyer for one of the sugar factories. There is adequate evidence of significant financial assistance by the sugar millowners to the local, state, and national Congress organizations and to some individual Congress leaders.

[15] Interview in Padrauna on July 17, 1962.
[16] Interview with a millowner in Padrauna on July 17, 1962.
[17] Interview in Padrauna on July 17, 1962.

The charge of harassment of millowners for failure to pay the Congress contribution cannot be proved.

However, there is some evidence against the opposition argument that the state government supports the millowners on policy issues. It is true that the sugar mills in east Uttar Pradesh owe quite considerable arrears of taxes, that some of the arrears have been written off, and that little progress is being made in clearing up the balances. On the other hand, in the present state of the sugar industry in eastern Uttar Pradesh, the millowners refuse to be coerced into paying their arrears and often would rather give up their mills than pay their taxes. Of the fourteen sugar mills in Deoria district, three have been auctioned off for realization of arrears and three others have been put under Government of India controllers in recent years. As for the charge that the state government has supported a lower cane price to the growers and favored the recent linkage of the cane price to the quality of the cane, former Chief Minister Gupta stated in the Uttar Pradesh Assembly that both he and the Chief Minister of Bihar had objected to the linkage established by the central government.[18] The former Chief Minister of Uttar Pradesh was known to have had good relations with the prominent industrialists of the state, but he was also known to be quite blunt in his remarks and in his policy towards the millowners when necessary. The former Chief Minister squarely and publicly placed a large part of the blame for the present condition of the sugar industry in eastern Uttar Pradesh upon the "short-sighted" policy of the millowners, who made huge profits in the early years of their factories, but put very little of the profits back into the plants for modernization.[19]

The fact is that no Congress government could openly sacrifice the interests of the growers to those of the millowners without endangering its electoral strength. Throughout the state, there are five or six million cultivators growing some cane. When the families of the cultivators are counted, the number of people who are affected by the government's policies on sugar approaches a third or more of the total population of the state. Besides, the millowners and all businessmen in the state are dependent upon government in countless ways—for licenses, permits, supplies of government-controlled commodities, and so on; it is on these matters that the government is most amenable to the pleas of industrialists and businessmen, but less so on basic policy issues.

The Congress and the millworkers

Before 1946, Deoria and Gorakhpur were one district. In undivided Gorakhpur, there were twenty-three sugar factories. The trade union

[18] *National Herald*, December 15, 1962.
[19] *National Herald*, October 22, 1962.

movement in the sugar industry was begun in the factories of Gorakhpur and Deoria districts. The trade union movement in the sugar industry suffers from multiple unionism, a by-product of Congress factionalism and fragmented political party opposition. The origin of multiple unionism in the sugar industry stems largely from a factional struggle which took place within the Uttar Pradesh Congress party and among Congress trade union workers in both textiles and sugar in the immediate post-Independence period.

After Independence, there were three broad groups in the Uttar Pradesh Congress and in the Congress-sponsored trade union movement. Only one group had an ideological basis, the Congress Socialist Party. The other two groups were strictly personal in character—one led by Rafi Ahmad Kidwai and the other by the Chief Minister, Pandit Pant, and his party manager, C. B. Gupta.[20] In 1948, the Congress Socialists left the party. From 1948 until 1950-1951, the Kidwai and Pant-Gupta groups struggled for power in the Uttar Pradesh Congress and in the trade union movement. Throughout the struggle, which ended in the victory of the Pant-Gupta group in party affairs, the followers of Kidwai in the party and in the trade unions operated as a dissident group.

In the Congress trade union movement in Uttar Pradesh, the two main protagonists were Harihar Nath Shastri, whose base was in the Kanpur textile industry, and Shibban Lal Saksena, from Gorakhpur, whose influence was in the trade union movement in the sugar industry. In May, 1947, when the Congress-sponsored Indian National Trade Union Congress (INTUC) was formed, Harihar Nath Shastri became the President of the Uttar Pradesh branch. Shastri's opponents in the Congress trade union movement either refused to work with him or were refused prominent positions in the Uttar Pradesh INTUC organization. Harihar Nath Shastri was the leader of the Pant-Gupta group and Shibban Lal Saksena was the leader of the dissident group in Congress trade union politics.

Each of the two protagonists had allies in the other's home base. Shibban Lal Saksena had an ally in the Kanpur textile unions, opposed to the Shastri leadership, and Harihar Nath Shastri had an ally in the sugar unions, opposed to the leadership of Shibban Lal. The conflict in the Kanpur textile industry will be discussed in chapter viii. Here, only the conflict in the sugar industry will be treated.

Shibban Lal Saksena's opponent in the sugar trade unions was Kashi Nath Pande, a Congress labor worker of Deoria district. Kashi Nath Pande had been employed in the sugar factories at Kathkuiyan and Chhitauni in Padrauna tahsil for some time before he began trade union organization work. The first registered trade union in the sugar industry was organized

[20] See chap. iii.

by him at Kathkuiyan in October, 1939. In 1940, Kashi Nath Pande helped
to organize strikes in a number of sugar factories of Gorakhpur-Deoria district and was jailed for his activities. In 1945, 'he was largely responsible for
the formation of the Gorakhpur Zila Chini Mill Mazdoor Federation
(CMMF), a federation of trade unions in the factories of Gorakhpur-
Deoria district. In November, 1946, a larger federation of unions was
formed which, after several changes in name, eventually became the
Indian National Sugar Mill Workers Federation (INSMWF), affiliated to
INTUC. In 1948, when the Socialist split from the Congress occurred, a
rival federation of Socialist trade unions in the industry was formed.

The Socialist federation had little following in the sugar industry. The
main rival of the INTUC-affiliated federation was the Uttar Pradesh and
Bihar Chini Mill Mazdoor Federation of Shibban Lal Saksena. Shibban Lal
Saksena has spent most of his life working among both factory workers and
cane growers in the sugar industry of Uttar Pradesh. Though he never
worked in a factory, as Kashi Nath Pande did, and was an "outsider" to the
trade union movement, Shibban Lal developed a large personal following
among the millworkers and cane growers in all the sugar districts of the
state. Though a much better-known Congressman than Kashi Nath Pande,
Shibban Lal belonged to the dissident group in the Uttar Pradesh Congress
and was bypassed when the INSMWF was formed. In the INTUC federation, Harihar Nath Shastri was elected president and Kashi Nath Pande
the general secretary. Shibban Lal Saksena remained the president of his
CMMF and remained a member of the Congress, though his federation was
not affiliated to INTUC and though he was engaged in a bitter struggle
with the INTUC federation for control over the trade union movement in
the sugar industry.

Although many important issues were raised during the struggle between
the two rival federations, the origin of the struggle was purely personal and
related to factional conflicts within the Uttar Pradesh Congress. Both federation leaders proclaimed their belief in single unionism, but neither leadership was willing to sacrifice personal prestige for the sake of trade union
unity. The struggle between the two rival federations began in 1947-1948
and came to a head early in 1950. In the final outcome, the members of
the Shastri-Pande group continued to hold their positions of dominance
in the Congress labor movement, but Shibban Lal Saksena was able to
demonstrate convincingly that he and his federation had much greater support among sugar millworkers, even in Deoria district, where Kashi Nath
Pande had his greatest personal influence.

The climax of the struggle between the rival federations came in February and March, 1950, when Shibban Lal Saksena and one of his colleagues

began a fast which lasted thirty days, for the satisfaction of certain alleged demands of the sugar workers in general and of the members of his federation in particular. The four main demands of the fasting men were: a wage increase, democratic election of Works Committees in each mill, official recognition of the most representative unions to be determined by a census of sugar workers, and reinstatement of workers of the CMMF allegedly victimized by the factory managers for their trade union activities. The fast and the demands were directed against the government of Uttar Pradesh, which has the authority and responsibility for fixing wages, supervising employer-employee relations, and granting recognition to trade unions. According to the fasters, the method of fasting, rather than a general strike, was resorted to because the INTUC federation had earlier submitted some demands to adjudication, thus making a strike illegal. The fast ended, as most political fasts do in contemporary Indian politics, with the government agreeing to appoint inquiry committees to go into the major demands. However, the most important demand of the fasting men, for a census to determine the representative character of the two federations, was conceded. The census, held on March 15, 1950, was an overwhelming victory for the CMMF of Shibban Lal Saksena. In 66 factories in Uttar Pradesh, 68,142 men cast their votes for one of the two federations; the CMMF received 47,691 votes against 20,449 for the INTUC federation.[21] The CMMF was successful in 48 of the 66 sugar factories, thus winning recognition as the most representative union in these 48 factories and in the state as a whole. The victory meant that CMMF union members replaced INSMWF union members on the Works Committees of the 48 factories and on the labor Conciliation Boards of the Uttar Pradesh government. The results in Deoria district were particularly pleasant for Shibban Lal Saksena. The CMMF was successful in 10 of the 14 sugar mills in Deoria, including the factories at Kathkuiyan and Chhitauni, where Kashi Nath Pande had begun his trade union career.

The trade union movement in the sugar industry has never recovered from this battle for recognition. Despite the success of the CMMF, rival unions continued to function in each mill and to work against each other and, since the census, the number of rival unions in the mills has increased. Now, almost all the major political parties—Congress, Socialists, PSP, and even the Jan Sangh—have fostered rival unions wherever they could do so. Together Shibban Lal Saskena and Kashi Nath Pande could easily have prevented the splintering of the trade union movement in the industry.

[21] The results of the census, by factory, are contained in a compendium of documents relating to the fast compiled by Shibban Lal Saksena, entitled *Justice Demanded to the Sugar Workers of U. P.: Why the Fast Was Resumed* (New Delhi, 1950), pp. 138-140.

Only the internal factional and personal struggles of the Uttar Pradesh Congress prevented cooperation between the rival federations. The statements of Shibban Lal Saksena in the dispute indicate clearly the personal and factional nature of the struggle. In a letter to the Deputy Prime Minister during his fast, Shibban Lal Saksena remarked that "INTUC in my province has discredited Congress. It has become a group affair and is no longer serving the ideals for which it was formed."[22] After the fast and the census, Shibban Lal again wrote to the Deputy Prime Minister, in a rather caustic vein, about the character and the activities of Harihar Nath Shastri:

The result of the census . . . has clearly proved what I have been urging upon you so far that you have placed the INTUC in the hands of persons like Shri Hariharnath Shastri, who are discredited among the labour . . . Shri Hariharnath Shastri became the sole dictator of the INTUC for these 2½ years, and he deceived you with bogus registers and 'paper unions' . . . Gandhiji wanted to serve labour for its own sake, and not for ulterior motives such as exploitation for party ends or personal greed. But Mr. Hariharnath Shastri has made the INTUC an instrument for satisfying personal ambitions, and the workers' welfare and contact with them has never mattered to him. . . . Can Congress prestige on the labour front be safe in the hands of such ungrateful persons, and opportunist adventurers? [23]

Although Shibban Lal Saksena scored a great personal victory over his opponents in the trade union movement, this victory had no effect on the internal balance of power in the Uttar Pradesh Congress. Harihar Nath Shastri and Kashi Nath Pande remained dominant in the Congress labor movement and Shibban Lal Saksena, along with many other dissidents in the state Congress party, resigned from the Congress before the 1952 General Elections. Since the great struggle of 1950, no important factional conflicts have occurred within the Congress labor movement in the sugar industry. After the departure of Shibban Lal Saksena from the Congress, Kashi Nath Pande became the only prominent Congressman actively involved in trade union organization in the sugar factories.

However, there has been conflict between Kashi Nath Pande and the dominant faction in the Deoria Congress on many issues. Technically, the Congress organization and INTUC are entirely separate organizations. However, Kashi Nath Pande is a member of the Executive Committee of the Deoria DCC; he also has influence with some national party leaders and, thus, can secure a few Congress tickets for his people in the general

[22] Letter to the Deputy Prime Minister, Sardar Vallabhbhai Patel, dated February 23, 1950. *Ibid.*, pp. 17-18.

[23] Letter to the Deputy Prime Minister, Sardar Vallabhbhai Patel, dated March 26, 1950. *Ibid.*, pp. 178-180.

elections in Deoria. Conflict between Kashi Nath Pande and the dominant faction in the Deoria Congress has related to real conflicts of interest as well as to personal differences. The INTUC people are concerned primarily with the grievances of the sugar workers. The leadership of the district Congress must be concerned primarily with the interests of the cane growers who are, of course, the largest group of people involved in the politics of sugar.

The Congress and the cane growers

Among the most powerful of local institutions in Uttar Pradesh are the cooperative cane unions, which are semi-official agencies representing the cane growers to the sugar factories. The cane unions perform three major functions—the distribution of *purzis* (requisition forms) to each grower, requisitioning a certain number of carts to bring the grower's cane to the factories; collection and distribution of the payment due to each grower from the factories; and, the distribution of loans to the cultivators. The major sugar districts are divided into cane supply zones. Each zone is controlled by a cooperative union, which contracts on behalf of the growers in its zone to supply a certain amount of cane each season to the factories which it serves. In Deoria district alone, there are twenty-five zones and, thus, twenty-five cooperative cane unions.

Most of the cane unions in Deoria district are dominated either by Congressmen or by "Congress-minded" independents. A few of the unions in the PSP and Socialist strongholds are controlled by the opposition parties. However, the boards of directors of most of the cane unions in Deoria include Congressmen, opposition party members, and independents. The directors are partly elected from special constituencies of members of the union and partly appointed. Opposition party men claim that there is a clear class division in the cane unions between those "who are with the factory-wallahs and people who are advocates of the cane growers."[24] The opposition party leaders manage continually to keep the Congress on the defensive by agitating periodically for an increase in the cane price. However, the fact is that most of the cane unions are dominated by the big growers, whatever their party affiliations.

The Deoria P. Cooperative Cane Union is an example. This union is one of the largest in the district, serving 49,407 growers from 485 villages. The union supplied a total of 1,006,140.82 quintals of cane to three sugar factories in Deoria district in the 1961-1962 season. The average quantity of cane supplied by each grower works out to just over 20 quintals. In contrast, the average amount of cane supplied by the eleven directors of the

[24] Interview in Lucknow on May 17, 1962.

cane union works out to 510 quintals each, better than 25 times the amount of cane supplied by an "average" grower. Of the two Socialist party members on the Board of Directors, one provided 201 and the other 826 quintals of cane.[25]

The dominance of the cane unions by the big growers makes it difficult for opposition party leaders to enlist the support of the cane unions in agitations for a higher cane price. A higher cane price would be welcomed by all growers, but it would mean much more to the grower who brings in two or three bullock-carts of cane and must live upon the cane price he receives for the next year. The difficulties of organizing the cane growers are, of course, tremendous. Only Shibban Lal Saksena has made a serious attempt to organize the cane growers and to lead strikes, that is, refusals by the growers to supply cane to the factories. However, even Shibban Lal Saksena has had very little success in this field.

Another problem of political organization in the sugar industry is the conflict of interest between the growers and the millworkers. No strike in a sugar mill can be successful unless the growers agree not to supply cane to a struck factory. However, unless the growers can dispose of their cane to another factory and that quickly (because of the rapid deterioration of cut cane), they are not likely to support the striking workers. In 1957, there was a 33-day INTUC strike at the Chhitauni factory in Deoria district, which illustrates the dilemmas of the Congress in this kind of situation and the conflict of interests between the local Congress organization and INTUC. One Congress labor worker, commenting on the Chhitauni strike, said that INTUC ran into opposition from some of the directors of the cane unions during the strike, but that it was the big growers who opposed the strike, not the small. The District Congress Committee, of which Ram Dhari Pande was president at the time, also opposed the strike. Some Congressmen appealed to government and to the ministers concerned to argue that the INTUC leaders were in the wrong. According to this Congress labor worker, the Congressmen who opposed the strike did so for two reasons: "they wanted the big growers to be contented because that was the election time; secondly, they were in favor of the management."[26] However, C. B. Gupta, who was Industries Minister at the time of the strike, intervened on behalf of INTUC and, so the story goes, told the employers to settle the strike in favor of INTUC or give up their factory.

The same labor worker summed up the problems of conflict between the mill unions and the cane unions in this way:

[25] Information supplied by the office of the Deoria P. Cooperative Cane Union.
[26] Interview in Padrauna on July 17, 1962.

The Cane Unions are controlled by the big growers, but there are today many small growers in these Unions as well. We need, if not the active support, at least the moral and passive help of the Unions when there is a trade union action. Usually, we are not together. There are employees of the Cane Unions and we have got the Uttar Pradesh Cane Unions' Employees' Federation. Kashi Nath Pande is the President of this Federation. It is an industrial union of the whole of Uttar Pradesh and these local Cane Unions are the branches. That way, we are in conflict with the Cane Unions always. But, in times of trade union action, we appeal to the Cane Unions to cooperate with us by not supplying cane because, if they bring their carts to the gate, we fight with the growers and there is a possibility of failure of the strike. Then, the seasonal workers who come from adjacent villages are also growers; while in the factory, they are employees; while at home, they are growers. When there are rival unions and only one union gives a strike notice, then the growers come to the gates and then the factory needs the support of the Cane Unions. At Chhitauni, the Cane Unions supported the strike. Only two of the Directors went against the strike. . . . Towards the end of the strike, they wanted to create some disturbance and were harassing the workers. . . . The rest of the directors supported the strike. None brought their carts to the gates, except those under the influence of [the two Directors].[27]

At Chhitauni, INTUC was able to win over a majority of the directors. However, on the whole, relations between the cane unions and INTUC are precarious. Of course, noncooperation can work both ways, especially since the political parties are actively involved in strikes of either cane growers or millworkers. A Congress trade union may get the support of Congressmen on the cane unions in case of a strike, but not of opposition party members. The same is true for the opposition parties. For example, at the Ramkola Punjab factory in Deoria district, there was a cane growers' strike in 1958 in connection with an agitation led by Shibban Lal Saksena for an increase in the cane price. The Socialist union in the factory tried to help the cane growers by going on a "go slow." However, INTUC refused to support the strike and it failed completely.[28]

The combination of conflict between cane growers and millworkers, on the one hand, with the conflict between the political parties militates against any really effective political organization among either the millworkers or the growers. Even within the Congress, as has been seen, there is conflict between INTUC workers and Congressmen who support the big growers and the factory owners. The result is a splintered trade union movement and a hopelessly disorganized and sporadic expression of the demands of the cane growers.

[27] Interview in Padrauna on July 18, 1962.
[28] *Ibid.*

THE 1962 GENERAL ELECTIONS:
VOTING BEHAVIOR AND VILLAGE FACTIONS

The varieties of interparty competition are as great as the forms of Congress factionalism. In Gonda, the main opposition to the Congress was from conservative parties, Swatantra and Jan Sangh, an opposition largely based upon the influences and resources of the traditional landed estates of the district. In Aligarh, opposition to the Congress came from the opposite end of the economic spectrum, primarily from landless, agricultural laborers, who supported the Republican party. In Deoria, the major opposition parties are the two moderate leftist parties, the PSP and the Socialists. Together, these two parties won eight of the fourteen Assembly seats in the district, leaving the remaining six for the Congress.

Party politics in the districts of Uttar Pradesh reflect the diversities of society and economy in different parts of the state. The conservative parties are strongest in Oudh, where the great *talukdars* have dominated the rural economy. The Republican party has its strength in a few districts only, where there are heavy concentrations of landless Chamars. The center of leftist opposition to the Congress has been in the eastern districts of the state—among the most backward, poverty-stricken, famine- and flood-ridden districts in Uttar Pradesh and in all of India.

More than in any other rural district in Uttar Pradesh, appeals to voters based upon economic issues have an equal place in Deoria with appeals based upon caste, community, kinship, or personal influence. Opposition politicians in Deoria are quick to engage in demonstrations, *satyagrahas* (non-violent civil disobedience movements), and fasts during the periodical famine crises and the nearly annual sugar crises which affect the cultivators of the district. Genda Singh, the leader of the PSP in Deoria district, has been in and out of jail since Independence for his part in various agitations in the district. Ugra Sen, the leader of the Socialist party in the district (and for a time in the Uttar Pradesh Assembly), was jailed during an agitation in the district in 1956 and has extended his activities to the floor of the Uttar Pradesh Assembly, from which he and his party colleagues have been expelled and suspended on numerous occasions.

Economic issues are important in the elections in Deoria district. However, even the opposition leaders admit that there are many noneconomic factors operating in any election. One of the strongest PSP constituencies is Padrauna South. This constituency has been handed down from father to son and has been a successful PSP constituency in all three general elections. The PSP MLA from Padrauna South attributed his re-election from this constituency in 1962 to a number of different causes. He stressed the

idea that the people of the constituency in general were with the PSP because the party had always advocated an increase in the cane price. Some
of the reasons given for his success were peculiar to the candidate and the
constituency—the long public service record of the candidate and his
father, contrasted with the fact that his Congress opponent was new to
the constituency; the good organization which the PSP has established in
the constituency in three successful contests; the bad leadership and reputation of Ram Dhari Pande, the most prominent Congressman in this part
of the district. Other reasons are those commonly given by successful candidates in all parts of the state—the purely personal factor, the contacts and
friends which the candidate has built up among locally influential people
of the constituency; his help to the people of the constituency by getting
jobs for students and providing services of various sorts to the villagers.[29]

Caste voting was not very important in Padrauna South. The largest
communities in the constituency are Muslims, Chanaus (an agricultural
caste), Brahmans, and Scheduled Castes in that order. Four candidates contested the election. Of the four, one was a Brahman, two were Bhuinhars,
and the fourth was a Muslim. Though Bhuinhars account for less than 2
percent of the voters in the constituency, the two Bhuinhar candidates
(PSP and Jan Sangh) together polled close to 70 percent of the vote. The
Congress candidate, a Muslim, polled under 30 percent of the vote. The
Brahman candidate polled insignificantly.

Most party workers will exploit caste and community loyalties when
these loyalties will help their candidate. However, all candidates in almost
every constituency in the state realize that the vote of a single caste is not
enough. Sometimes, a combination of two communities, as in the elections
in Aligarh, can be politically effective. However, in many constituencies
in Uttar Pradesh, local factions are as important as community loyalties or
village, economic, and kinship ties in influencing voting behavior in the
rural areas. The introduction of *panchayati raj* in Uttar Pradesh has had
the effect of broadening and intensifying factionalism in the villages. The
PSP candidate from Padrauna South remarked that, in his constituency,
"every caste was divided." Before the general elections, elections of the
village panchayats had been held, so that there were "distinct groups in
every village."

Possibilities are present in the politics of Deoria district for the transformation of factional conflicts in the villages to economic and class conflicts. Factions in Deoria villages tend to follow economic divisions. Another PSP MLA remarked that most government services are ". . . given
to friends of the Congress, to the headmen and important people of the
village. Thus, we have to galvanize the support of those who are below

[29] Interview in Lucknow on May 17, 1962.

the *chaudhuri* [headman]. The traditional vested interests in the villages exploit the landless laborers and the common villagers. If the *chaudhuri* is a good man, we become weak. If he is a bad man, we thrive because of his evil and generally they are bad men."[30] This same MLA, also a Bhuinhar, remarked that his own caste fellows refused to support him in this last election and voted instead for the Congress candidate, who was a Brahman. Bhuinhars are landowners and are among "the traditional vested interests in the villages."

In the southern part of the district, where the Socialists have their strength, a conscious effort is being made to organize the "backward" or middle castes of agriculturalists against the elite Brahman and Rajput ex-*zamindars*. Interestingly enough, the leadership of the Socialist party in Deoria is predominantly Rajput. One of the major platforms in the All-India Socialist party manifesto is reservation of 60 percent of the posts in the administrative services for members of "backward" castes. As yet, these middle castes have not developed an autonomous political leadership. However, the Rajput leadership of the Deoria Socialist party has applied the 60 percent policy to its own party positions and has given important offices in the district party organization to members of the middle castes.

Salempur West is the constituency of Ugra Sen, the Socialist party leader. Ugra Sen is a Rajput, but he has established good relations with all castes in his constituency. However, his strongest support comes from the middle agriculturalist caste of Ahirs. Village A in Salempur West is typical of many of the villages in this constituency. The village has a fair amount of land in proportion to population for the area. There are 110 households in the village and about 500 acres of land. Brahmans are the dominant caste in the village; there are between 40 and 50 Brahman households. Before *zamindari* abolition, Brahmans of the village owned all the land. Now, the Brahman families own approximately half the land. There are eight other castes in the village, but only the Ahirs, who form approximately 10 percent of the population, own much land. The biggest *zamindar* in the village before *zamindari* abolition is now the panchayat president. He was elected president without contest in both panchayat elections. The panchayat president and his family voted for the Congress candidates for both Assembly and Parliament; the Congress Assembly candidate was a Rajput and the parliamentary candidate a Brahman. The panchayat president commented on voting behavior in his village in this way: "Most Brahmans voted for both Congress candidates, the other castes distributed their votes among various condidates. However, most of the Ahirs and other low castes voted for Ugra Sen. The Brahmans wanted everybody to

[30] Interview in Lucknow on May 18, 1962.

vote for the Congress; if the Ahirs had, it would have been a good thing.
. . . [But], if somebody wants to go one way, someone else wants to go
another way." [31] The panchayat president thought "it would have been a
good thing" if the Ahirs had voted for the Congress not because he has
any particular attachment to the Congress, but because the Ahir vote represents a rebellion against the authority of the traditional village leaders.
The reasons which the panchayat president gave for voting Congress do not
even relate to favors done him by the Congress. In fact, the panchayat
president remarked that the Congress had not done a thing for the village.
However, the president voted Congress because he "wanted to vote for the
strongest party, the ruling party . . . at least we know the Congress, whereas
others may be worse. . . . Everybody comes to the village only for votes
and not for any other reason." [32] The panchayat president's remarks contain a curious mixture of fatalism and cynicism. Though the panchayat
president and the Brahmans of village A in general represent the "vested
interests" of the village, they themselves are far from happy with their
present condition. The nephew of the panchayat president, noting that the
yield of the land was so low that the crops they grow are not sufficient
even for their own food, went on to say that "we have to live like animals."
The persistence of the tradition among the locally influential of voting
for "the Government," whatever government is in power, simply out of fear
of a worse government, is an important element in Congress strength in
Uttar Pradesh. In many districts, including Deoria still, the locally influential can often carry a good part of the village with them; but the development of factions in village politics means that opposition parties do not
have to rely upon the support of the dominant faction, but can attempt to
win the support of opposing village factions. It is in the nature of factional
politics that, as the panchayat president remarked, "if somebody wants to
go one way, someone else wants to go another way."

Though the possibilities are present in Deoria district for the transformation of factional conflicts into class divisions, there is no trend in this direction with respect to voting behavior. Deoria politics is presently in a
chaotic state, with no clear alignments perceptible in voting behavior. The
growth of factional politics in the villages, the development of conflict
between ex-*zamindars* and middle agricultural castes, the rise in the political consciousness of the backward classes in general are some of the more
important influences which affected voting behavior in the 1962 election
in this district. Only one thing is clear from the conflicting trends operating in Deoria politics: the economic and political dominance of elite, proprietary castes is being challenged. Any opposition party which could

[31] Interview in a village in Salempur tahsil on July 7, 1962.
[32] *Ibid.*

channel this protest into disciplined voting behavior would transform the nature of party politics in the district. However, the irrationalities of factional politics are a major obstacle to the development of party loyalties. At present, the major determinant of voting behavior in Deoria district is not party loyalty, certainly not ideology, and not even self-interest. What determines how an individual votes is most often what one's opponents are planning; if one factional opponent in the village plans to vote Congress, then the other votes Socialist. If, in the next election, the same opponent votes Socialist, the other will vote Congress.

The absence of party loyalties in Uttar Pradesh politics clearly affects both the Congress and the opposition parties. The difference between the Congress and the opposition parties is that the Congress has an established network of influence among the locally dominant elements in the village communities. The leftist opposition parties in Deoria district have attempted to appeal to local factions opposed to the traditional "vested interests"; but whatever success they have had has depended more upon temporary factional alignments in the villages than upon the development of a feeling of identification by local factions with opposition parties.

CONCLUSION

Opposition parties in Deoria district have raised important issues and have given an economic content to the language of political debate. It is certainly partly wishful thinking on the part of opposition leaders when they claim that the big cane growers and the ex-*zamindars* are with the Congress, whereas the smaller cane growers and the middle agricultural castes are with the opposition parties. As has been seen, these economic and class divisions are not the most important determinants of voting behavior. Nevertheless, economic and class divisions really exist in Deoria politics. They reveal themselves in conflicts of interest between millworkers and cane growers or between big and small cane growers in the strikes and agitations which have become a permanent feature of politics in Deoria district. Economic divisions also exist in many individual villages in the conflicts between ex-*zamindars* and the middle class of agriculturalists.

At present, politics in Deoria district lies somewhere in between a politics of issues and a politics of factional bargains. The language of politics in the district revolves around the major issues—the cane price, wages of factory workers, the demands of the middle castes for increased political participation. Economic issues even have a bearing upon factional conflicts within the Deoria Congress. The dominant faction in the local Congress has been identified with the "sugar magnates" and with the big cane growers by some Congressmen, as well as by opposition party leaders. The

INTUC people in the local Congress have worked against the dominant faction in internal party matters.

Factional alignments in Deoria sometimes correspond with economic divisions. However, in Deoria politics, factional conflicts and economic conflicts are independent variables; neither one determines the form of the other. It is tempting to consider the possibility that factional politics is a transitional form of politics and that issues will eventually replace factional antagonisms as the primary determinants of political behavior. The missing link, which makes it impossible to predict such a transition, is the absence of party loyalties among either faction leaders or voters.

Party loyalties will be difficult for opposition parties to develop among the voters. For one thing, the village voter in Uttar Pradesh is covered with a thick layer of fatalism and cynicism, bred partly by religion and philosophy and partly by hard experience that no matter what government is in power, one's condition remains unchanged. Opposition party fragmentation reinforces these attitudes. At election time, the villages of Uttar Pradesh are besieged by the party workers of ten, twelve, or twenty candidates. Village leaders feel that there are too many candidates and that most candidates are self-seeking; villagers are perceptive about individual candidates, but care little for party labels. In one village, the panchayat president remarked that he did not vote for the Congress candidate for the Assembly because the candidate was "a duffer and an illiterate man"; he voted for the Socialist candidate who, though he had not done anything for the village, "is a good worker and has done much for the area." [33]

Another obstacle to the development of party loyalties is the nature of the opposition parties themselves. With the exception of the Communist party and the Jan Sangh, the major political parties in Uttar Pradesh are little more than coalitions of local factions. Factions within the Congress struggle against each other and bargain amongst themselves for the distribution of patronage; alliances change, factions come and go, but the Congress organization goes on as long as there is patronage to distribute. Opposition parties have little patronage to distribute; local factions opposed to the Congress ally now with the PSP, now with the Socialists or with any other political party which will offer the faction leader a prominent position in the party organization or an Assembly ticket. Many opposition faction leaders eventually return to the Congress. In every district in Uttar Pradesh, there are prominent faction leaders who left the Congress in 1948 with the Socialists or in 1950-1951 with the KMPP and who have returned to the Congress after failing to find position and prestige in opposition suitable to their aspirations.

As long as factional considerations dominate party politics, the Congress

[33] Interview in a village in Salempur tahsil on July 14, 1962.

has every advantage. The Congress is the only party which has sufficient resources in the form of patronage and positions of status to induce factional leaders to remain in the Congress and fight for power within the party rather than against it. Opposition parties may be able to defeat the Congress occasionally when issues arise or events occur, whose importance transcends local factionalisms—the communal riot in Aligarh, strikes and agitations in Deoria. But in the absence of political loyalties among the voters, such opposition successes can be only temporary. When political tension decreases and factional antagonisms again prevail, the Congress organization emerges with new strength.

VII.

Meerut: Caste and the Congress

THE ENVIRONMENT

Meerut district is of particular importance in modern Indian history, for it was here that the famous Mutiny of 1857 began. Even before 1857, Meerut had been an important battleground. The proximity of the district to Delhi has meant that Meerut has been influenced by all the major events of north Indian history. It suffered from the early Muslim invasions, from the invasion of Timur in the late fourteenth century, and later on "was ravaged by Sikhs, Mahrattas and Rohillas."[1]

The prosperity of the district does not seem to have been affected by its constant use as a battleground, for Meerut is one of the most prosperous districts in Uttar Pradesh. The relative prosperity of the district stems from the agricultural skills of the peasant-proprietor castes of Meerut, among whom the Jats are the most important and the most enterprising. The district's favorable economic condition is, however, threatened by the increasing pressure of population on the land. Meerut's population of 2,712,-960 is the largest of any district in Uttar Pradesh; density per square mile is 1,168, the third largest in the state.[2]

Some industrialization has been taking place in Meerut district, which now has eight large sugar mills spread throughout the district and some small and medium-sized industries in the two major towns of Meerut and Ghaziabad. The district has an "urban" or town population of over half a million, but only three towns are of importance—Meerut (with a population of 283,997), Ghaziabad (70,438), and Hapur (55,248).[3] Despite some

[1] *District Gazetteers of the United Provinces of Agra and Oudh,* Vol. IV: *Meerut,* by H. R. Nevill (Allahabad: Government Press, 1904), p. 154.
[2] *Census of India, 1961, Paper No. 1 of 1962, Final Population Totals,* p. 348.
[3] *Ibid.,* pp. 236-237.

137

industrialization and a relatively large town population, Meerut district remains overwhelmingly rural; the urban population is only 20.6 percent of the total.[4] The major crops grown in the district are sugar cane, corn, wheat, *juar*, and *bajra*.

Like the rest of the districts in northwestern Uttar Pradesh, Meerut has a large proportion of Muslims, who form close to 25 percent of the total population. Among Hindus, Chamars predominate numerically, followed by Jats, Brahmans, Rajputs, Banias, Gujars, Tyagis, and Ahirs. Before *zamindari* abolition, the major proprietary castes were Jats, Banias, Tyagis, Rajputs, Gujars, Brahmans, and Muslims. All of these latter communities, except Banias, have also been the leading cultivating castes and thus remain the influential communities of the district.

Meerut district differs from the three previous districts studied in many ways. Its relative prosperity stands in sharp contrast to the extreme poverty of Deoria. Though it has eight sugar mills and though sugarcane is the major crop in Meerut, the sugar industry is flourishing here rather than declining, as in Deoria district. There are more Muslims proportionately in Meerut district than in Aligarh, but Hindu-Muslim differences do not have as profound an effect upon politics in Meerut district as in Aligarh. As Gonda district was an area of great estates, Meerut district has always been essentially an area of independent peasant proprietors.[5] Before *zamindari* abolition, Meerut district contained only four *zamindars* paying a land revenue of Rs. 10,000 or above, compared to ten in Gonda, eleven in Deoria, and twenty-three in Aligarh district.[6] As a *mahalvari* area,[7] with very few large proprietors and a relatively prosperous peasantry, political power in rural Meerut tends much more than in most other Uttar Pradesh districts to be in the hands of the leaders of the locally dominant castes.

Another difference between Meerut and the other districts analyzed above, which is important to this case study, is the special caste composition of the people of the district. The political and economic life of Gonda, Deoria, and Aligarh has been dominated by the elite proprietary castes of Brahmans and Rajputs. In Deoria district, the failure of the Brahman-dominated leadership of the local Congress organization to open leadership positions in the party to the middle agricultural castes gives the Socialists an

[4] *Ibid.*, p. 349.
[5] With a population approximately 20 percent greater than Gonda's, Meerut district in 1948 contained more than seven times the number of small zamindars, i.e., those paying a land revenue of Rs. 250 or less (165,729 for Meerut, 23,608 for Gonda district). *Report of the United Provinces Zamindari Abolition Committee* (Allahabad: Superintendent, Printing and Stationery, 1948), II, 14.
[6] *Ibid.*
[7] On the *mahalvari* land system, see chap. ii, p. 11 above.

important political rallying cry and a potential mass base. In Meerut district, the two most important proprietary communities are nonelite castes in terms of traditional ritual hierarchies. In their local environments, these two castes—Jats and Tyagis—have high social status commensurate with their economic power. Yet, both communities aspire to more generalized recognition as "elite" castes: the Jats aspire to Rajput status and the Tyagis to Brahman status.

Since most Rajputs reject the Jat claims and most Brahmans the Tyagi claims, the potential for caste conflict in Meerut district would appear great. Within the local Congress, internal political conflicts do partially reflect caste antagonisms. However, it will be argued in this case study that the Congress has shown a great ability to integrate diverse castes into the local party organization without significant friction. The Congress has been able to do this because of the integrative functions of its system of factional politics. Much attention has been given to the disintegrative impact of factionalism upon party organization in the preceding studies. This case study examines the integrative aspects of factionalism.

THE MEERUT CONGRESS:
THE ENEMY OF AN ENEMY IS A FRIEND

The "Dictatorship" of Chaudhuri Charan Singh

According to many Congressmen in Meerut, the people of the district are living under a "dictatorship." The "dictator" is the leader of the district Congress organization, Chaudhuri Charan Singh. Chaudhuri Charan Singh, currently Minister for Agriculture in the Uttar Pradesh Government, has dominated the district Congress and district politics since the early forties and has successfully resisted numerous challenges to his leadership during his long rule. Chaudhuri Sahib, as he is reverentially called by his followers, has been an unusually successful faction leader in Uttar Pradesh politics. Inspired less by a desire for power than by an invincible belief in the rightness of his actions and policies, Charan Singh seeks neither friend nor favor and gives no quarter to those who oppose him. A look at the elements of Charan Singh's power will throw more light on the requirements for factional leadership and political influence in contemporary Uttar Pradesh politics.

Charan Singh is not exactly an intellectual in politics, but he is a well-read man, with an incisive intelligence which he has devoted to a continuing study of agricultural problems in Uttar Pradesh. Charan Singh is the leading ideologist in Uttar Pradesh of the peasant proprietor. As a prominent member of the United Provinces Zamindari Abolition Committee, he worked hard to ensure that the Zamindari Abolition Act would contain no loopholes, which would permit the continued dominance of the *zamindars* in the rural economy of the state, and to make certain "that landlordism may not raise its head again."[8] In his most recent publication, *Joint Farming X-Rayed: The Problem and Its Solution*,[9] Charan Singh has opposed—partly on technical grounds, but also because of his belief in the values of peasant proprietorship—the new government policy of fostering cooperative farming. In the 1962 factional struggle within the Uttar Pradesh Congress over the question of placing a surcharge on the land tax in Uttar Pradesh, Chaudhuri Charan Singh provided the intellectual opposition to the tax in a confidential government memorandum, which reportedly objected to the burden which the tax would lay upon the small proprietors of the state.

Charan Singh's devotion to the cause of the peasant proprietor reflects his personal and community background. Charan Singh was born in 1902 in a Jat family of small proprietors in Noorpur village of Meerut district. The agricultural skills of the Jats are well known in northern India. The *Final Settlement Report of the Meerut District* notes that "the Jats are hard thrifty men, and, it is hardly necessary to say, admirable cultivators. . . . It is remarkable . . . that in nearly all parganas they have succeeded in getting the best tracts. Whenever possible they have chosen the naturally fertile soil to start with, and when they find that they have to work on a poorer basis they make the best of it."[10]

The Jats are a proud people, with a martial history. The major Jat settlements are in Rajasthan and in the eastern districts of the Punjab. Jats have prospered in peace and in war. In the periods of empire in the middle ages, the Jats maintained their independence; in wartime, they extended their domains. The Jats were an important military power in the entire northern Doab in the late eighteenth century, after the final breakdown of the Delhi Empire.[11] They are now the most influential community in the Meerut division, particularly in the districts of Saharanpur, Muzzafarnagar, Meerut, and Bulandshahr.

In Meerut district, Jats are the third largest community after Muslims and Chamars, but are by far the most influential rural community in the district. In 1940, Jats cultivated more than 30 percent of the land in the

[8] Charan Singh, *Agrarian Revolution in Uttar Pradesh* (Uttar Pradesh: Publications Bureau, Information Department), p. 13.

[9] Charan Singh, *Joint Farming X-Rayed: The Problem and Its Solution* (Bombay: Bharatiya Vidya Bhavan, 1959).

[10] *Final Settlement Report of the Meerut District*, by R. W. Gillan (1901), p. 10, cited in *Meerut, op. cit.*, p. 89.

[11] A brief account of Jat military activities in the Ganges-Jumna Doab in this period is given in W. Crooke, *The North-Western Provinces of India: Their History, Ethnology, and Administration* (London: Methuen and Co., 1897), p. 117.

district; no other community cultivated more than 11 percent of the land.[12] The settlement report of 1940 notes of the Jats that "on the whole, there are few big landlords among them, and their strength lies mainly in numerous communities of thrifty hard-working small farmers who cultivate their own land and are generally in comfortable, if not prosperous, circumstances."[13]

Chaudhuri Charan Singh has made the Jat way of life his political creed. As the only Jat cabinet minister in the state government, his popularity among the members of his community in Meerut and adjacent districts has been great. It has been reported that the resignation of Charan Singh from the Sampurnanand government in 1959[14] "was taken as an insult to the caste" and that "anti-Congress feeling was high among the Jats" at the time.[15] Charan Singh has successfully contested the Assembly elections in his Jat-dominated constituency three times; in 1962, he polled close to 70 percent of the vote in the constituency against four independent candidates.

Charan Singh's place as the undisputed leader of the most important community in the district is one factor in his long domination over district politics. Another factor, perhaps even more important, has been his position in the state government. Charan Singh joined the Pant government as a parliamentary secretary in 1946. He became a cabinet minister in 1951 and has remained a minister since then, with a break in 1959-1960 during the factional conflict which led to the downfall of the Sampurnanand government. Charan Singh was a favorite of Pandit Pant and enjoyed Pant's patronage until the latter's death in 1960. As long as Pandit Pant lived, there were no disputes over the distribution of Congress tickets for Meerut district. In 1946, 1952, and 1957, no Congressman who did not enjoy the favor of Charan Singh received a Congress ticket from any rural constituency in Meerut. Thus, thanks to his position in the state government and his special relationship with Pandit Pant, both party and government patronage for Meerut district filtered through the hands of Charan Singh and through his hands only.

Charan Singh has many of the qualities of the ideal Indian faction leader. He is known for his intellectual abilities and has a reputation for integrity. No one has ever charged him with a desire for material advantages for himself. The major criticisms levelled against Charan Singh as a party

---

[12] *Final Settlement Report of the Meerut District,* by C. H. Cooke (Allahabad: Superintendent, Printing and Stationery, 1940), p. 15.

[13] *Ibid.,* p. 13.

[14] See chap. iii above.

[15] Mahesh Chandra Pradhan, "Socio-political Organization of the Jats of Meerut Division" (unpublished Ph.D. dissertation, University of London, School of Oriental and African Studies, 1961), p. 343.

leader are that he is proud by nature and uncompromising in his relations with others. The following description of Charan Singh by a Congressman of Meerut district is typical of the comments made about him by his opponents:

He is not accommodating; not being accommodating is not a virtue of a politician. He is not even accommodating to his own people to the extent he should be. Moreover, once he forms an opinion about a man, he's not likely to change it; he has very strong likes and dislikes. . . . Charan Singh wants abject loyalty. You must bow down and then accept some small grace from the omnipotent Chaudhuri Charan Singh. . . . Charan Singh wanted that no leader should come to Meerut except he alone; he wanted it [Meerut] as his own *jagir* [estate]. He wanted to be the undisputed leader of Meerut district, whom all would obey.[16]

Charan Singh is faithful to his friends, provided their requests for favors are both reasonable and just to his satisfaction. He is ruthless towards those he considers his enemies—even unto the second generation. One young Congressman of Meerut, the son of a large ex-*zamindar* with considerable influence in the area of the family estate, claims that he could be "of much use" to Charan Singh. But Charan Singh, who long ago struggled against the father, refuses to have anything to do with the son.

The cohesiveness of a faction depends upon the personal qualities of the leader and his ability to distribute goods and services to his followers. Most faction leaders can only hope that the favors they distribute will be returned by the loyalty of the beneficiary to the leader in a time of crisis and contest. Some faction leaders have enough power to withhold favors also—not only to grant favors to their followers, but to prevent favors from being granted to their enemies. It is a rare faction leader in Uttar Pradesh who has the full armory of powers of the American party boss— the power not only to give or to withhold, but the power to take away. At the peak of his control over Meerut politics, Charan Singh had even the power to take away. The Mool Chand Shastri episode is an example.

Mool Chand Shastri is also a Jat and came under the patronage of Charan Singh in 1953, when the latter saw to it that Mool Chand was elected president of the District Board. However, Mool Chand had ambitions of his own and tried to run the District Board and distribute its patronage in the way he thought fit. According to Mool Chand, Charan Singh resented the fact that the District Board President did not "act according to his [Charan Singh's] wishes and he resented that a man whom he gave the chance of the Chairmanship was not following his advice."[17] Early in 1954, the followers of Charan Singh brought a motion of no-confidence against Mool

[16] Interview in Lucknow on October 18, 1962.
[17] Interview in Lucknow on October 19, 1962.

Chand Shastri, which failed to carry. However, Charan Singh does not accept defeat easily. Three years later, Charan Singh succeeded in having a resolution passed by the state Parliamentary Board, ordering Mool Chand to resign. Since this episode, Charan Singh has placed the chairmanship of the District Board in more reliable hands. He also saw to it that Mool Chand Shastri was refused the Congress ticket in the 1957 elections in Meerut district. It is from actions such as these that Chaudhuri Charan Singh has acquired the reputation of a "dictator."

Charan Singh has been a more successful faction leader than most others in the districts of Uttar Pradesh in the sense that he has wielded nearly exclusive power in Meerut district for an unbroken period of close to twenty years. Some of the elements of Charan Singh's power have been illustrated —his personal character, his relations with the Jat community, and his long tenure of office in the state government. Charan Singh's personal syndrome of power illustrates the requirements for political influence in local and state politics. His position as the undisputed leader of the most influential rural community in the district enabled him to gain political control over the district Congress and the District Board. Control over the district has guaranteed him an important place in the state party organization and in the government. In turn, Charan Singh's influence in state party and government councils reinforces his political control over the district.

Jats, Tyagis, and other castes

An additional source of strength for Chaudhuri Charan Singh has been an alliance with the leaders of another influential rural community of Meerut district—the Tyagis. The Tyagis are a highly localized Hindu caste, found only in the northwestern districts of Uttar Pradesh, in Delhi, and in two eastern districts of the Punjab. Only in Meerut district, however, are the Tyagis in considerable numbers. Before *zamindari* abolition, Tyagis were, after Jats, the leading landed proprietors of the district. In parts of Hapur and Ghaziabad tahsils and in a few other areas of the district, the Tyagis hold more land than Jats.

Tyagis generally are less enterprising than Jats and have been motivated more by an aspiration for status commensurate with their economic power than by the desire to increase their economic prosperity. Tyagis claim descent from Gaur Brahmans, but few Brahmans are willing to recognize this claim. Some intermarriages between Tyagis and Gaur Brahmans have taken place in Meerut and adjacent districts, but not on any large scale.

Before *zamindari* abolition, the leading Tyagi family of the district was that of Chaudhuri Raghubir Narayan Singh of Asaura. Chaudhuri Raghubir Singh farmed the revenue of 27 villages in Meerut district and paid a land revenue of Rs. 18,000. He joined the Congress in 1905 and participated in all the civil disobedience movements. In fact, Chaudhuri Raghubir Singh was the first prominent rural leader of the Congress movement in Meerut district and the Tyagi caste formed the first wave of the nationalist movement in the rural areas of the district.

The Tyagis are proud of the role of Chaudhuri Raghubir Singh and of the Tyagi caste in the nationalist movement. Their pride is mixed with some resentment at the later entry of the Jats into Congress politics and the rise to prominence of Chaudhuri Charan Singh. This mixture of pride and resentment is evident in a comparison between the two leaders, which appeared in the July, 1959, issue of the *Tyagi Brahman,* a community monthly magazine. Part of the comparison is reproduced below:

Chaudhuri Raghubir Narayan Singh was born in a great landlord family. The atmosphere in which he was brought up was very aristocratic. At the call of Mahatma Gandhi, our Chaudhuri Sahib from a great landlord became a nationalist. From then on, he considered himself an enemy of the British and, in the view of the British Government, the Tyagi caste became a traitor caste because of Chaudhuri Raghubir Narayan Singh. When the British Government was pushing back the Tyagi caste, at that time the Jat people came into the good books of the British, and, under their rule, were acquiring high position; whereas we, because of being in the caste of Chaudhuri Sahib, were thrown away like a fly from milk. But the Tyagi caste never gave way and it became a nationalist caste. At that time, the Tyagi caste was considered a Congress caste.

When our people were locked up in jails, the followers of Chaudhuri Charan Singh were enjoying the *Raj*. Times changed and Independence came to the country. Chaudhuri Charan Singh was a capable person. Because he was born in an ordinary family, he had ambitions to be a big man and, because of his determination, he tried to become a big man and cleared all the obstacles in his way one by one, like a clever diplomat, and the majority of Jat votes in the district brought him into the limelight.[18]

The leadership of the Tyagi community has remained with the House of Asaura. Despite some resentment amongst Tyagis at the new leadership of the Jats, Tyagis and Jats have generally worked together in local Congress affairs. In 1956, the son of Chaudhuri Raghubir Singh was elected DCC president, with the support of Charan Singh. In 1958, the grandson of Chaudhuri Raghubir Singh was elected to the same position, again with the support of Charan Singh.

The important position of Jats and Tyagis in the district Congress organization is evident from table 7. Jats or Tyagis are the single largest community in almost every segment of the district organization. Generally, the positions of the two communities are complementary; that is, in a

[18] *Tyagi Brahman* (July, 1959), p. 5; translated from Hindi with the assistance of D. P. S. Dwarikesh.

given tahsil, one or the other community holds the dominant position, while the other has few members. The nearly equal place of Tyagis with Jats in the district Congress organization reflects the early political consciousness of the Tyagis and their important role in the Meerut Congress before the entry of the Jats into the Congress. In the rural institutions of the district, Jat dominance is much more pronounced. Ten of the 26 Block Development Committee presidents are Jats, compared to only 4 Tyagis.

TABLE 7

CASTE COMPOSITION OF DISTRICT CONGRESS COMMITTEE AND
OF PCC DELEGATES FROM MEERUT DISTRICT, 1962

Position		Jats	Tya-gis	Brah-mans	Vaish[a]	Raj-put	Hari-jan[b]	Guj-ars	Mus-lim	Others	Not Known
DCC Executive	(18)	3	6	4	3	0	1	1	0	0	0
DCC Members	(19)	4	1	3	2	3	0	2	1	1	2
MCC Presidents											
Ghaziabad	(23)	1	5	3	2	3	1	2	1	2	3
Baghpat	(20)	8	0	5	2	0	0	0	0	2	3
Sardhana	(14)	6	1	1	0	1	3	1	1	0	0
Meerut	(11)	3	2	2	1	0	2	0	0	1	0
Hapur	(18)	1	10	4	2	0	0	0	0	0	1
Mawana	(12)	2	2	0	2	1	0	0	2	1	2
PCC Delegates	(17)	7	5	1	1	0	0	0	1	1	1
Total[c]	(152)	35	32	23	15	8	7	6	6	8	12

[a] Bania, Bishnoi, and Jain.
[b] All Scheduled Castes, including Chamars.
[c] Since there are a few cases of overlapping memberships, the totals refer to the number of positions in the party organization held by members of various communities—not the actual number of individuals of each community in the district Congress.

On the District Board of 108 (nonofficial) members, 35 are Jats and only 11 are Tyagis. The Executive Committee of the District Cane Committee, which contains 9 members, has 7 Jats, but no Tyagis. Six of the chairmen of the 8 cooperative cane unions in Meerut are Jats; the remaining 2 are Tyagis. Since 1950, Fateh Singh Rana, a Jat and an important ally of Charan Singh, has been chairman of the powerful District Cooperative Development Federation.

The data on the caste composition of the Meerut Congress also support the more general proposition that the local Congress organizations are dominated by the major proprietary castes. The influence and position of a particular community in the district Congress organization is more in proportion to land ownership and social status than numbers. Table 8 shows the percentages of land owned and land cultivated by the major proprietary and cultivating castes at the last land settlement (in 1940) before *zamindari* abolition. Chamars and Muslims, though numerically the largest communities in the district, have very little representation (in proportion to their population) in the local Congress and almost no real influence—this despite the fact that, in Meerut, as in most other districts (excluding Aligarh, of course), these two communities are considered major Congress supporters in the general elections.

The political alliance between the leaders of the Jat and Tyagi communities has not been designed to exclude other communities from political participation. Chaudhuri Charan Singh is not a community leader only. Some of his major supporters in the past have been Brahmans. In 1962, the President of the DCC was a Brahman and an ally of Charan Singh. In the 1963

TABLE 8

PERCENTAGES OF LAND HELD AND LAND CULTIVATED BY COMMUNITY,
MEERUT DISTRICT, 1940

	Jat	Vaish	Tyagi	Rajput	Gujar	Brahman	Muslim	Others
Land held	24.7	14.7	11.8	7.5	6.0	4.7	15.2	15.4
Land cultivated	30.7	. . .[a]	10.8	10.1	11.0	7.1	7.8	22.5

Source: *Final Settlement Report of the Meerut District,* by C. H. Cooke (Allahabad: Superintendent, Printing and Stationery, 1940), Statement 5, p. 15 and Statement 4, p. 13.

[a] The area cultivated by Vaish castes is insignificant and is included under "Others."

elections for president of the District Board, Charan Singh successfully supported another old ally in district politics, who happens to be a Vaishya. Relations between Jats and Rajputs, Gujars, Ahirs, and Rawas in district social life have traditionally been good. The Jats also aspire to higher status and claim recognition as Rajputs. However, unlike the Tyagis, the Jat aspirations for higher status are tempered by a more equalitarian ethic. Jats will take food from and smoke with both Rajputs and the middle castes of Gujars, Ahirs, and Rawas.

In a recent study of social and political organization among the Jats of Meerut division, Mahesh Chandra Pradhan claims that traditional Jat sociopolitical institutions, like the *khap* and *sarv-khap* (clan and interclan) councils are being used to unite for social and political purposes the various Jat clan groups and other castes of similar ritual status, such as Ahirs, Gujars, and Rajputs. Pradhan reports that, at two meetings of the *sarv-khap* council in the last decade, "it was emphasized by various leaders in their speeches, that these castes stand in the relationship of brothers to each other; have the same cultural and historical background; and, therefore, should unite under the banner of the *sarv-khap* council. Inter-caste marriages between these castes were also suggested by various speakers." He even suggests that "these castes may come to form one cultural-political group to maintain their political dominance within their respective *khap* areas and in the area of the Meerut Division." [19] In fact, there is no evidence in the politics of Meerut district that such a political alliance of these castes is developing. Approaches by politicians to Jats and these other castes are not through the traditional caste councils, whose meetings are too rare to be of significance in any case, but through local influential leaders in each village, who themselves act quite independently and according to their own political interests.

Local party leaders claim that political tension between Jats and Rajputs, Gujars, and other middle castes, as well as among different groups of Jats, is increasing. One Jat political leader remarked that, in his constituency, relations between Jats and Rajputs have been particularly bad, since Jats make a claim for Rajput status, which is not conceded by Rajputs. As for the relations between Jats and other middle castes, he remarked that " . . . there were good relations among Jats, Gujars, and Rawas at one time because they [Gujars and Rawas] were also considered to be on the same level as Jats. Now, casteism is so [prevalent that] there is hatred; even among Jats, there is groupism. [Twenty years ago], there was peace in the villages and good relations among castes, with no quarrels; now, [even families] are quarreling with each other." [20] Nevertheless, the equalitarian attitude of the Jats toward other castes of similar status reduces the intensity of caste antagonisms and makes the political leadership of the Jats more acceptable than, for example, the leadership of the Tyagis, who aspire to more exclusive status as Brahmans.

In fact, one of the reasons for the transfer of political leadership in Meerut from the Tyagi family of Asaura to Chaudhuri Charan Singh was a temperamental difference in the character of the two leaders, which arose from their different cultural and economic backgrounds. Charan Singh was "a man of the people," with no desire for enhanced status in the ritual hierarchy. Before joining the Congress, Charan Singh was a member of the Arya Samaj, a Hindu religious revivalist organization which favored social reform measures, opposed the dominance of Brahmans over ritual Hinduism, and generally adopted an equalitarian approach in social matters, opening its organization to all castes. Many Jats, like Charan Singh, became Arya Samajists. One Jat politician claims that the Arya Samaj movement, many of whose tenets later became integrated into the nationalist creed and the creed of progressive leaders of all castes, was adopted first by Jats

[19] Mahesh Chandra Pradhan, *op. cit.*, p. 344.
[20] Interview in Meerut on December 14, 1962.

because the movement suited the Jats who, "by custom and habit . . . are reformers." [21]

The Tyagis also early sought social reform measures, but the aspiration for Brahman status is clearly exclusive, rather than egalitarian. Even the *Tyagi Brahman*, previously cited, admits that the transfer of leadership from Chaudhuri Raghubir Singh to Charan Singh was partly a result of a "weakness" in the character of the Tyagi leader who, "being from an aristocratic family, . . . could not make his place in the hearts of the people" because "he could not get rid of his aristocratic tendencies." Chaudhuri Charan Singh, on the other hand, was not inhibited in his relations with the people by "aristocratic tendencies"; he had neither the prestige derived from ownership of a large estate nor the desire to enhance his status in traditional Hindu society.

Brahmans and Banias

Opposition to the long rule of Chaudhuri Charan Singh has come largely from the political leaders of the Brahman and Bania castes in Meerut district. Superficially, one may receive the impression that factional conflicts in the Meerut Congress are based upon caste antagonisms or upon rivalry between rural-based communities and urban castes. Both caste antagonisms and rural-urban differences play a role in factional conflicts in the Meerut Congress. However, as in the other districts that have been discussed above, all factions in Meerut politics are multicaste in composition. The diversity of castes in Meerut, as elsewhere in Uttar Pradesh, makes it impossible for a faction seriously interested in obtaining power to restrict its membership to particular social groups. Every important community in Meerut district has its own political leaders, but faction leaders of different communities are oriented towards obtaining political power for themselves and not necessarily towards advancing the claims of their communities. Moreover, political leadership conflicts within each community lead to defections of Jats to Brahman-led factions, of Brahmans to Jat-led factions, and so forth. Faction leaders welcome such defectors from opposing factions and are willing to offer important positions in the local party organization and in local government institutions in exchange for the political support of influential leaders of different communities. Even more important in reducing the influence of caste antagonisms upon political behavior is the necessity for alliances among factions whose caste composition is different. The alliance between Jat and Tyagi political leaders has been mentioned. Here, the political alliance of Brahman and Bania political leaders in the Meerut Congress will be discussed.

Factional alignments in the Meerut Congress are more complex than in

[21] *Ibid.*

most districts in Uttar Pradesh. The reason for this complexity lies in the special political role of Charan Singh in state politics. Charan Singh is the only prominent leader in the state government who has refused to identify himself with either of the two large groups which have been struggling for control of the state party organization and the government since 1955. Charan Singh has a small following in the state party organization and among some of the legislators from the "backward" or middle castes, which enables him to act independently and forces the leaders of the two main groups to bargain for his political support. Thus, in 1959, when nine ministers of the Sampurnanand government resigned to show their solidarity with and loyalty to the party manager, C. B. Gupta, Charan Singh was not among them. Although he had differences with the members of the Sampurnanand group, Charan Singh chose to act alone and wait until his defection would prove of decisive importance to the Gupta group. It has been widely reported that, when Charan Singh resigned a few months later to join the dissident Gupta group, it was with the promise that he would be supported by C. B. Gupta for the chief ministership. The close balance between the two main groups in the state Congress has made Charan Singh and his small following a valuable prize for both sides. Yet the leaders of both sides would prefer to remove the unpredictable Charan Singh from his central role in state Congress politics.

Because Charan Singh's defection to C. B. Gupta was decisive in the downfall of the Sampurnanand government, the followers of the former Chief Minister have opposed Charan Singh in state Congress politics and have tried to help his political rivals in Meerut district. Relations between C. B. Gupta and Charan Singh have been equally bad. For various reasons, C. B. Gupta was not able to keep his promise to support Charan Singh for the chief ministership. In fact, C. B. Gupta was careful to see that Charan Singh, though Minister for Agriculture in an overwhelmingly agricultural state, had little political power. Most of the normal responsibilities of the Minister of Agriculture were taken away and divided among other ministries, whose portfolios were given to more reliable supporters of C. B. Gupta. Relations between C. B. Gupta and Charan Singh deteriorated still further when the latter joined the Gautam-Tripathi group in November-December, 1962, in opposition to the Government's proposal to levy a surcharge on the land tax in Uttar Pradesh. C. B. Gupta has also sought to undermine Charan Singh's power in Meerut district by helping the latter's political opponents. What gives factional alignments their peculiar complexity in Meerut district is that the followers of Gupta and the followers of Gautam and Tripathi are fighting each other as well as Charan Singh.

Charan Singh's oldest rival in Meerut politics is Kailash Prakash, like C. B. Gupta a Bania. Banias, who have traditionally been moneylenders, shopkeepers, and merchants, form the bulk of the business and merchant class in the towns and cities of Uttar Pradesh. In Meerut and in many other districts of the state, Banias acquired quite considerable *zamindaris* in the rural areas also. By 1940, the Vaish or commercial castes (mostly Banias) had become the second largest class of rural proprietors in Meerut district (see table 8). However, most of the rural influence of the Banias disappeared with *zamindari* abolition, since hardly any Banias cultivate their own land.

Kailash Prakash was born in 1909 in a small town in Meerut district. His father was a moneylender and a *zamindar*. Kailash Prakash joined the Congress in 1930 and was jailed four times in the various Congress movements. In 1948, he was elected to the Legislative Council and in 1952 and 1957, he was elected to the Assembly from the Meerut City constituency. In 1962, he contested from Hapur constituency, but was defeated. Kailash Prakash 'has long been a loyal ally of C. B. Gupta. The latter brought Kailash Prakash into the Government in 1955 as a deputy minister. Kailash Prakash served as a deputy minister until 1959, when he resigned from the Government along with eight other ministers who were loyal to C. B. Gupta. He became a Minister of State in the Gupta government, formed in 1960. However, his defeat in the 1962 election prevented his return to the government after the election.

Kailash Prakash has little personal influence outside of his home town of Parikshitghar and the two major towns of the district—Meerut and Hapur. Meerut and Hapur towns have been two important enclaves where opposition to the leadership of Charan Singh and the Tyagi family of Asaura has been strong. In Meerut City, which became a separate Congress Committee in 1956, factional conflicts have been primarily intraurban in character and have related only secondarily to the struggle for power in Meerut district as a whole. However, the influence which Kailash Prakash has in Meerut City has provided him with the necessary political base to challenge the leadership of Charan Singh.

From his base in Meerut and Hapur towns, Kailash Prakash has tried to build a coalition capable of defeating Charan Singh. The difficulty facing Kailash Prakash is that he 'has little following in the rural areas of the district. In fact, Kailash Prakash is more of a symbol of challenge to Charan Singh than a powerful factional leader in his own right. It has been his close relationship with C. B. Gupta, the former Chief Minister of the state which has given him access to patronage and the ability to gather around him all those who have personal differences with Charan Singh.

The main rural opposition to Charan Singh comes from the Brahman leadership of the district Congress, who are allied with the Brahman-led, Gautam-Tripathi group in state politics. However, to oppose Charan Singh in district politics, the Brahman leaders are forced to ally with the Kailash Prakash group, whose members in turn are allied with the Gupta group in state politics. One Brahman leader described the situation in this way:

Now I am with Kailash Prakash. For a certain duration, I was with Kamlapati Tripathi. However, at present, in our district, that group cannot make any headway and I am seriously pitted against Chaudhuri Charan Singh. In 1960, I supported Uma Dutt Sharma for DCC President; he belonged to the Kamlapati Tripathi group. In the state, Kamlapati Tripathi is the dominant opposition group. In the district, most of us have decided to join hands with Kailash Prakash. . . . He too [Kamlapati Tripathi] recognizes the special circumstances prevailing in the district.[22]

Thus, the necessities and the intricacies of factional politics make apparently inconsistent alliances essential. Brahmans of Meerut have affinities with the Brahman-led group in state politics, as Banias have with the Bania-led group. However, Brahmans and Banias find it possible to combine when their political interests are identical. In short, it is the quest for power, not caste antagonisms, which ultimately motivates community leaders. The ultimate principle of politics in Meerut district is that the enemy of an enemy is a friend.

The alliance of Brahman and Bania leaders in Meerut district is strictly *ad hoc*. If one faction could win power without the other, the alliance would immediately be ended. Even within some of the local institutions in Meerut district, the alliance does not operate where it is not of mutual benefit to both sides. In fact, in the District Bank, alliances are reversed. The District Bank is one of the few important local institutions which the Kailash Prakash faction has been able to capture. So, on the Bank, Brahmans allied with Kamlapati Tripathi work with Jats allied with Charan Singh against a mixed group allied with Kailash Prakash. It is useless to probe into such alliances for any communal or economic principles of alignment. Factional and personal interests take precedence over all other ties.

Even Charan Singh and Kailash Prakash joined together for a short time, after both had resigned from the Sampurnanand government. Then these two old rivals worked together against the followers of Kamlapati Tripathi in the district.

The maze of factional politics in Meerut district illustrates sharply a fundamental feature of factional politics in Uttar Pradesh, which so far has prevented the development of any faction into a stable political "machine." This feature is the instability of both factional membership and of alliances between factional leaders. The instability of factional member-

[22] Interview in Meerut on December 16, 1962.

ship and of factional alliances has two primary causes—the availability of alternative sources of patronage and the status motivations of individual faction members and leaders. The effect of an unstable factional system is to produce continually a situation of parity or near parity between opposing groups of factions.

For example, in 1956 and in 1960, factional alignments in the contest for president of the Meerut DCC were completely different. Charan Singh and Kailash Prakash worked against each other in 1956 and worked together in 1960. Yet, in 1956, the vote for DCC president was a draw and the decision had to be taken by lot. In 1960, the vote was 73 to 70. The reason for the near parity between opposing groups of factions is that almost every shift of allegiance produces a counter-shift. If one side acquires the support of one factional leader, those who have antagonisms with the latter will join the opposite side. The situation is precisely the same as in Deoria, where the dominant faction leader lost "old friends" whenever he sought new alliances.

In recent years, Charan Singh has lost his nearly exclusive control over party and government patronage for Meerut district. For the first time since Independence, the selection of Congress candidates for the 1962 election in Meerut was bitterly disputed and several of Charan Singh's recommendations were not accepted. The existence of an alternate source of party and government patronage through Kailash Prakash undermines the cohesiveness of Charan Singh's faction.

Equally unstabilizing are the aspirations of faction members for leadership positions. Many of the defectors from Charan Singh have left or have been forced to leave the faction because they aspired to recognition and desired the right of independent decision and action which Charan Singh would not concede. Among the opponents of Charan Singh, the difficulties are just as great. Almost every minor factional leader in the opposition group claims to be the "real" leader of the entire opposition contingent. If the opposition group should achieve a victory over Charan Singh, these faction leaders would immediately begin to fight among themselves for the limelight and for the power to decide on behalf of the whole group.

Thus the existence of factional politics prevents the development of party loyalties. The availability of alternative sources of patronage and the pervasiveness of status motivations among faction leaders prevents the development of stable political machines in the districts of Uttar Pradesh. In the absence of either party loyalties or machine politics, there is an inevitable deterioration in the electoral strength of the party organization. Until 1962, the Congress organization in Meerut district had been one of the strongest in the state. Out of fifteen Assembly seats, the Congress lost none in 1952, only one in 1957, and three in the 1962 election. All three of the seats lost in 1962 were lost as a direct result of internal factional conflicts in the local party organization. The Meerut Congress is still among the strongest Congress organizations in Uttar Pradesh. However, it seems clear that the Meerut Congress organization is beginning to be affected by the disintegrative impact of factional politics.

Rural-urban differences

Meerut district contains three towns with a population over 50,000—Meerut City, Ghaziabad, and Hapur. The growth rate in both Meerut and Hapur has declined, but that of Ghaziabad has increased in the last decade. Since 1951, Ghaziabad has replaced Hapur as the second town of the district. The prospects for a continued increase in the urbanization of Ghaziabad are good, since major plans are being put into operation for the industrialization of the town. Industry has for some time been spilling over from Delhi (only seventeen miles away) into Ghaziabad and there is every possibility that the entire area from Delhi to Ghaziabad will one day be a large industrial complex. Yet it is unlikely that the development of Ghaziabad will be so rapid as to alter significantly the rural-urban population proportions for some time to come.

Rural-urban conflicts have affected politics and the Congress organization in Meerut district in two ways. One kind of conflict developed during the nationalist movement in the 1920s and 1930s when the center of political activity and of political leadership began to shift from the towns to the rural areas. One old Congressman from a subdivisional town in Meerut described the transition from urban to rural political leadership which has taken place in the district in the following way:

Before the noncooperation movement [of 1921], there were no branches of the Congress in the rural areas; the only branches were in the cities and they were led by eminent lawyers. . . . Pyarelal Sharma [a Brahman and a lawyer from Meerut City] was the father of the Congress organization in this district. After we went to jail in 1922, then Chaudhuri Raghubir Narayan Singh, the biggest *zamindar* of the district and a title-holder, gave up his title, was arrested, and took up the leadership of the district.[23]

Still, until the end of the 1930s, Chaudhuri Raghubir Narayan Singh shared the political leadership of the district with the "eminent lawyers" of the towns. The decisive change from urban to rural political leadership in Meerut district came in the late 1930s and early 1940s when the Jats began to participate in the Congress movements. Since 1940, no DCC president in Meerut has come from an urban area.

At the same time that the shift from urban to rural political leaders was

---

[23] Interview in Meerut on December 12, 1962.

taking place, the leadership of the Congress in the cities and towns also was changing. In the towns, there was a gradual shift of leadership from the "eminent lawyers" and professional men to the middle class of business-men, merchants, and shopkeepers. In short, in both town and country, the leadership of the Congress passed from the hands of the British-trained, Western-educated elite in the cities and towns to the rural and urban middle classes.

Although the notion of rural-urban conflict is kept alive in contemporary factional struggles between the Kailash Prakash and Charan Singh groups, the differences are largely coincidental and temperamental, rather than indicative of any real conflicts of interest between the rural and urban middle class. The state and national Congress leaderships have carefuly sought to avoid such conflicts by separating all large towns and cities from their rural surroundings and raising them to the status of independent Congress Committees. Meerut City acquired this status in 1956. The separation does not prevent attempts by opposing factional leaders from Meerut to undermine their rural rivals in the DCC or rural faction leaders from undermining urban rivals in the City Congress Committee. Nevertheless, the conflict which does exist, as has been seen in the previous section, relates to broader factional alignments and not to real conflicts of interest between urban and rural political leaders.

The kind of confrontation between rural and urban economic interests which one expects to see in an industrializing country has only begun to develop in Meerut district, primarily with respect to the industrial development of Ghaziabad. The major political problems which have arisen in connection with the development of Ghaziabad have been over the question of acquisition of village lands from the surrounding areas for residential and industrial development. Approximately fifty villages are affected by land acquisition proceedings for the development of the town. Peasants from these villages, usually assisted by opposition party leaders, have swamped state ministers who have visited the town with complaints against the acquisition proceedings and against alleged cases of exploitation of peasants by "colonisers" who purchase lands for profiteering purposes.[24] Largely as a result of the political pressures by rural interests against the land acquisition proceedings, the Government of Uttar Pradesh decided to reduce the amount of land to be acquired from 35,000 to 6,000 acres only.[25] In the final plan, some major shifts of location of industries were made also.[26] Numerous other minor concessions for landowners have been granted.

[24] *Hindustan Times* (Kanpur Supplement), January 17, 1961.
[25] *Statesman*, May 14, 1962.
[26] *National Herald*, August 12, 1962.

Although there has been considerable conflict over the development of the town of Ghaziabad, this conflict has had no effect on factional struggles in the district Congress for several reasons. In the first place, pressure has been directed against the state government, which has had the responsibility for preparing the master plan of Ghaziabad and for notifying acquisition proceedings. Second, political pressures on the issues involved have been strictly *ad hoc* and have reflected primarily the desire on the part of peasants either to save their land or at least get a better price for it. Finally, and most important, is the fact that the town of Ghaziabad, whatever its future prospects, is still a very small and insignificant place, a little town in a large rural district. The rural focus of Meerut politics is unlikely to be altered by the development of Ghaziabad for a long time.

THE 1962 GENERAL ELECTIONS: CASTE, COMMUNITY, AND THE CONGRESS

The role of caste in elections is easily the most discussed aspect of contemporary Indian political behavior. Among journalists in India, a common notion prevails that very little else matters in an Indian election but the caste of the candidates. It is often argued that the Congress has been so successful in winning elections in post-Independence Indian politics because it has carefully analyzed the caste composition of every constituency and has selected candidates from the largest or most influential community in each case. Very little systematic scholarly work has been done on the subject. A pioneering study by Selig Harrison appeared in 1956, which sought "to establish the crucial importance of caste manipulation as a source of Andhra Communist strength." Harrison went on to say more generally that "the institution of caste, so peculiarly integral to all Hindu social organization, pervades the entire political system in predominantly Hindu India. Whether caste in India lends itself more readily to political manipulation than do social factors elsewhere has not yet been explored. But Hindu caste discipline clearly wields a measure of political influence in India that cries for serious study."[27] In a later study, Harrison argues that caste is not only important in each constituency, but that "caste lobbies function coherently on the basis of entire linguistic regions."[28] Although the development "of regional caste lobbies is most noticeable in the south," Harrison claims that even in the "sprawling unit" of Uttar

[27] Selig S. Harrison, "Caste and the Andhra Communists," *American Political Science Review*, L, No. 2 (June, 1956), 378.
[28] Selig S. Harrison, *India: The Most Dangerous Decades* (Princeton: Princeton University Press, 1960), p. 109.

Pradesh, "smaller castes that do not loom large separately . . . can through coalitions find political strength." Harrison refers specifically to an alleged alliance of Ahirs, Jats, and Gadariyas in Uttar Pradesh politics.[29]

Harrison's comments on caste and politics have been criticized in an unpublished paper by Baldev Raj Nayar, in which it is argued that Harrison has not been able to prove his thesis statistically and that he has been forced to bring in other factors, such as "appeals to patriotism, nationalism and economic programs," whose relative weight in determining voting behavior has not been established.[30] Nayar points to evidence in another study that an election does not necessarily solidify castes, but that it may also disrupt caste solidarity when contesting candidates belong to the same caste.[31] Still another survey of the role of caste in politics, however, tends to support Harrison's thesis and claims that, "for the greater part of India . . . caste-loyalty comes usually before party sentiment and ideological alignments."[32]

A recent series of studies of individual constituencies in India's third General Elections provides evidence to support both sides. Myron Weiner, the editor of the series, notes that, "in some constituencies the political cohesion of ethnic groups was high, but in others factional and leadership conflicts within the community made it possible for candidates of many parties to win some support." In general, the studies revealed that many different factors influence an election in India, as elsewhere in the world, and that Indian voters have "many loyalties to choose from," not only loyalties to caste but to "kin groups, factions, . . . and individual leaders."[33]

Clearly, there is room for more precision about the extent and limits of community voting in India. In this section, an attempt will be made to analyze the conditions under which "solid" community voting does or does not take place, the effect of community solidarity upon the election outcome, the role of intercaste alliances, and the role of noncaste factors in determining the election outcome in individual constituencies in Meerut district. It will be argued on the basis of statistics and interviews from three rural constituencies in Meerut district that the success or failure of individual Congress candidates depends more upon the ability of the can-

[29] *Ibid.*, p. 135. The alliance referred to is reported to have operated during the 1951-1952 General Elections (in unspecified constituencies), but there is no evidence in contemporary Uttar Pradesh politics to support Harrison's assertion on the same page that this alliance "twines its coils in and out of state political life."

[30] "The Study of Voting Behavior in India," n.d., p. 7. (Mimeographed.)

[31] *Ibid.*, p. 16.

[32] C. Von Fürer-Haimendorf, "Caste and Politics in South Asia," in C. H. Philips, ed., *Politics and Society in India* (New York: Frederick A. Praeger, 1962), p. 65.

[33] Myron Weiner, "The Third General Elections, Studies in Voting Behaviour I: Introduction," *Economic Weekly*, XIV, Nos. 28-30 (July, 1962), 1109-1110.

didate to win support from many castes rather than upon the ability of
the candidate to win support from his caste fellows only.

Baghpat

It should be apparent from the material on the selection of candidates
presented in the other district case studies that Congress tickets are usually
distributed through the processes of factional bargaining and that the tickets are not always given to candidates who belong to the largest or most influential community in the constituency. For example, for Baghpat constituency in Meerut district, there were two claimants for the Congress
ticket. Although the constituency is dominated by Gujars, one of the claimants was a Tyagi and the other a Muslim. The Tyagi claimant was the
incumbent MLA and had the support of Chaudhuri Charan Singh. However, the ticket was given to the Muslim, who succeeded in winning the
favor of the Uttar Pradesh Congress President and the Union Home Minister.

The constituency is almost wholly rural, containing only two small
towns, in which are situated 13 of the 90 polling stations. As in every
rural constituency in Uttar Pradesh, there is a great diversity of castes in
Baghpat. Gujars are by far the largest caste in the constituency, comprising about 25 percent of the total population. Gujars are clearly dominant
in 18 polling stations in the constituency. Jats come next with 11 polling
stations clearly under their influence. After the Jats come Tyagis, who
dominate in 9 polling stations. Three polling stations are dominated by
Rajputs, 2 by Rors, and 1 by Ahirs. However, the largest number of polling stations are of mixed composition, with no particular community
dominant. There are significant numbers of Muslims in several polling
stations; but in none are Muslims numerically dominant.

Seven candidates contested the Assembly election in Baghpat, but there
were only 3 main contenders—the Congress candidate, who was a Muslim;
a Communist Jat candidate; and an independent Gujar candidate. The other
4 candidates (1 Jat, 1 Gujar, 2 not known) polled insignificantly, although
one of them polled a plurality in 3 polling stations in or near his home
village. Table 9 shows the distribution of the vote for the main candidates
in Baghpat constituency, that is, the number of polling stations (by category) in which each candidate won a plurality of the total votes polled.
In this constituency, the vote of all castes was divided to some extent. However, it is clear from the table that the independent Gujar candidate had
significant strength primarily in polling stations dominated by Gujars. The
Jat candidate won 15 of his 31 pluralities in polling stations dominated by
Jats or Tyagis. The Congress Muslim candidate had no significant strength

among any of the three most influential communities in the constituency,
but won the election on the basis of broad support from all other communities—Brahmans, Muslims, and Chamars primarily.

The Congress candidate himself gave the following analysis of the

TABLE 9

ELECTION RESULTS BY POLLING STATION FOR BAGHPAT ASSEMBLY CONSTITUENCY
IN MEERUT DISTRICT, 1962

| | Polling Stations Dominated[a] | | Number & Percentage of Total Pluralities Won | | | | | | |
| | | | Cong.(Muslim) | | Communist(Jat) | | Ind.(Gujar) | | Other |
Community	No.	Pct.	No.	Pct.	No.	Pct.	No.	Pct.	No.
1. Gujar	18	20.0	3	9.4	1	3.2	13	54.2	1
2. Jat	11	12.2	2	6.3	9	29.0	...	...	...
3. Tyagi	9	10.0	3	9.4	6	19.4	...	...	...
4. Other castes[b]	6	6.7	2	6.3	1	3.2	2	8.3	1
5. Mixed[c]	24	26.6	14	43.8	4	12.9	5	20.8	1
6. Urban	13	14.4	7	21.8	6	19.4	...	...	...
7. Information incomplete	9	10.0	1	3.1	4	12.9	4	16.7	...
Total	90	99.9	32	100.1	31	100.0	24	100.0	3

Source for caste composition of polling stations: *Census of India, 1891, District Census Statistics, N.-W. Province and Oudh, Meerut Division* (Allahabad: Government
Press, 1896).

[a] A polling station may contain a single village or part of a village or as many as five
or six villages. I have classified a polling station as "dominated" by a particular caste
where the 1891 census lists that caste as the largest in the village or villages. Where
there is any doubt, the polling stations have been classified as "mixed." I have spot-
tested the accuracy of the 1891 census data on village caste in a number of villages in
several districts in Uttar Pradesh—villages which I have personally visited or whose
caste composition has been given to me by candidates. However, the accuracy of the
census data has not been checked systematically. For this reason and because of the
age of the census data, I have not tried to correlate exact percentages of caste populations by village with the votes for various candidates. The proportion of the population of Gujars in a "Gujar-dominated" polling station, for example, probably has
changed over the decades. However, it is much less likely that Gujar influence has
disappeared entirely from the village.

[b] Rajput 3, Ror 2, Ahir 1.

[c] Polling stations containing villages where there are two large castes or containing
two or more villages, each dominated by a different caste. For example, polling station
number 3, containing three villages, one with a large population of Rors, another of
Brahmans, another of Bhangis, has been classified as "mixed."

election outcome in this constituency: (1) the Gujar candidate "made
things difficult because he took most of the Congress supporters [among
Gujars] away from me in the name of the *baradari* [caste brotherhood]."
(2) The major reason for his success was that there was no Brahman or
Bania[34] candidate against him to draw votes from these communities. (3)

[34] The Bania vote comes from the two towns, but statistics are not available to isolate
the Bania localities.

He received a majority of the Jat votes because his uncle, who had been a big *zamindar* and a member of the Assembly for thirty years, had developed good relations with Jats by "serving them as an MLA and as a Nawab, getting them jobs, etc." [35] The statistics support the Congress candidate's analysis in every respect but the support he received from Jats. Although he achieved a plurality in two of the eleven Jat-dominated polling stations, the remaining nine went to the Jat candidate.

Left out of the explanation is any reason for the Tyagi vote, which went largely to the Jat candidate. A possible explanation is that the Tyagis were dissatisfied with the failure of the Congress to give the ticket to a Tyagi, as in the past; but this explanation does not account for the Tyagis voting for the Jat candidate rather than for the Gujar. Since no depth analysis was made in this constituency, no other explanations can be offered.

The Congress candidate's analysis and the statistics do lead to some interesting conclusions, however. In the first place, it is clear that contradictory tendencies may operate in a constituency simultaneously. There is evidence of some caste solidarity influencing voting behavior—Gujars voting for the Gujar candidate and Jats for the Jat candidate. Yet it is most significant that the successful candidate and the runner-up both combined votes from different communities and that the successful Congress candidate had much greater diversity of support in the constituency than either of his opponents. In this constituency, electoral success depended upon the ability of the Congress candidate to combine votes of different communities.

Barnawa

In Baghpat, the candidate of the largest and most inflential community in the constituency polled third because he was unable to win support from other communities. An even more dramatic illustration of the failure of a "dominant" caste in a constituency to elect a candidate of the community is provided by the election results from Barnawa constituency. Barnawa is the only constituency in the entire state in which the majority of voters belongs to a single caste. Sixty percent of the population of Barnawa are Jats. The rest of the population is divided among various castes, of which the largest are Rajputs, followed by Rors, with a sprinkling of Muslims, Gujars, and Tyagis. Yet in 1962 a Jat candidate on a Congress ticket lost to an independent Rajput candidate.

The losing Congress candidate gave these reasons for his failure in the 1962 election from Barnawa: (1) There were nine candidates, of whom seven were Jats, thus dividing the Jat votes. (2) The Jats worked for Jat candidates, so that all other communities combined against them. (3) Re-

[35] Interview in Lucknow on October 18, 1962.

lations between Jats and other castes in the constituency are not good because of caste antagonisms. (4) There was "groupism" among Jats.[36] The election results support statistically the Congress candidate's analysis (see table 10). Thirty-nine of the polling stations in which the Congress candidate was successful were dominated by or influenced by Jats. The other Jat candidates drew just enough support away from the Congress to turn the balance in the election. Finally, 35 out of 48 of the Rajput candidate's

TABLE 10

ELECTION RESULTS BY POLLING STATION FOR BARNAWA ASSEMBLY CONSTITUENCY
IN MEERUT DISTRICT, 1962

Community	Polling Stations Dominated No.	Pct.	Number & Percentage of Total Pluralities Won Congress (Jat) No.	Pct.	Other Jats No.	Pct.	Ind. (Rajput) No.	Pct.	Other No:
1. Jats	43	43.4	28	68.3	8	88.9	6	12.5	1
2. Mixed (some Jats)	15	15.2	11	26.8	1	11.1	3	6.3	...
3. Rajput	9	9.1	...	...	...	...	9	18.7	...
4. Ror	7	7.1	...	...	...	...	7	14.6	...
5. Other castes^a	5	5.0	...	...	...	...	5	10.5	...
6. Mixed (no Jats)	16	16.2	2	4.9	...	...	14	29.2	...
7. Information incomplete	4	4.0	...	...	...	...	4	8.3	...
Total	99	100.0	41	100.0	9	100.0	48	100.1	1

aMuslim 2, Gujar 2, Tyagi 1.

pluralities were in non-Jat polling stations. In every polling station clearly dominated by non-Jats—whether Rajputs, Rors, Muslims, Gujars, or Tyagis—the Rajput candidate won a plurality of the votes.

Again, opposing tendencies operated in the same constituency. Jats voted for Jat candidates, but the winning candidate succeeded by drawing support from different communities. A comparison of Baghpat and Barnawa constituencies reveals that there is no common voting pattern in the two constituencies. In Baghpat, it was the Congress candidate who drew support from diverse castes; in Barnawa, it was an opposition candidate who had broader intercaste support. In Baghpat, most Jats voted for the Communist Jat candidate; in Barnawa, most Jats voted for the Congress. A tentative conclusion from the election results in these two constituencies is that electoral success depends less upon selecting a candidate of the "dominant" community in the constituency than upon selecting a candidate who can gather diverse support from various communities. In Barnawa constituency, factionalism in the majority community and intercaste alliances among the minority communities determined the election outcome.

36 Interview in Meerut on December 14, 1962.

Dasna

Religion is often a more powerful divider in Uttar Pradesh elections than caste. Hindu-Muslim rivalries are sharpest in the urban areas where there are large concentrations of Muslims, as in Aligarh town for example. However, there are many rural constituencies in Uttar Pradesh where Muslims are numerically and economically the most important community. Dasna constituency in Meerut district is one. More than 30 percent of the population of Dasna constituency is Muslim. Muslims too are divided into caste groups. In fact, every major caste in Meerut district, except Brahmans, has both Hindu and Muslim sections. In Dasna constituency, the most prominent caste of Muslims are the Muslim Rajputs who dominate or are in significant numbers in 12 of the 77 rural polling stations in the constituency; all Muslim castes together have significant influence in 28 polling stations. The largest single ethnic group in the constituency, however, are Hindu Rajputs who alone are influential in 25 polling stations. Seven polling stations are dominated by Jats, two by Chamars, and one each by Ahirs, Tyagis, and Brahmans; nine polling stations are of mixed composition and thirteen fall in two small towns.

Five candidates contested the election from Dasna constituency. The Congress candidate was a Muslim. The winning candidate was a Congress "rebel," a Hindu Rajput on an independent ticket. Only one of the other three candidates, a Chamar on a Socialist ticket, succeeded in winning a plurality in any of the polling stations in the constituency. The results of the election by polling stations are given in table 11.

The voting figures in the Hindu and Muslim Rajput polling stations are most striking. Every one of the 19 Hindu Rajput polling stations was captured by the Hindu Rajput candidate and all 8 of the Muslim Rajput polling stations were captured by the Congress Muslim candidate. More generally, the Hindu Rajput candidate scored an overwhelming majority of his successes in rural polling stations among Hindus; 38 of his 44 rural victories were in Hindu-dominated polling stations and 24 of his victories were in polling stations where Hindu Rajputs are numerous. In contrast, 21 out of 26 of the Congress Muslim candidate's rural successes were in polling stations where Muslims are in large numbers. Put in another way, the Hindu candidate polled a plurality in 38 of the 46 or 83 percent of the Hindu polling stations, whereas the Congress Muslim won a plurality in 21 of the 28 or 75 percent of the Muslim polling stations.

The successful candidate analyzed the election outcome in the following way: (1) He claimed that he received "about 90 percent of the Hindu Rajput vote." (2) Although there were two Muslim candidates, "not a single Muslim" voted for the non-Congress Muslim candidate "because they [the Muslims] did not want to lose their votes." (3) In the predominantly Muslim polling stations, "I was utterly defeated." [37] All three of the candidate's perceptions are supported by the statistics. However, he denied that communal voting was the reason for his success. Instead, he claimed that those who supported him did so because he was a local man, whereas the Congress candidate was an outsider. Although the Congress candidate was the incumbent MLA, he "did not visit even a single village during his five years and does not even know the names of the polling stations." The successful candidate remarked that if the Congress candidate had been a Muslim from the constituency, he himself and the public in general would have supported such a candidate. To prove his point, he noted that some

TABLE 11

ELECTION RESULTS BY POLLING STATION FOR DASNA ASSEMBLY CONSTITUENCY
IN MEERUT DISTRICT, 1962

	Number & Percentage of Total Pluralities Won						
	Polling Stations Dominated		Ind. (Hindu Rajput)		Cong. (Muslim)		Other
Community	No.	Pct.	No.	Pct.	No.	Pct.	No.
1. Hindu Rajput	19	21.1	19	36.6	...	...	...
2. Mixed (some Hindu Rajput)	6	6.7	5	9.6	...	...	1
3. Muslim Rajput	8	8.9	...	...	8	23.5	...
4. Mixed (some Muslim Rajput)	4	4.4	1	1.9	2	5.9	1
5. Other Muslim	4	4.4	2	3.8	2	5.9	...
6. Mixed (some Muslim)	12	13.3	3	5.8	9	26.4	...
7. Jat	7	7.8	5	9.6	1	2.9	1
8. Other castes[a]	5	5.6	3	5.8	2	5.9	...
9. Mixed	9	10.0	6	11.5	2	5.9	1
10. Information incomplete	3	3.3	3	5.8	...	...	...
11. Urban	13	14.4	5	9.6	8	23.5	...
Total	90	99.9	52	100.0	34	99.9	4

a Chamar 2, Ahir 1, Tyagi 1, Brahman 1.

of his best election workers were Muslims, whereas some prominent Hindu Rajputs worked for the Congress. He also noted that some Hindu polling stations were carried by the Congress. Finally, he commented upon the importance of village factionalism; in most villages, one group supported him and the other supported the Congress candidate.[38]

It is likely that all the factors mentioned in the successful candidate's analysis had some effect upon the voting behavior of different groups in the constituency. Unlike the elections in Aligarh, communal issues did not pervade the campaign in Meerut district. Nevertheless, both the candi-

[37] Interview in Lucknow on October 24, 1962.
[38] *Ibid.*

date's remarks and the statistics support the conclusion that most Hindus voted for him and most Muslims for the Congress candidate. Clearly, communal voting, whatever the reasons, was the most important factor in the election outcome in Dasna.

Summary

Selig Harrison has remarked, in presenting his argument about the crucial importance of caste in Indian elections, that "invariably, the most perplexing election surprises become crystal-clear when the caste factors in a constituency come to light." [39] There is a great deal of truth in this statement. However, most of Harrison's data and his assumptions about the value of caste "manipulation" for political success are based on the notion, which may be true for the Andhra delta or other parts of south India, that victory goes to the candidate who can best mobilize the votes of the dominant community in a constituency. Some of the districts in the Andhra delta, for example, appear to have large Kamma majorities. In such districts, Congress and Communists pit Kamma against Kamma; the candidate who can win the most support from the Kammas succeeds. However, as Nayar points out and as Harrison's own analysis reveals, when Kamma is pitted against Kamma, caste solidarity is disrupted and appeals to noncaste factors become important.

The three constituencies analyzed above and the previous data presented on the Aligarh elections suggest some more precise conclusions. First, there is a definite tendency for an overwhelming majority of caste members to vote for candidates of their own community, irrespective of party label. However, the real test of the effects of caste solidarity or caste discipline in an election is what happens when caste or community members are presented with more than one candidate from their community in a particular election contest. Here, there is conflicting evidence. In Baghpat, there were two Jat and two Gujar candidates, but only one Jat and only one Gujar candidate secured the votes of their respective communities. In Dasna, where there were two Muslim candidates, only one was able to acquire community support because the Muslims "did not want to lose their votes." However, in Barnawa a multiplicity of Jat candidates and "groupism" among Jats created enough of a division of caste votes to give the victory to a non-Jat candidate, even though Jats are in an absolute majority in the constituency.

The election result in Barnawa points to the increasing importance of factionalism in elections in Uttar Pradesh, not only to the divisive impact of factionalism, but to its integrative aspects. For, in Barnawa, while the majority caste was divided by factionalism, the minority castes united in

[39] Harrison, *India: The Most Dangerous Decades*, p. 109.

a multicaste alliance to defeat the Jats. It is hardly surprising to find that the previously cited statement that "caste loyalty comes before party sentiment and ideological alignments" is largely true. Nor is it likely that party sentiment or ideology will play much of a role in local politics in India for some time to come, if ever. However, it is quite likely that factionalism will play a continuously increasing role in Indian elections, just as it has already come to dominate party politics not only in Uttar Pradesh, but in other Indian states as well. Thus, Harrison's statement about the importance of "caste factors" in a constituency must be qualified to take account of the increasing role of factionalism in Indian elections. Election results can be interpreted only when one knows which castes are united behind particular candidates, which castes are divided by internal factions, and which castes will ally with other castes for election purposes. The introduction of factional considerations in any constituency makes many other factors important. For the ties between a candidate and his factional supporters in a constituency are many and various—involving caste, community, and kinship loyalties, as well as loyalties based upon favors and services done or promised.

It is important to recognize that both "caste factors" and factional alliances vary from constituency to constituency and election to election. Members of a caste which votes Congress in one constituency may vote Communist in a neighboring constituency. Intercaste or intercommunity alliances rarely extend beyond the limits of a parliamentary constituency. Factions in party organizations, in separate constituencies, and in individual villages all operate autonomously and are only tied together by temporary alliances of mutual interest. The development of party loyalties among large sections of voters, which would give some stability to voting patterns, is not in sight.

The *ad hoc* character of factional and intercaste alliances makes unlikely Harrison's predictions, arrived at during the height of the linguistic states controversy, that "caste lobbies" operating "coherently on the basis of entire linguistic regions" will dominate Indian politics in the foreseeable future. There is increasing evidence, not only from Uttar Pradesh, but from Andhra itself [40] and from other states that, with the controversy over linguistic reorganization of states now settled, factional politics is coming into its own all over India.

[40] In Ponnur constituency in Andhra, Myron Weiner found that, in the 1962 election, "factional loyalties within Congress proved to be more powerful than party loyalties" and that "multi-caste village factions were the basic working units for each of the Assembly candidates," in "The Third General Elections, Studies in Voting Behaviour IX, Village and Party Factionalism in Andhra: Ponnur Constituency," *Economic Weekly*, XIV, No. 38 (September 22, 1962), 1517-1518.

CONCLUSION

Congress politics in Meerut district reveals another facet of factional politics in the Uttar Pradesh Congress party, which has been touched upon only briefly in the other district studies. This aspect of factional politics is the relationship between factions and the parochial social groups of Indian society. It is a major contention of this study that the strength of the Congress in Meerut district, in Uttar Pradesh in general, and increasingly in the rest of India lies in its proven ability to integrate and accommodate different caste groups and to tolerate intraparty factionalism. The integration of local caste groups into the internal factional system of the district and state Congress organizations prevents either the dominance of a particular caste or community over others in the Congress or the development of polarized conflict between large caste groups or between Hindus and Muslims.

The growth of political consciousness among an increasing number of different caste groups is making diversity a political as well as a social fact in contemporary Indian life. Any caste group or caste leader seriously interested in obtaining political concessions must bargain with other caste groups and leaders to get them. Simultaneously, the growth of factional politics limits caste solidarity and encourages intercaste alliances. The "dominant" castes split and the smaller castes join together in an endless process of fission and fusion, which makes every political coalition inherently unstable.

Most faction leaders in the district and state Congress party use their community ties as a stepping-stone to political power. Still, the reputation that a politician has within his own community is only a prerequisite for power. In addition the aspiring faction leader must be able to talk to and share power with faction leaders from other social groups. Thus, in Meerut district, Chaudhuri Charan Singh initially came to prominence as a leader of his Jat community. But, Charan Singh cannot control the Meerut Congress on the basis of Jat support alone. To maintain power, Charan Singh has allied with other community leaders. Those who have opposed Charan Singh have also had to seek inter-community alliances.

The same pattern of fission and fusion, alliance and counteralliance is evident among the electorate of Meerut district. It is useless to seek consistent and persistent patterns in these processes. Factional politics reveals neither consistent communal divisions nor meaningful economic divisions.

The ability of the Congress to integrate new caste groups and their leaders into its factional system gives the Congress great diversity of leadership and electoral support. Those who wish to oppose the Congress must match that diversity. Strangely enough, it is this diversity of leadership and support operating in an ever-shifting system of factional alliances which, though it prevents the development of political "machines" in the districts of Uttar Pradesh, gives the Congress organization a resilience which explains its past ability to gain and maintain power and guarantees that the Congress will retain that ability for a long time to come.

VIII.

Kanpur: The Congress Party in an Urban Industrial Setting

THE ENVIRONMENT

Kanpur, with a population of 947,000 according to the 1961 census, is the largest city in Uttar Pradesh and one of the major industrial cities in the Indian Union. Ranking as one of the three great textile centers in the country (after Bombay and Ahmedabad), Kanpur has also a wide variety of large and small factories in almost every sphere of industrial production —the most important in ordnance, leather goods, iron and steel, chemicals, metal products, engineering, and food and tobacco. In 1953, there were 273 factories in Kanpur, providing employment to 68,832 workers; the textile industry provided the bulk of this industrial employment, 288 factories providing employment to 51,084 workers.[1] In the earning population of the city, industrial workers constitute the largest category, accounting for 22 percent of the total work force. Manual workers in general, both industrial and non-industrial, account for 30 percent of the earning population. The next largest category of earners (20 percent) are those engaged in trade and commerce—13 percent as petty traders and hawkers and 7 percent "with a considerable business turnover." Also included in the commercial population of the city are the middlemen (2 percent) and the shop assistants (5 percent). Other important economic categories in the city are the white collar workers—scribes, typists, and stenographes—(9 percent), professional occupations (5 percent), artisans (12 percent), and the "executive, managerial, and technical" class (3 percent).[2]

[1] D. N. Majumdar, *Social Contours of an Industrial City: Social Survey of Kanpur, 1954-56* (Bombay: Asia Publishing House, 1960), pp. 51-52.
[2] *Ibid.*, pp. 111-114.

Ethnically, the population of the city is predominantly Hindu, although Muslims constitute a large minority, with over 20 percent of the population of the city. Scheduled Castes are only a little over 5 percent, according to the 1951 census. A large proportion of industrial and manual labor comes from the Muslims and the Scheduled Castes. Among caste Hindus, Brahmans predominate, with Banias, Kayasthas, and Khatris following in descending order.[3] Banias and Khatris provide a large proportion of the shopkeeping and trading class, but no generalizations can be made about other castes. Most of the castes are spread over the city and do not dominate any particular geographical area; only some Khatris and some Thakurs live in geographically compact areas. The same is more or less true of the Scheduled Castes, but there are large concentrations of Scheduled Castes in a number of industrial areas of the city. The Muslim population of the city is partially scattered; but, in many areas, Muslims are in an overwhelming majority and in others they constitute a very large minority. Kanpur has also a highly localized population of Sindhi and Punjabi refugees from Pakistan in two or three areas of the city.

This chapter presents a case study of the functioning of the Congress in an urban industrial environment. It is a study of the relationships between class and community groups, on the one hand, and Congress factions, on the other hand. It will be argued that the leadership of the Congress in Kanpur comes from the socially and economically dominant groups in the population of the city. Factional conflicts take place among members of these groups and reflect personal quarrels unrelated to social and economic conflicts which exist in the life of the city. As a result, Congress strength in the electorate has steadily declined since Independence. The effect of Congress factionalism on the public life of the city, as elsewhere in Uttar Pradesh, has been the paralysis of local institutions of self-government.

THE KANPUR CONGRESS: THE POLITICS OF PERSONAL ENMITY

The political life of Kanpur City has been dominated in the last decade by conflicts, based solely upon personal enmity, between two of the most dynamic, colorful, and vituperative Congress politicians in Uttar Pradesh. It is said that the personal conflict between Ram Ratan Gupta and Shiv Narain Tandon began in primary school, when the two boys used to fight each other. The source of their enmity is of little interest. It is sufficient to note that the two men hate each other and have hated each other as long as they or their contemporaries can remember. A look at the motivations

[3] *Ibid.*, p. 67.

and aspirations of these two men and at the factional conflicts which their conflicting aspirations have engendered will illustrate further the nature of contemporary Congress political leadership and political organization in the districts of Uttar Prade\'sh.

Shiv Narain Tandon

Shiv Narain Tandon comes from a Khatri family of cloth dealers from the predominantly Khatri area of Kanpur, known as Philkhana. He joined the Congress in 1926 at the age of eighteen, under the inspiration of Ganesh Shankar Vidyarthi, the most important leader of the Kanpur Congress at the time. By 1930, Shiv Narain was a well-known Congressman of Kanpur and he was elected president of the City Congress Committee (CCC) in that year.

In the early days of the Congress in Kanpur, there were two clealy defined factions. One, led by Ganesh Shankar Vidyarthi, was called the "Pratap" group, after the name of the well-known Congress Hindi newspaper of the city, founded by Ganesh Shankar. It was this group which Shiv Narain joined and which controlled the affairs of the City Congress throughout most of the nationalist period and for some time after Independence.

The second important faction in the Kanpur Congress was known as the "Rashtriya Vidyalaya" group and was led by Guru Raghubar Dayal Misra, the master of the Rashtriya Vidyalaya, a nationalist school of Kanpur. The differences between the two factions will be discussed below. Here, it is necessary to note only that Ram Ratan Gupta was a member of the "Rashtriya Vidyalaya" group.

Babu Shiv Narain Tandon has wanted only one reward from his participation in the political life of Kanpur—recognition as the first citizen of the city, the righter of all wrongs, champion of the underdog. For a time, Shiv Narain Tandon occupied this position in fact. After the end of World War II, Shiv Narain emerged as the undisputed leader of the Kanpur Congress and was unanimously elected President of the CCC. During his two-year regime, from 1946 to 1948, he dominated the civic life of Kanpur. The patronage at his disposal was enormous and was liberally dispensed. In addition to his private resources as a partner in the great Kanpur cloth firm of Jwala Prasad Radhakrishna, he controlled the most important local body in the city, the Development Board, and brought the entire administration of Kanpur under his control through his influence with the District Magistrate. His power was so great that the leading millowners of the city, some willingly and others reluctantly, were forced to bow to his wishes. Under the regime of Shiv Narain Tandon, a "Spindle Tax" was imposed upon the millowners of Kanpur at the rate of two annas per spindle as a contribution to the city Congress funds.[4] Two of the most important textile millowners of Kanpur have paid heavy penalties for failing to cooperate with Shiv Narain Tandon. Under his tenure as City Congress president, a long and bitter strike was carried on by Congress labor leaders, aided and abetted by Shiv Narain himself, against Ram Ratan Gupta's Lakshmi Ratan Cotton Mill. Shiv Narain personally attended gate meetings, helped to feed the workers and, most important, organized a boycott of cloth from the Lakshmi Ratan Mill by the cloth dealers of the city. On another occasion, the Jaipurias, proprietors of the largest cotton textile mill in the city, had to face a similar boycott led by Shiv Narain.

Shiv Narain Tandon is a man of fiery temperament, with strong and often harsh opinions of other people, subject to sudden changes of mood which make his actions wholly unpredictable. Often moved by impulses, he has suddenly publicized bold and generous schemes, which are just as suddenly forgotten. Shiv Narain's actions have become more unpredictable as his real influence in civic affairs has waned. As his claim to be first citizen has more and more become an untenable one, Shiv Narain has engaged in stunts designed to prove his claim. In 1954, 'he was elected to Parliament from Kanpur in a bye-election; nine months later he resigned both from Parliament and from the Congress, ostensibly because of his disagreement with state party and government leaders on the issue of rationalization in the Kanpur textile industry. Opinions differ sharply on the actual reasons for the resignation. In fact, it is said that Shiv Narain himself gave different reasons to different people. One Kanpur Congressman provides an explanation which, if it does not accurately describe Shiv Narain's reasons, gives some insight into his character:

Shiv Narain Tandon . . . told his family he had resigned to take charge of the family business, which became his responsibility on the death of his elder brother; he told me that he had resigned on the rationalization issue; and he gave other reasons to other people. Actually, I think he resigned because he had no idea of what being an MP involved. When he was elected, he announced that he would be available at Tilak Hall [the City Congress office] for four hours every day, from 9:00 to 1:00 in the morning, to satisfy any request and he hired a steno for the purpose. In a short time, the work became so great that he was forced to hire three stenos to do the typing and three to do the dictating, while he sat and signed all the letters. Shiv Narain Tandon would send letters to anybody, even on local matters such as allotment of houses. He sent out such a large number of letters of this sort that the local officials went to their ministers and said they were not able to act for fear of displeasing Shiv Narain Tandon. The situation was such that Pantji [the Chief Minister of Uttar Pradesh] began to apply pressure on Tandon. Then there was a letter that Shiv Narain Tandon sent out on

---

[4] *National Herald*, May 12 and 20, 1949.

behalf of an oil magnate on a tax matter. This letter was sent all the way up to C. D. Deshmukh, the then [Central] Finance Minister who, as an old ICS [Indian Civil Service] man, would not tolerate this kind of nonsense and he also applied pressure on Shiv Narain Tandon.[5]

The picture of Shiv Narain Tandon sitting in the Congress office, righting all wrongs and satisfying all grievances with the stroke of a pen is quite in character. Another explanation, also in character, is that his resignation was meant to draw attention to factional quarrels in the Kanpur Congress and force state Congress leaders to intervene on his behalf. Reportedly, a little "persuasion" would have been sufficient to make Shiv Narain withdraw his resignation. One local Congressman remarked at the time that the resignation was "purely meant to create dramatic and spectacular effect and to focus the attention of the PCC towards the Kanpur Congress disputes." [6]

Shiv Narain's own explanation of his resignation is most revealing about his personal character. In many ways, Shiv Narain is representative of a type of politician who has come to prominence in Uttar Pradesh politics since Independence. In a politics of open struggle for personal power, prestige, and self-advancement, most Uttar Pradesh politicians still find it necessary to disavow any self-seeking motivations on their own part and to attribute their difficulties to the evil machinations of others. Shiv Narain sees himself as unself-seeking, but if he is not consulted on every issue of importance affecting the city's public life, he feels insulted and must retaliate against such an insult and demonstrate his power and his indispensability. He feels that the people of money and power in the city are his enemies, but that the "people" adore him. All these elements of Shiv Narain's personal character and psychology appear in his own explanation of the resignation:

I resigned because of differences with C. B. Gupta. The question arose of rationalization. About 22,000 laborers were to be retrenched. *I didn't ask for the ticket, but they have always asked me*, since 1937. Then, Pantji sent his emissary and said, I'll give you the ticket and you should not refuse. Even C. B. Gupta supported me. Then, I stood; but, on the question of rationalization, I said I cannot side with the Government on rationalization, I am with labor. When I was President in 1946-48, Arjun Arora, Ganesh Datt Bajpai, and Ganga Sahai Chaube [Congress labor leaders], we all worked together. Every day, we had 200 workers in Tilak Hall and we always sided with . . . the millworkers. *Since then, the millowners have been against me. Labor loved me*. . . . Then, Mr. Sampurnanand called a conference on rationalization at Naini Tal, in which he called

[5] Interview in Kanpur on February 27 and 28, 1962.
[6] *Advance*, September 1, 1954.

the MLAs, *but I was not called because, before me, none of them would have stood* ... I immediately sent a letter to Pantji and Sampurnanand—*how could you take a decision without me?* They sent a notice to me, if you don't behave, you will be expelled. I issued a statement condemning the Naini Tal decision. I received a notice that I have become intolerable. *Mr. C. B. Gupta has always wanted to expel me; he says, Shiv Narain Tandon is my enemy.* I am not, but he should side with the workers, not with the millowners. *Therefore, they [the millowners] become against me. Even in my election, Jaipurias spent Rs. 50,000 against me. Even the shopkeepers voted against me;* they were told by the mill-owners they would be chucked off if they voted for me. I resigned from the Congress and it was only logical I should resign from Parliament, since I was elected on the Congress ticket.[7]

If Shiv Narain Tandon expected to be "persuaded" against resigning, he was sorely disappointed, for the bluff was called. For two years, Shiv Narain remained politically inactive. Then, suddenly in 1956, a major campaign was launched for the re-entry of Shiv Narain into the Congress. It would, of course, be wholly inappropriate for the indispensable man simply to re-enter the Congress by depositing his membership fee at the Congress office. In fact, when a "great man" re-enters the Congress, the ritual of face-saving calls for an appearance of reluctance on the part of the returning prodigal. With a man of so colorful a temperament as Shiv Narain, the return was bound to be particularly unusual. Thus, Shiv Narain heralded his return to active politics by leading a full-scale agitation by the traders of the city against a sales tax imposed by the Congress Government. A threat also was announced that the organization of traders would oppose Congress candidates in the forthcoming general elections. Simultaneously, the Parade Ward Congress Committee (in a major trading area of the city) passed a resolution demanding the re-entry of Shiv Narain Tandon into the Congress; a signature campaign was also launched for the same purpose.

Still, the proper opportunity for the re-entry did not come until 1958. An invariable condition for the return of a prominent local politician to the Congress is a personal request from the great national leaders of the country for him to do so. There are literally hundreds of politicians in Uttar Pradesh of strictly local influence who have re-entered the Congress from the political wilderness because "Nehru needed me." Shiv Narain himself describes his own re-entry in this way:

I remained outside the Congress for about three years. Then Dhebar [national Congress President], Chaturbhuj Sharma [state Congress President] came to Kanpur; Jageshwar Trivedi was CCC President. They all caught my throat and made me take a four-anna membership. Pantji [Union Home Minister at the time] was actually my leader; I couldn't refuse when he asked me. But, active

[7] Interview in Kanpur on November 23, 1962. Italics supplied.

membership I have not joined so far. Otherwise I would be an ex-officio member of the Executive Committee automatically, but I have not given my Rs. 11.[8]

The appropriate circumstances for Shiv Narain's return to the Congress came none too soon, for the first elections to the newly-formed Kanpur Corporation were scheduled for 1959. It had been widely known since 1956 that Shiv Narain would be a candidate for the mayorship of the city. However, Ram Ratan Gupta had so effectively consolidated his hold on the Congress organization in the period of Tandon's withdrawal that the former was elected Mayor of the Kanpur Corporation with little difficulty. But, by a strange turn of factional politics, Ram Ratan was unable to bring about the election of one of his supporters to the position of Deputy Mayor; instead, he was forced reluctantly to accept Shiv Narain Tandon as his Deputy Mayor. The result was what one local newspaper editor called a "cruelly comic situation. Two men who detest . . . each other are now called upon to work together to save their face[s] and to serve the city." [9] The situation lasted less than four months, during which time each man blocked the other's actions until a showdown finally was called in which the Tandon group attempted, but failed, to bring a motion of no-confidence against the Mayor and the Gupta group succeeded in passing a resolution of censure against the Deputy Mayor, which led to the latter's resignation. This time there could be no reason for mystery surrounding the resignation; the resolution of censure was obviously a humiliating experience which Shiv Narain could not tolerate.

Although Shiv Narain resigned from the deputy mayorship, this time he remained a member of the Congress and the Corporation. Since the resolution of censure was passed against him in May, 1960, Shiv Narain's influence has declined even further from its former heights. Although Shiv Narain has long ceased to occupy his once omnipotent position in the city's politics, his main rival has not been wholly successful in filling the breach. Before analyzing the present factional position in the Kanpur Congress, a look at Ram Ratan Gupta's political career is necessary.

Ram Ratan Gupta

Although Ram Ratan Gupta joined the Congress about the same time as Shiv Narain Tandon, Ram Ratan soon turned to industry and opposition to the Congress. Ram Ratan Gupta comes originally from a Bania family of Kanpur cloth dealers; however, after his release from jail in 1930, he joined the J. K. enterprises and formed the Lakshmi Ratan Cotton Mills in partnership with the Singhania family. Ram Ratan remained with the

[8] *Ibid.*
[9] *Citizen*, February 13, 1960.

Singhanias until 1944, when long-smoldering differences between him and the family finally led to a break. Ram Ratan had prepared himself financially for the break, so that when the split did occur, he had the beginnings of a modest, independent industrial empire. Today, Ram Ratan's enterprises include the original cotton textile mill, engineering works, a glass and miniature bulb industry, enamels, a construction firm, and banking interests in Kanpur, Aurangabad, and Bombay.

During the period when he was building his industrial empire, Ram Ratan found it neecssary to oppose the Congress and Congress candidates in various election contests in Kanpur. He was responsible for the organization of a Hindu Sangh in Kanpur, affiliated to the Hindu communal party, the All-India Hindu Mahasabha. Ram Ratan has also taken pride in his struggles against Congress labor workers in the 1930s. In fact, Ram Ratan's revived interest in the Congress began in 1947 when his Lakshmi Ratan Mill was facing one of the most bitter strikes ever witnessed in the Kanpur textile industry. The strike in the Lakshmi Ratan Mill, on the question of rationalization, occurred during the regime of Shiv Narain Tandon as CCC president. In fact, it is said that Shiv Narain Tandon himself was the moving force behind the strike.

Despite the efforts of Shiv Narain, the Lakshmi Ratan Mill survived the long strike and became the first textile mill in the city to introduce a significant measure of rationalization. However, the strike taught Ram Ratan the lesson that the CCC could be a very dangerous weapon in the hands of his opponents and Ram Ratan immediately began to work to oust Shiv Narain and his friends from control of the City Congress and to replace them with men of his own choosing. In this struggle between one of the richest cloth merchants of the city and a wealthy industrialist, men were bought and sold and money and jobs were available for the asking at Jwala Prasad Radhakrishna, the cloth firm of Shiv Narain, and in the many enterprises of Ram Ratan. Today it is a matter of great pride for a Congressman of Kanpur to say, "I have never taken anything" from the moneyed men of the city.

Although Ram Ratan has more resources than Shiv Narain, the struggle for control of the CCC was carried on for five years, from 1948 to 1953, without a definitive victory for either side. Finally, by 1953, the struggle had become so bitter that the state Congress was forced to intervene in the dispute, dissolve the CCC, and appoint an *ad hoc* Congress Committee in its place. In the following year, Shiv Narain committed the tactical blunder of resigning from the Congress. By the time Shiv Narain rejoined the Congress in 1958, shortly before the CCC was again permitted to function democratically, Ram Ratan had so effectively consolidated his position in the City Congress that Shiv Narain Tandon and his followers were almost completely excluded from the new CCC elected in 1958.

There is much that is similar in the political careers and in the psychological makeup of Shiv Narain Tandon and Ram Ratan Gupta. Perhaps the only major difference politically is that Ram Ratan Gupta is a man of much greater personal ambition than Shiv Narain. The latter has wanted only recognition within his home town. Ram Ratan's ambitions, on the other hand, have always been all-India in scope—both industrially and politically. If Shiv Narain has been fired by the desire to be Mayor of Kanpur, Ram Ratan has always wanted a seat in the national Parliament. Ram Ratan's cherished goal eluded him for more than a decade; but in 1962 he was elected MP from Gonda.[10]

Although Ram Ratan Gupta has never been convicted in a court of law for any of his industrial or political activities, the breath of scandal seems to accompany him wherever he goes and to whatever activity he puts his hand. In 1936, one of his associates was imprisoned for participating in a scheme of manipulating the electoral rolls of Kanpur, a scheme for which Ram Ratan takes full credit. In an extraordinarily candid autobiographical sketch, Ram Ratan declares of this incident that "had not Mr. G. C. Jog [the convicted man] played the gentleman, many of us would have been publicly disgraced and jailed." [11] In March, 1963, the alleged default of one of Ram Ratan's firms of a large debt owed to the Life Insurance Corporation of India (a government concern) became a *cause célèbre* in the national Parliament.[12] Another suit was brought against Ram Ratan by a Kanpur Corporator, alleging that the former had some valuable land of the Corporation transferred to the Lakshmi Ratan Cotton Mills on favorable terms during his tenure as Mayor. Also in the courts is an election petition against Ram Ratan charging that he succeeded in winning the election to Parliament from Gonda by enlisting the aid of the District Magistrate and tampering with the ballot papers before the election recount.[13]

Whether any or all of the charges against Ram Ratan are legally valid, the political significance of the many suits against him is great. In a politics of status, the enhancement of one's own prestige and the discrediting of the moral character of one's opponents through accusation and character assassination are everyday political weapons. His enemies will see only poetic justice in the many accusations currently being brought against Ram

[10] See chap. iv above.
[11] *Citizen*, April 8, 1961.
[12] *Statesman*, March 19, 1963.
[13] The charge that tampering with the ballot papers occurred in the Gonda election was established by an Election Tribunal in August, 1964. Ram Ratan has since been deprived of his seat in the Lok Sabha. See p. 77, fn. 24, above.

Ratan and the possibility of his public disgrace. Aside from the usual political enemies any politician collects in his career, Ram Ratan weekly establishes new enemies through the attacks of his Delhi newspaper, the *Flame*, upon national political leaders who incur his wrath. The continual insinuations and vituperative attacks upon important national Congress leaders brought the activities of the paper to the attention of both Congress party leaders and the members of Parliament. In a discussion on the activities of the paper in Parliament, Pandit Nehru described the *Flame* as "a newspaper which is singularly unreliable and irresponsible." [14]

Like any politician, Ram Ratan Gupta has sought political power. Even more than power, Ram Ratan values the political influence which he wields with state party leaders. He cherishes the personal friendship which he has long had with C. B. Gupta, the former Chief Minister of Uttar Pradesh. He has contributed generously to state Congress party funds and has received liberal concessions for his industrial enterprises from the state Congress government. More than anything else, however, Ram Ratan values the esteem of his fellow men. In his autobiographical sketch, the overwhelming desire for esteem and the obsessive fear of public or private humiliation fills every paragraph. Every event mentioned in his life story ends either in the enhancement of his personal prestige and the recognition of his status as a leader among men or in humiliation or near humiliation. In one particularly revealing paragraph, Ram Ratan sums up the essential quality of his personality: talking about his relations with the Singhania family, Ram Ratan remarks, "I had imbibed a habit from early age that I would not approach and contact with even the greatest personage unless I was sure of an honourable reception and from the beginning I had made it clear to Bhai Saheb [Sir Padampat Singhania] that I must be treated as an equal, that I was very sensitive and my sensitiveness should not be hurt. Still he would often boss over me and throw indignities on me and humiliate me before others." [15]

Both Shiv Narain Tandon and Ram Ratan Gupta seek the esteem of their fellow men above all else. Both men feel that evil and immoral men have blocked their schemes and ambitions. Both men picture themselves as uninterested in power, but at the same time powerful and indispensable. In 1953, an investigator was sent to Kanpur by the High Command to inquire into charges of bogus voting in Kanpur Congress elections. The investigator, a man from another state, uninterested in and in no way involved in local disputes, was somewhat taken aback by this particular contradiction in the character of Ram Ratan Gupta. In his report of an interview with the latter, the investigator remarked:

[14] *Citizen*, October 20, 1962.
[15] Published in the *Citizen*, May 6, 1961.

I had a long interview with Ram Ratan Gupta whom I met for the first time. He began by telling me that he took no interest in the party politics of the city and that his sole interest lay in constructive work. . . . But towards the end of a two hour monologue he somewhat changed his tune and tried to impress upon me the important part he played in the Congress politics of the city and the Province. He showed me with evident pleasure a copy of an agreement between Shri Algurai Shastri (President of the PCC), Shri Shiva Narayan Tandon and himself regarding the election of the President of the City Congress Committee. He also told me that he was mostly responsible for collecting quite a few lakhs of rupees for the Congress in the last election. The fact of my being a complete stranger did not stand in the way of his talking about respected Congress leaders.[16]

Both men have tried to be simultaneously king and kingmaker, have tried to combine political power with a desire to be in the limelight. Unlike the classical boss politician, neither man has been willing to pull the strings from behind the scenes and let others receive the honors. During the height of his power over the Kanpur Congress, it was said of Ram Ratan that he "paid the piper and called the tune"; however, when Ram Ratan emerged from behind the scenes to lead the orchestra, his power began to wane. It is well known that the ability of the classical boss politician to rule a city's politics has traditionally rested upon his relative anonymity and immunity from public criticism. When the boss politician steps out into public view himself, it requires extraordinary political control and finesse to remain in power. Ram Ratan's troubles date from his acceptance of the mayorship of Kanpur and have increased with his election to Parliament.

The differences between Shiv Narain Tandon and Ram Ratan Gupta relate to the extent of their ambitions and their reactions to political setbacks. Shiv Narain Tandon has had less ambition than Ram Ratan and less trouble. Moreover, Shiv Narain's reactions to political difficulties have made him much less of an object for public criticism. When Shiv Narain feels that his prestige is threatened, he resigns in a huff and, as the Indian saying puts it, goes "underground" for a while. Ram Ratan is both more ambitious and more aggressive. When Ram Ratan sees "disgrace" coming, he reacts violently, struggles to maintain his position, and lashes out at his critics through his newspaper. Still, the similarities between the two men are more important than the differences. Both want not only the power, but the glory of politics; since glory cannot be attained in present-day Uttar Pradesh politics without participation in the kind of struggle for political power which mars one's reputation, the boss politician who steps into the limelight often finds that the esteem he has sought from his fellowmen is irretrievably lost.

[16] Cited in the *Citizen*, June 8, 1963.

Time	Group 1	Group 2	Group 3	Group 4
1. Pre-Independence	*Pratap Group*	*Rashtriya Vidyalaya Group*		
	G. S. Vidyarthi	Guru R. D. Misra		
	B. K. Sharma	R. P. Misra		
	Dr. Jawaharlal	V. P. Misra		
	S. N. Tandon	H. N. Shastri		
	R. D. Bhatta	R. R. Shastri		
	J. P. Trivedi	R. R. Gupta		
	H. S. Vidyarthi	S. R. Shukla		
	P. L. Agarwal			
2. 1946 to 1948	B. K. Sharma	V. P. Misra	C. B. Kantak	
	S. N. Tandon		Dr. Jawaharlal	
	H. S. Vidyarthi		P. L. Agarwal	
3. 1948 CCC Election	1	+ 2	*vs.* 3	
		Pres.: R. D. Bhatta		
		Sec.: V. P. Misra		
4. 1950 CCC Election	1	*vs.* 2	+ 3	
			Pres.: V. P. Misra	
			Sec.: C. B. Kantak	
5. 1952 CCC Election	*Tandon Group*	*Gupta Group*	3	
	1	+ 2		
		Pres.: Dr. Banerji		
6. November, 1952: PCC Election	1	*vs.* 2	+ 3	
			V. P. Misra	
			H. N. Shastri	
			C. B. Kantak	
			D. S. Bajpai	
7. June, 1953: Ad Hoc CCC	*Tandon Group*	*Gupta Group*	3	
	1	*vs.* 2	+	
			R. R. Gupta	
			Pres.: D. S. Bajpai	
			Dr. Jawaharlal	
			C. B. Kantak	
8. September, 1955		2	*vs.* 3	
		R. R. Gupta	C. B. Kantak	
		V. P. Misra	Dr. Jawaharlal	
		D. S. Bajpai	P. L. Agarwal	
9. 1958 CCC Election	1	+ 2	+ 3	+ 4
	S. N. Tandon	R. R. Gupta	Dr. Jawaharlal	D. S. Bajpai
	J. Bajpai	S. R. Shukla	P. L. Agarwal	J. Jatav
			Pres.: J. P. Trivedi	
10. 1960 Mayoral & Deputy-Mayoral Contests	1	2	3	4
	S. N. Tandon	R. R. Gupta	C. B. Kantak	D. S. Bajpai
	Dy. Mayor: S. N. Tandon		Mayor: R. R. Gupta	
11. 1960 CCC Election		2		
		Pres.: C. P. Tripathi		

Fig. 5. Diagram-history of factional conflict in the Kanpur Congress.

The nature of factional conflict

It has been stressed in the other case studies that, among most Congressmen in Uttar Pradesh district politics, factional loyalty and personal self-interest take precedence over party loyalty and party interest. The following quotation illustrates one view of these developments in the Kanpur Congress:

Many on top, in the middle and even below in the Congress organization in the city fancy and act as if the Congress is made for their good, and not for the country's good, and that they owed no obligation to the party that gave them everything. . . .

Every such Congressman is himself a party. He makes alliances within Congress as well as with those outside for his narrow personal interest, and breaks them at his convenience. Loyalty to the Congress organization has become a thing of the past. With impunity Congressmen support and encourage anti-Congress groups.[17]

Contemporary factional politics in Uttar Pradesh is characterized by three important features, all of which are clearly illustrated in Kanpur. First, ideological or economic issues are completely absent. Splits and mergers, alliances and conflicts among factions are generally traceable to specific incidents involving either a loss of actual or potential power or prestige by individual faction leaders or the possibility of a gain of power or prestige by faction leaders. A second feature of factional politics in Uttar Pradesh is the instability of factional groups and of alliances between factional leaders. Third, faction leaders move out of the Congress into opposition when the threat to the leader's power and prestige is particularly strong and may involve a loss of face, but return again when opportunities for the recapture of power and prestige present themselves. Figure 5 represents a simplification of the history of factional politics in the Kanpur Congress, which is useful in illustrating some of the main features of Congress party factionalism.

The organizing principle of factional conflict.—It has been mentioned before that the only permanent organizing principle for factional conflicts in a local or in the state political system of the Congress party in Uttar Pradesh is personal enmity between two people. Leaving aside the present political position in the Kanpur Congress, the only relatively stable feature in the history of splits, mergers, alliances, and conflicts among the members of the major factional groups is the opposition between Shiv Narain Tandon and Ram Ratan Gupta, that is, between groups 1 and 2. In 1948, as figure 5 shows, groups 1 and 2 did come together in a political alliance

[17] *Citizen*, July 7, 1956.

opposed to group 3. However, at that time, Ram Ratan Gupta was not involved in Congress disputes directly. In 1952 again, the two groups came together. However, this was not an alliance, but a temporary agreement on a cease-fire. In 1952, Dr. Dhirendranath Banerji, a respected, wholly neutral, and totally powerless Congressman was elected president of the CCC while the two main groups took a temporary respite before the final showdown.

Thus the enmity between Shiv Narain and Ram Ratan has provided the basic framework for factional conflict in the Kanpur Congress. If it were possible to present more detail in the diagram, other equally strong personal enmities between some less important factional leaders could be shown. In any case, the boundaries of factional conflict are formed by personal enmities. Within these boundaries, there remains great fluidity. The fluidity that does exist in the system takes place through mergers and alliances among faction leaders who hold no mutual grudges, but share a dislike for a third party. As the chart shows, this kind of fluidity is of great importance and no alliance lasts very long. Almost every new contest brings forth switches of allegiance and alliance.

The composition of factional groups.—The impossibility of finding any ideological or economic principles of association among faction members can be illustrated by examining the composition of the two important pre-Independence groups. One Congressman of the Rashtriya Vidyalaya group described his group as a "laborite and kisan group" and the Pratap group as a group of "people from the commercial and business classes." [18] In fact, this description is only partly true. Although the Pratap group was composed primarily of traders and businessmen, it was led by a journalist. In the Rashtriya Vidyalaya group, only one member had rural connections. It would be more accurate to describe the Rashtriya Vidyalaya group as a labor-industrial group, composed of labor leaders like Harihar Nath Shastri and Raja Ram Shastri and men associated with the J. K. group of industries—Ram Ratan Gupta and Sri Ratan Shukla. Ideologically, it was composed of anti-capitalists and pro-capitalists, Congress Socialists and right-wing Congressmen. This combination of incompatibles arose solely out of personal differences between individuals—between Shiv Narain Tandon and Ram Ratan Gupta and between Ganesh Shankar Vidyarthi and Harihar Nath Shastri.

Neither is it possible to find any persistent caste or communal basis for factional alignments. Shiv Narain Tandon is a Khatri, but not a single one of the other twenty people shown on the chart is a Khatri. Although Ram Ratan is a Bania, only two of the other twenty leaders—Dr. Jawaharlal and Piyarelal Agarwal—are Banias; nor have the three Banias ever been together

18 Interview in Kanpur on November 29, 1962.

for very long. The largest single caste group in the Congress organization is the Brahmans, who form close to a third of the active membership of the Congress and eleven of the twenty-one faction leaders shown in the chart. This Brahman predominance in numbers has not been used to take control of the Congress organization. Brahman leaders have usually either formed separate groups, as in the case of Vasudeo Prasad Misra and Chhail Bihari Kantak, or they have been members of the larger Tandon and Gupta groups.

Thus, although no persistent principles of factional alignment exist, it is possible to illustrate clearly the proposition that factions split, merge, ally, or conflict when a faction leader faces a gain or loss of power or prestige. Only a few examples need be given. The first split, illustrated on the diagram, of Dr. Jawaharlal and Piyarelal Agarwal, took place in 1948 and related to conflicts over appointments to the Kanpur Development Board, the most important civic institution in the city at that time. The split occurred because Dr. Jawaharlal expected to be appointed to the presidency of the Board as a senior member of the Congress and of the Pratap group. Shiv Narain Tandon, who made all the appointments to the Board, in a typically whimsical manner decided to commemorate the memory of Ganesh Shankar Vidyarthi by giving the presidency to the latter's son, Hari Shankar Vidyarthi. Similarly, after 1950, the alliance between groups 2 and 3 was broken because the leader of group 2, Vasudeo Prasad Misra, was denied Congress backing to contest the presidency of the Municipal Board. In 1955, groups 2 and 3 split because Chhail Bihari Kantak felt that the Gupta group had not given him sufficient backing in his contest for Parliament in the 1955 bye-election.

As for alliances, the motivations are obvious in most cases from the chart itself. In 1948, Vasudeo Prasad Misra was given the position of General Secretary as part of the bargain for allying with group 1 against group 3. In 1950, the same Congressman was elected president of the CCC, after allying with group 3 against group 1. Groups 1 and 3 came together for the 1960 mayoral election, after twelve years of noncooperation, because of the split that occurred between groups 2 and 3 in 1955. And so on.

Clearly, the factional system of the Kanpur Congress is marked by a great deal of fluidity, with incessant bargaining among different factional groups and constant shifts of alliance. Whatever structure the system has is provided by personal antagonisms between individual leaders. These antagonisms set the boundaries or limits within which bargains and compromises may be arranged.

The continuance of factional conflict in opposition.—This final point about factional conflict needs little comment. The resignation of Shiv Narain Tandon from the Congress in 1954, his anti-Congress activities in leading an agitation of traders against a Sales Tax Act, and his return to the Congress in 1958 have already been discussed. As the chart shows, Tandon's re-entry into the Congress complicated the factional struggle, which had temporarily become polarized between two groups. Tandon re-entered the Congress at a time when new opportunities for realignments 'had developed, which offered him the chance to regain some of his previous power and prestige in the struggle for Congress tickets to the Kanpur Corporation and for the mayorship of the Corporation.

The example of Shiv Narain Tandon is by no means unique. Many lesser figures have traveled a far more circuitous route, seeking position appropriate to their estimation of themselves in various opposition parties, but eventually returning to the Congress party for the sake of a position on the party executive or a Congress ticket to the legislature. The difference between Shiv Narain and these other Congressmen is that the former identifies very strongly with the Congress organization. The Congress represents a way of life for Tandon, as for many other men who sacrificed in the nationalist movement, and it is in the Congress that they seek recognition.

The leadership of the Kanpur Congress

The nonideological and noneconomic character of factional disputes in the Kanpur Congress is partially explained by the character of the leadership of the organization. As a socially diverse industrial city, Kanpur has experienced many bitter conflicts between social and economic groups, between Hindus and Muslims, laborers and employers. The city's diversity is fairly well represented in the active membership of the Congress. An analysis of 847 active members of the Kanpur Congress reveals the figures shown in table 12 for caste, community, and occupation. The figures show a very strong overrepresentation of Brahmans, on the one hand, and of traders, businessmen, and shopkeepers on the other. No statistics are available on the caste composition of the City. Although Brahmans form the largest caste in Kanpur, their numbers do not approach a third of the total population. Muslims are underrepresented; they form 12.6 percent of the active membership of the Congress, compared to over 20 percent of the total population of the city. For other castes, it is difficult to make any comparisons. Among caste Hindus, the order of numerical predominance in the city is estimated as Brahmans first, followed by Banias, Rajputs, Kayasthas, and Khatris.[19] The unknowns in the table probably contain many Rajputs and Scheduled Castes, since it is rarely possible to identify these castes by name alone. In other respects, however, the numerical ordering of castes among the active members of the Congress corresponds roughly to that of the general population of caste Hindus in the city.

[19] Majumdar, *loc. cit.*

With respect to the economic categories, only the business community is heavily overrepresented; over 40 percent of the active membership of the Congress is composed of businessmen, a little less than double their actual proportion in the city as a whole. Employees of all sorts, listed under "service and labor," form 35.2 percent of the active membership of the Congress, a figure which is only slightly less than the proportion of employees in the general population of the city. Professionals are also slightly overrepresented—7 percent of the active membership, compared to an estimated 5 percent of the population.

Thus, although there is an imbalance in the active membership of the

TABLE 12

ACTIVE MEMBERS[a] OF THE KANPUR CITY CONGRESS: CASTE, COMMUNITY, AND OCCUPATION

Caste and Community			Occupation		
Social Group	No.	Pct.	Category	No.	Pct.
Brahman	275	32.4	Trade, Business,		
Muslim	107	12.6	Shopkeeping	349	41.2
Bania	70	8.3	Service & Labor	298	35.2
Kayastha	29	3.4	Professional	59	7.0
Chamar	11	1.3	Social Work &		
Jain	10	1.2	Party Work	26	3.1
Ahir	9	1.1	Other	80	9.4
Rajput	9	1.1	Not Given	35	4.1
Others	23	2.7		—	—
Not Known	304	35.9		847	100.0
	—	—			
	847	100.0			

Source: Official register of active members of the Kanpur City Congress for the years 1960-1962.

[a] The data in the table are for 847 out of somewhat over 1,000 members of the Kanpur City Congress. It was not possible to complete the transcription of the membership list.

Kanpur Congress favoring Brahmans and businessmen, all the important social and economic categories in the city are fairly well represented. This is not so of the leadership of the city Congress. Among the 21 leaders shown on the diagram of factions, all the imbalances are accentuated. Thirteen of the 21 or 62 percent of the faction leaders are Brahmans; for the rest, there are 3 Banias, 3 Kayasthas, 1 Khatri, and 1 Chamar. Of the economic categories, 10 or nearly half of the leaders are businessmen or traders and 8 or close to 40 percent are professional people (doctors, lawyers, journalists); 2 are social or party workers, and 1 is unknown. These statistics are for all the important faction leaders in the history of the Kanpur Congress, including 8 men who have passed away.

A more contemporary breakdown of 26 Congress leaders, taken from the 1960 Congress register, including current faction leaders, MLAs, MLCs, prominent labor leaders, and others shows few differences—13 Brahmans, 2 Muslims (1 ex-MLA, 1 sitting MLA), 3 Banias, 3 Kayasthas, 1 Sikh, 1 Christian, 1 Khatri, 1 Chamar. For economic categories, the breakdown shows 10 businessmen, 8 social workers or party workers, 6 professionals, and 2 employees.

Significantly absent from any important leadership positions in the Congress are Muslims and Chamars or other low castes on the one hand, and employees on the other. The Congress is clearly dominated by caste Hindus, particularly Brahmans, from the middle and upper middle class of the population. The major divisions in the population of the city, which find expression in social and economic conflicts, simply do not exist at the leadership level of the Kanpur Congress. Few Congress leaders belong to or represent the discontented groups in the city. Factional conflicts in the Kanpur Congress take place within an elite group and largely reflect issues of status among members of the elite rather than the broader social and economic issues which divide majority and minority communities or elite and mass in Kanpur.

THE CONGRESS AND THE KANPUR MUNICIPAL CORPORATION: STALEMATE AND CORRUPTION

The struggle between Shiv Narain Tandon and Ram Ratan Gupta has not been confined within the local Congress party organization. Control over the local Congress organization has been, for both men, only a precondition for control over and recognition in the broader public life of the city. From 1959, with the coming into operation of the municipal corporations in Kanpur and other Uttar Pradesh cities, the struggle between these two men and, in fact, the arena of local Congress politics as a whole shifted to the Kanpur Municipal Corporation. The effects of the antagonism between Ram Ratan and Shiv Narain and of Congress factionalism in general upon the working of local self-government in Kanpur have been great. The effects can be summed up in two words—stalemate and corruption.

In fairness, it should be noted that the whole question of local self-government in Kanpur and other large cities in India is most complex and has a long history. The problems which exist in Kanpur municipal affairs cannot be traced to contemporary Congress factions alone. The record of local self-government in Kanpur had been largely a dismal one long before the Congress came to power. Moreover, there are defects in the structure of municipal self-government itself, which have caused considerable difficulty. To place the recent functioning of the Kanpur Corporation in proper perspective, a brief review of the history of local self-government in Kanpur and a summary of the main features of the Corporation Act are necessary.

Municipal Government in Kanpur

Kanpur has had some form of modern local government since 1861 when the Municipal Committee of the Cawnpore Civil Station came into being. From 1861 until 1916, however, the Municipal Committee or Board was under official control. In 1916, with the passage of the Uttar Pradesh Municipalities Act, the Board, already predominantly elective, was granted the right of electing its own Chairman; only five members out of thirty-six were nominated by Chambers of Commerce and two by the Government. Under the reconstituted Municipal Board, education received the most attention, but to the neglect of other aspects of civic administration, particularly public health and sanitation.[20] The general development of the city had, since 1919, been the responsibility of an Improvement Trust, a separate body whose function was to alleviate congestion by developing new areas of the city. Unfortunately, the growth of population in Kanpur throughout the twentieth century and especially during the World War II years far outstripped the pace of development. By 1945, conditions in the city were such that a committee appointed by the government to examine the functioning of local government in Kanpur reported "that they were impressed by the hundred percent unanimity of opinion regarding the deplorable state of general civic administration of Cawnpore, the utterly inadequate and out-of-date systems of drainage and sewage and sewage disposal, the badly maintained system of roads and transport facilities, and the lack of coordination between the Municipal Board, the Cantonment Board, and the Improvement Trust." [21]

As a long-term solution to the problems of civic administration and government in Kanpur, the Committee was in favor of establishing a municipal corporation in the city modelled upon the highly successful Bombay Corporation. However, civic affairs in Kanpur were in such a chaotic state at that time that the Committee recommended the establishment of a new authority, wholly nominated, which would set things right before a corporation was created for the city. The new authority, called the Development Board, absorbed the old Improvement Trust and took over many of the functions of the Municipal Board as well, although the latter was not abolished.

[20] Most of the material on the constitutional history of local self-government in Kanpur up to 1952 presented in this section comes from S. P. Mehra, *Cawnpore Civic Problems: A Critical and Historical Review of City Government in Cawnpore* (Cawnpore: The Citizen Press, 1952).

[21] Cited *ibid.*, p. 50.

The Development Board had a relatively short and controversial existence; it was established in 1945 and was superseded in July, 1953. Two serious problems plagued the Development Board throughout most of its short existence. Both problems arose partly as a result of the return of local Congressmen from jail to participation in the public life of the city, now as representatives of a Congress government. The existence of the Development Board when the Congress came to power made it relatively easy for local Congressmen to take control of the administration of the city. Until 1948, the Development Board Chairman was a Scotsman, Sir Edward Souter. However, by increasing the number of members of the Board and appointing local Congressmen to the new positions, the state government created a Congress majority, which made an uncomfortable situation for Sir Edward. The latter resigned in March, 1948, and was replaced by a Congress chairman.

The first difficulty of the Development Board, which marred its effective functioning, was caused by factional conflicts among local Congressmen. From the beginnings of the reconstituted Board, it remained completely in the hands of Shiv Narain Tandon. Shiv Narain and his closest associates nominated all the members of the Board and Shiv Narain announced in November, 1948, that the resignations of all the new members were in his "pocket." [22] The appointments to the Development Board and his control over it gave Shiv Narain a very powerful source of political patronage. However, simultaneously, the appointments split the Congress party in half —between the "Development Board Party" and the regular Congress party, between the "haves" and "have-nots."

The second difficulty arose over the dyarchical division of city government between the nominated, Congress-dominated Development Board and the elected, non-Congress-controlled Municipal Board. A most peculiar situation existed in the relations between the two Boards, in that the Municipal Board remained responsible for financing certain aspects of civic maintenance and development while the Development Board was entrusted with the actual operations and expenditure. The fact that the Municipal Board was controlled by non-Congressmen made cooperation between the two local bodies even more difficult than might have been expected from such an arrangement.[23] Inevitably, there was delay in the payment of dues from the Municipal Board to the Development Board to the detriment of civic administration. For several years, local Congressmen who were associated with the Development Board prevailed upon the state government

[22] *Ibid.*, p. 68.
[23] Relations between the two local bodies were strained even before the Congress gained control over the Development Board. The renewed participation of Congressmen in civic affairs added another element of conflict to an already difficult situation.

to supersede the Municipal Board and entrust the entire civic administration to the former. For various reasons, the state government was unable or unwilling to comply with this request and the two Boards were forced to tolerate each other reluctantly until both were superseded in July, 1953.

It should not be surprising, therefore, that the Development Board was able to accomplish very little in its seven-year existence. A master plan was prepared, but never published or followed; almost nothing was done to increase the urgently needed water supply of the city or to improve drainage and sewage disposal; roads which should have been torn up and replaced were merely patched up; the public transportation system was inadequate and lost money. The major achievement of the Board was the construction of 2,400 workmen's quarters, half of which had to be let out to Punjabi refugees from Pakistan after the partition, hardly a dent in the housing problem of the city. The Board also spent some money in the improvement of workers' *ahatas* (compounds); however, when Pandit Nehru was conducted on a tour of these "improved" *ahatas* in 1952, he burst into a rage and reportedly advocated the burning down of the quarters and the hanging of the Development Board President.[24]

In July of 1953, the two Boards were superseded and replaced by a Civic Administrator, while the state government prepared a Corporation Act for the five cities of Uttar Pradesh. A Corporation Act was promised in "about a year," but was not enacted until 1959. Elections to the new corporations were held in the same year and the Kanpur Corporation began work in February, 1960. This brief outline of the history of local government in Kanpur reveals that civic government and administration in the city have been plagued by both constitutional and political difficulties. The Act of 1959 was designed to prevent their recurrence and to launch civic government in the five cities of Uttar Pradesh upon the successful path of local self-government, which had been tried and tested in Bombay.

The Corporation Act

The main features of the Uttar Pradesh Corporation Act of 1959, as applied to Kanpur, can be outlined very briefly. The Corporation is a wholly elective body. Seventy-two councillors are elected from thirty-six wards of the city; the councillors then elect eight additional members to the Corporation, called aldermen; councillors and aldermen together elect a mayor and deputy mayor. The Corporation also elects members to the two most important and the only statutory committees of the Corporation—the Executive Committee and the Development Committee.

Two features of the Act must be specially mentioned since they have caused the greatest difficulties in the successful working of the Corpora-

[24] Mehra, *op. cit.,* p. 185.

tion. The first feature is the position and powers of the mayor and deputy mayor. It was clearly the intent of the Act that the office of mayor should be largely ceremonial and that the chief function of the mayor should be merely to convene and preside over the meetings of the Corporation, whereas the deputy mayor should be the effective leader of the House. Thus, the mayor does not have to be a member of the Corporation, whereas the deputy mayor must. The mayor is elected for one year, the deputy mayor for five years. Finally, the mayor has no legislative responsibilities other than convening and presiding over the general meetings of the Corporation, whereas the deputy mayor is ex-officio chairman of the two statutory committees.

The second feature of the Act which requires special comment is the nearly complete separation of legislative and executive functions. The Corporation's responsibilities end with the enactment of legislation; implementation is the responsibility of the chief executive officer (the commissioner). The commissioner is appointed by the state government and is responsible only to his superior administrative officers and to the rules specifying his duties. The Corporation and the mayor have very limited control over the executive branch. The Corporation may remove a chief executive officer by a five-eighths vote and it may create new administrative positions. Appointments to senior executive posts, except that of the commission, are made by the mayor in consultation with the state Public Service Commission.

On the whole, the Act lodged really effective power nowhere. It was clearly intended that the deputy mayor would be the most important corporator; but, whatever limited control over the administration was provided in the Act vests with the mayor, who is otherwise not very powerful. Separation of the executive and deliberative functions followed the Bombay pattern, but the traditions of local self-government in Bombay and Kanpur have been quite different. What has been good for Bombay is not necessarily good for Kanpur.

The Kanpur Corporation in action: The
Election of the Mayor and Deputy Mayor

Although the balance of real power and the advantage of a long term to consolidate power in the Corporation clearly rests in the office of deputy mayor, the coveted position in Kanpur has been the mayorship. To make the Corporation Act work, it is clearly essential that either the mayor restrict himself to the merely formal duties of the office or that the mayor and deputy mayor work together harmoniously. The personality of Kanpur's first mayor eliminated the first possibility and factional rivalries in the Congress eliminated the second.

Although the Congress lacked a clear majority in the Kanpur Corporation at first, it emerged from the civic elections as the largest party in the Corporation faced with a totally fragmented opposition. In addition, it could count upon the support of a number of independent and opposition councillors. The only important division in the Corporation was that within the Congress party, between the Gupta and Tandon groups. Within the Congress party, the supporters of Ram Ratan Gupta had a decisive majority, sufficient to ensure his nomination as the official Congress candidate. Ram Ratan's majority in the party was so clear that Shiv Narain did not contest against him personally in the party caucus, but supported another Congressman who was defeated. In the Corporation itself, Ram Ratan was elected mayor by fifty-one votes to twenty-one against an opposition party candidate.

Ram Ratan's decisive victory both in the party and in the Corporation masked the essential instability of the structure of power he commanded. Although he was able to count upon the support of a varied group of Congressmen and non-Congressmen for his own election, he could not transfer this support to others. Two of his most important followers in the Congress party each had their own factional followings and each desired the post of deputy mayor. Neither faction leader would tolerate the election of the other to the deputy mayorship. The result was that, in order to prevent the division of his following, Ram Ratan was unable to choose between the two men and was forced to accept Shiv Narain Tandon as his deputy mayor. The inability of a faction leader to transfer his personal support to others prevents the transformation of a faction into a stable political machine capable of effectively exercising political power.

The Mayor and the Deputy Mayor: The Battle of the Budgets

Although some effort at reconciliation between the Mayor and the Deputy Mayor was made, it soon became clear that peaceful coexistence between the two was impossible. Shortly after his election as mayor, Ram Ratan made a major policy speech, outlining a twenty-five-point program for civic improvement; it was clear from the beginning that Ram Ratan did not intend to perform ceremonial functions only. Ram Ratan's program involved nothing less than a comprehensive reorganization and development of the city and its public amenities, which would require an ambitious and well-financed Five Year Plan. Not to be outdone, Shiv Narain Tandon, after his election, announced a fourteen-point program for civic improvement. Shiv Narain's program was more modest than the Mayor's and involved improvement in the city's public amenities, rather than a wholesale reorganization of the city.

Neither program received a full debate in the Corporation. Instead, a year-long constitutional struggle was waged within the Corporation and in the law courts over the passing of the budget of the local body. In this struggle, the two Congress factions worked against each other, both enlisting the aid of non-Congress councillors. Thus, in the Executive Committee of the Corporation, presided over by the Deputy Mayor, the Tandon faction compromised with non-Congress members to get each other's proposals accepted against the opposition of the Mayor's group. The Tandon budget was then sent to the floor of the Corporation where it was debated and passed item by item in a nine-hour session. At the end of the session, a resolution was moved for the final adoption of the budget as a whole. The Mayor, however, decided to hold over the resolution until the next meeting of the Corporation two days later. At this meeting, the budget which had been passed item by item two days previously was rejected by a vote of the whole House, by thirty-nine votes to thirty-five. It was clear that the rejection of the budget was the Mayor's intention in holding over the resolution. A prominent councillor commented on the reasons for the rejection of the budget:

Ram Ratan Gupta . . . wanted to have full control on municipal affairs. . . . He wanted to run it [the Corporation] like one of his mills. . . . Ram Ratan Gupta had the majority, so whatever decision was taken in the Executive Committee, he got it rectified in the Corporation. The Budget for 1960-61 was passed by the Executive Committee and was then passed item-wise by the Corporation; but, when the budget as a whole came up, he managed to get it rejected. . . . [Why did Ram Ratan want the budget rejected?] Shiv Narain Tandon wanted to put up a poor house, latrines for the poor classes, and wanted to spend money for conservancy. Ram Ratan Gupta wanted to have big schemes. He wanted to work on the lines of Western countries. He wanted to expand the city across the river. Wanted a big dairy farm. However, first, the people living in dirty mohallas should have been taken care of. He wanted to have a monopoly.[25]

The budget fiasco set the stage for a showdown between the Gupta and Tandon groups. The rejection of the budget had made the Corporation appear foolish before the public and each group blamed the other for the result. For the next two months, the two groups maneuvered in the Congress Corporation party and in the Corporation as a whole, seeking a majority for a censure motion against the Mayor or the Deputy Mayor. In the end, a resolution of censure was passed against the Deputy Mayor, who then retired to the Himalayas for a two-and-a-half month vacation to lick his wounds.

With the Deputy Mayor defeated and humiliated, the Mayor now was able to prepare his own budget. A special committee, with the Mayor as chairman, was established in August to prepare a new budget for 1960-1961,

[25] Interview in Kanpur on November 26, 1962.

even though the Commissioner was operating with the rejected budget.[26]
The Mayor's budget was presented to the Corporation on September 11,
1960 and was debated a month later. Although the debate on the budget
ended in pandemonium, the Mayor declared the budget passed. At this
point, a Tandon-group councillor moved the courts for an injunction
against the Corporation, restraining the local body from operating according to the new budget. On November 17, the City Munsif (judge) declared
the passing of the budget illegal and, in a sharply worded judgment which
went beyond the purely legal issue, condemned the functioning of the Corporation for most of its first year of existence. In concluding his judgment,
he remarked, "It will thus be seen that whatever was done all these six
months from April to October 11 in the Mahapalika [Corporation] of
Kanpur, though at the pains of committing illegalities and breach of rules,
has been sheer waste of energy, time and public money. Even today we
remain where we were on March 26. The minutes of the Corporation show
that there have been more exchanges of temper than real discussion for
the good of the public." [27]

Thus, as a result of division within its own ranks, the Congress was not
able to function effectively in the Kanpur Corporation. Both Ram Ratan
Gupta and Shiv Narain Tandon had prepared well-intentioned and ambitious programs for the welfare of the city. Their personal differences prevented the enactment of any programs at all and engaged the Corporation
in a fruitless struggle which led nowhere and benefited no one. Bipolar factionalism in Kanpur, as in Aligarh, prevents the Congress from operating
local government institutions effectively and leads to stalemate and immobilism.

The Mayor and the Chief Executive Officer

Factionalism is the major obstacle to effective local government by the
Congress in Kanpur and elsewhere, but it is not the only obstacle. The
structure of local institutions in Uttar Pradesh seems inevitably to foster
fragmented authority. In many cases, local institutions are purposely designed to permit intervention by state authorities in local affairs. Some of
these devices, such as the existence of Government nominees on otherwise
elected bodies and the right of superseding local institutions, are direct
legacies of British rule. The British used such devices as "safeguards" to
maintain a measure of control over the pace of advancement in local self-
government. The Congress uses such devices partly for similar reasons, but
often merely to maintain political leverage over local factions and opposition parties.

[26] *Citizen*, August 27, 1960.
[27] Cited in the *Citizen*, November 19, 1960.

In some respects, the Congress government in Uttar Pradesh has been even more reluctant to grant total self-government at the local level than the British. For example, under British rule, the Kanpur Municipal Board selected its own chief executive officer; under the present Corporation Act, the state government appoints the chief executive officer, who is responsible for executing the decisions of the Corporation, but is accountable only to the state government for his actions. This division of authority and responsibility at the local level created difficulties from the beginning, which have yet to be satisfactorily worked out. Conflict between the Corporation and the chief executive officer was so severe that Kanpur had its third chief executive officer in 1962, although a three-year term for each officer was the original intention.

Conflict between the Corporation and the commissioners began early in the first year of the functioning of the local body. The struggle on the Corporation side was led by the Mayor. The first open expression of difference occurred when the first Commissioner sought to interfere with the working of the Corporation by questioning the legal right of the local body to consider adjournment motions. This interference by the Executive Officer in the affairs of the legislative body led to retaliation by the latter in the form of a demand by the Corporation to consider proposed service rules for its employees.[28] Other differences between the Mayor and the Commissioner developed. By August, relations between the two men had become so strained that the Mayor began to think of attempting to have the Commissioner removed. In the meantime, a special committee on Administrative Reorganisation had been appointed with the Mayor as Chairman. Finally, in January, 1960, the state government transferred the Commissioner to another post.

Thus, the Mayor won both of the two contests—with the Deputy Mayor and with the Commissioner—which together occupied the entire first year of the Corporation. However, the Mayor's successes did not give him the kind of power over the Corporation and over the Congress organization which he sought. Although the Mayor secured the removal of both his opponents, his tactics antagonized a number of Congressmen who had previously supported him. In 1961, the party was so evenly divided that no official Congress candidate was sponsored for the mayoral elections of that year. Congressmen were granted a "free" vote. Ram Ratan was forced to contest against another Congressman and succeeded in defeating him by one vote only. However, this time, one of Ram Ratan's followers was elected deputy mayor. There no longer remained any important center of opposition to the Mayor either in the Corporation or in the administration. Neither did the Mayor have a working majority. The meetings of the Cor-

[28] *Citizen*, May 14, 1960.

poration increasingly degenerated into rowdy scenes, involving "walkouts, shouts, and use of almost abusive language," some of it directed at the Mayor. As one commentator put it, "The Mayor . . . now . . . finds that he has created a Frankenstein, which is beyond his powers to control. The so-called parties and groups exist only in name. The largest party, the Congress Party, remains divided into groups. In fact every member of the Corporation seems to be a party unto himself." [29]

The Plot Allotment Committee

After the defeat and resignation of Shiv Narain Tandon, the transfer of the Commissioner, and, finally, at the end of his second term, the departure of Ram Ratan Gupta to Delhi, a power vacuum existed in the Corporation. The mayors who have succeeded Ram Ratan have treated the office of mayor more in the spirit of the Act as an award to a leading citizen, an honor. Conflicts between the Corporation and the administration continue, but they center now around specific issues rather than around the whole concept of legislative and executive functions. The new Deputy Mayor is little more than one corporator among many. Although the Congress has now acquired a clear majority in the Corporation through the entrance of some independent and opposition corporators into the party, the Congress does not rule the Corporation since there is no one who can control the Congress.

In the absence of an effective center of power, a shifting coalition of six or seven influential corporators joined together to run the Corporation through control of the Executive Committee. Two of the leading members of the new group were formerly members of the Tandon group and two were members of the Gupta group. A fifth is a member of the Jan Sangh. These five men formed the core of the ruling group. To obtain a majority in the Executive Committee of thirteen, two other corporators were drawn in on specific matters. Two members of the committee, who are considered uncompromising, were usually left out of important decisions.

The new situation in the Corporation was described by the editor of a local newspaper:

Both Ram Ratan Gupta and Shiva Narayan Tandon, the two personalities round which major clashes took place in the first two years of the Corporation, now seem to have retired from . . . Corporation politics, leaving the field free to their followers. Of these, those who were so inclined have entered into opportunistic alliances with each other, to exploit the Corporation. If such agreements between two groups had taken place when both Ram Ratan and Shiva Narayan were active in the Corporation it might have done some good to the city. Today the understanding and agreement between a handful of persons from both the

[29] *Citizen*, May 20, 1961.

groups is being used not to help better the lot of the city but to secure what benefits individuals and groups can at the cost of the city and, as it were, to share in the loot.[30]

The major achievement of the new ruling group was the distribution of approximately 800 plots of Corporation land to applicants for house-building purposes. The members of the ruling group in the Executive Committee appointed themselves to a specially formed Plot Allotment Committee to expedite the allotment of plots which had been tied up in administrative red tape for years. The PAC cut through this tape with such speed and efficiency that charges of political jobbery—favoritism, nepotism, and outright graft—were immediately brought by the "out-group" in the Corporation, composed of both Congressmen and non-Congressmen. According to one member of the Executive Committee, people who had deposited money five or six years previously received no plots, while relatives of the committee members, who had made no deposits, did receive plots.[31] Members of the Allotment Committee claimed that there was no favoritism involved and that the Corporators who made such charges had divided plots amongst themselves in the previous year when they controlled the Executive Committee.[32] Thus, there was unanimous agreement that political jobbery had taken place, but differences only on who had committed the offenses. Some of the allotments were made with the best interests of the Corporators' constituents in mind. Across the street from the house of one of the members of the Allotment Committee, a library and a hospital were already in an advanced stage of construction when the controversy broke.

The failure of the Kanpur Corporation

The new Kanpur Corporation, in its first years of operation, failed to provide orderly, honest, and efficient government for the city of Kanpur. Little development work was taken up by the local body. Like several other local bodies in India, the Kanpur Corporation failed even to utilize funds available to it from the central government for slum clearance and housing.

Immobilism and log-rolling in civic government are not, however, found in all Indian cities. Several Indian cities have had long traditions of competent and effective self-government. There is a great need for comparative studies of problems of urban government and politics in India to reveal the conditions for effective urban local government.

Kanpur's difficulties do not stem from social or political conflicts within the population of the city. The failure of local self-government in Kanpur

[30] *Citizen*, September 29, 1962.
[31] Interview in Kanpur on November 28, 1962.
[32] Interview in Kanpur on November 26, 1962.

is a direct result of Congress factionalism and of an unworkable bifurcation of legislative and executive functions. The former cause is the most important, for a united Congress organization could overcome merely constitutional difficulties. The Kanpur Congress seems to suffer either from too many leaders or from too few. With Congress leaders in conflict, the Corporation cannot function at all; in the absence of Congress leadership, the Corporation has functioned largely as an instrument of political jobbery. The inability of the Congress to control the affairs of the Corporation also means that local government patronage is not available to strengthen the party organization, but is divided up among individuals.

THE DECLINE OF CONGRESS INFLUENCE IN THE KANPUR TEXTILE TRADE UNION MOVEMENT

There is hardly an aspect of the civic life of Kanpur which has escaped the disintegrative impact of factional politics. Perhaps the most extreme form of factional conflict in Kanpur or anywhere in Uttar Pradesh exists in the trade union movement in the city's industries. The ideas of industrial unionism, of one union for one industry, of strong unions able to bargain with industrial management for increased wages and benefits for workers are only dreams in the minds of a few devoted labor organizers. In fact, all of Kanpur's industries are plagued by multiple unionism, by the incapacity of union leaders to engage effectively in collective bargaining, and by "professionalism." [33]

The difficulties in developing effective trade unions in Indian industries are generally attributed to three separate causes—the interference of political parties in trade union organization, the predominance of "outsiders" in trade union leadership, and defects in trade union legislation.[34] A full analysis of the problems of trade union organization in Kanpur is beyond the scope of this book. In this section, it will be possible only to illustrate the decline of Congress influence in the trade union movement of Kanpur through a brief analysis of the major events in the history of trade unionism in Kanpur and of splits and mergers among various trade unions.

Since the textile industry is by far the largest and most important industry in Kanpur, the main focus will be on the trade union movement in

[33] A term used in Indian trade unionism to apply to trade unions and union leaders who devote most of their time defending workers before the labor tribunals, set up under the conciliation and adjudication machinery for the solution of labor-management disputes.

[34] Two very important defects in Uttar Pradesh trade union legislation are a law permitting any trade union with seven members to be registered with the state government and the absence of any law determining a "representative" union in any industry or factory. Both these defects clearly contribute to the proliferation of trade unions described in this section.

this industry. More precisely, it will be argued that the Congress has lost influence among textile laborers in the city for two reasons. First, intra-party factional considerations have taken precedence over the desire for trade union unity and too many Congress "outsiders" have sought personal prestige through trade union organization. Second, the policy of the Con-gress-affiliated Indian National Trade Union Congress (INTUC) against militant trade union action effectively isolated the local INTUC union from participation in the most important event in post-Independence labor history in Kanpur—the great rationalization controversy of 1954 and 1955.

Congress factions and the Kanpur Mazdur Sabha

Like Indian history as a whole, brief periods of unity in Kanpur's trade union movement have been separated by long periods of chaos and frag-mentation. At one time, the trade union movement in Kanpur was consid-ered the strongest and most militant in the country. In 1937-1938, a power-ful industrial union in Kanpur's textile industry, the Kanpur Mazdur Sabha, led a series of long, bitter, and successful strikes which attracted the atten-tion of the entire country. The Kanpur Mazdur Sabha (KMS) was formed by Congressmen, reached its peak of strength in a united front between Congressmen and Communists with the Congress as senior partners, was then lost to the Communists because of Congress factionalism, and was eventually destroyed by the Congress government.

The Mazdur Sabha was formed in 1928 by Ganesh Shankar Vidyarthi, the leader of the Kanpur Congress at the time. After the latter's death in 1930, the leadership of the organization passed to Harihar Nath Shastri, a Congressman who devoted his life to building up a Congress labor move-ment in Kanpur and in the rest of the country. In the early period of the KMS, there was close coordination between the Sabha and the City Con-gress Committee. For a time, this coordination gave strength both to the Congress organization and to the trade union movement. However, it also meant that Congress factions were projected into the affairs of the KMS.

Factional conflict within the KMS caused little difficulty for the Con-gress as long as the KMS remained exclusively a Congress instrument. How-ever, in 1937-1938, a united front was formed and local Communists entered the organization. During the period of the great strikes of 1937 and 1938, when the KMS achieved its peak of strength, Harihar Nath Shastri was its president and Sant Singh Yusuf, a Communist, became the general secretary. Although the Communists soon acquired a representa-tion of seventeen or eighteen members on the forty-member Council of the Sabha, the Congress still had a clear majority.

The primacy of factional interest over party interest among Congress-men soon asserted itself. In the 1938 elections, the Communists acquired complete control over the Sabha with the aid of the anti-Shastri group of Congressmen. Sant Singh Yusuf, who became the new president of the Sabha in 1938, attributed his success to the fact of division among Congressmen:

There were groups inside the Congress and the Sabha, one led by Harihar Nath Shastri, the other by Balkrishna Sharma. . . . Balkrishna Sharma had no followers [among laborers]; labor was under the influence of Harihar Nath Shastri. The main job of Harihar Nath Shastri was in the labor field and secondarily in the Congress, whereas Balkrishna Sharma was only secondarily a labor leader. . . . [In 1938], we [the Communists] captured both seats [President and General Secretary] . . . Harihar Nath Shastri wanted to remain President and give me the General Secretaryship, but the Communists didn't accept it. Moreover, the Balkrishna Sharma group didn't want Harihar Nath Shastri to be President. The Balkrishna Sharma group allied with us to defeat Shastri. We offered Balkrishna Sharma the Presidentship, but he didn't accept it.[35]

Thus, a Congress leader, whose primary interest was not in the labor movement and who was not interested in controlling the affairs of the Sabha, allied with the Communists for the sole purpose of defeating a factional opponent in the Congress.

The fragmentation of the Trade Union Movement: The struggle for personal prestige

During the war period, when most Congressmen were in jail, the Communists were left alone in control of the Mazdur Sabha. The advantages which the Communists gained in the war period were soon wiped out when Congressmen were released from jail and the Communists, during the Telengana period,[36] were in turn jailed by the Congress government. While leading Communists were removed from trade union activity, the Congress had an opportunity to regain its influence over the trade union movement in the textile industry. The opportunity was lost through factional conflicts among Congressmen.

From 1946 until 1949, a number of Congress leaders worked together and built up a strong and dynamic INTUC union in the textile industry. Then, largely for personal and factional reasons, a long process of fission was begun, until nearly every former Congress labor leader became President of a separate union. The splintering of the Kanpur trade union movement had very little to do with the splintering of the leftist political parties at the national level and the proliferation of national trade union Congresses. The splits in Kanpur invariably preceded or came some time after the splits

[35] Interview in Kanpur on October 7, 1962.
[36] The period of Communist militancy in India, between 1946 and 1949, named after an area now in Andhra Pradesh where military action took place between Indian Communist and central government forces.

at the national level. The process of fission continued until the beginnings of the great struggle over rationalization when all the various unions in the textile industry joined together long enough to wage an historic eighty-day general strike in 1955.

This complicated process of fission and fusion can be illustrated best in chart form (see fig. 6). Comments on the splits shown on the chart will be limited to those which developed because of differences among Congressmen. Unions which are now or once were Congress—that is INTUC-affiliated—unions are listed in the left-hand side of the chart, including the Kanpur Mazdur Sabha, the Suti Mill Mazdur Union, the Kanpur Mill Mazdur Union, the Rashtriya Textile Mazdur Union, and the Textile Labor Association. Each one of these unions, except for the relatively new Textile Labor Association, has suffered from internal conflicts among Congress labor leaders eventually leading to disaffiliation from the INTUC federation. With the exception of Suraj Prasad Awasthi and Prabhakar Tripathi, every labor leader shown on the chart is an "outsider" (has never actually worked in a textile mill in Kanpur or anywhere else).

Splits involving INTUC unions have generally had two causes—personal conflicts among local labor leaders tied up with factional conflicts in the INTUC federation at the state level and conflicts based upon attitudes toward militant trade union action. Personal-*cum*-factional conflicts have been by far the most frequent causes of the proliferation of trade unions in the Kanpur textile industry. A Congress labor leader, defeated in a struggle for control over the local INTUC-affiliated union has two possible strategies. He may resign from the Congress altogether, form a new union, and attempt to have his union affiliated to a rival federation. Or he may remain a Congressman, form a new union, and attempt to have the INTUC union disaffiliated and his new union affiliated to the INTUC federation.

Examples of both strategies are illustrated in the chart. Thus, in 1949, the Kanpur Mazdur Congress was formed by Ganesh Datt Bajpai because of personal differences between him and the President of the INTUC-affiliated Suti Mill Mazdur Union. Ganesh Datt Bajpai lacked influence with state INTUC leaders and therefore chose to resign from the Congress and affiliate his new union to the Socialist federation, the Hind Mazdur Sabha. A year later, the Suti Mill Mazdur Union itself was disaffiliated from INTUC because of internal differences between Ganga Sahai Chaube and Suraj Prasad Awasthi. The disaffiliation occurred because the latter had influence with the leader of the state branch of INTUC. A new union, the Kanpur Mill Mazdur Union, was then formed, led by Suraj Prasad Awasthi and affiliated to INTUC. This union too suffered from internal conflicts and was in turn disaffiliated when a new group gained control over it and brought it into the united front, formed in 1954 to fight rationalization.

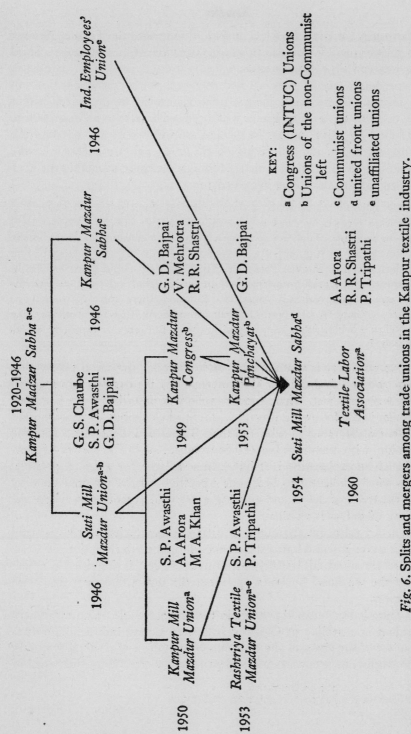

Fig. 6. Splits and mergers among trade unions in the Kanpur textile industry.

KEY:

[a] Congress (INTUC) Unions
[b] Unions of the non-Communist left
[c] Communist unions
[d] united front unions
[e] unaffiliated unions

1920-1946
Kanpur Madzar Sabba [a-c]

1946

Suti Mill Mazdur Union [a-b]

Kanpur Mazdur Sabba [c]

1946

G. S. Chaube
S. P. Awasthi
G. D. Bajpai

1946

Ind. Employees' Union [e]

Kanpur Mazdur Congress [b]

1949

G. D. Bajpai
V. Mehrotra
R. R. Shastri

Kanpur Mazdur Panchayat [b]

1953

G. D. Bajpai

1950

Kanpur Mill Mazdur Union [a]

S. P. Awasthi
A. Arora
M. A. Khan

1953

Rashtriya Textile Mazdur Union [a-e]

S. P. Awasthi
P. Tripathi

1954

Suti Mill Mazdur Sabba [d]

1960

Textile Labor Association [a]

A. Arora
R. R. Shastri
P. Tripathi

Simultaneously, a new INTUC union, the Rashtriya Textile Mazdur Union, was formed, which was in its turn disaffiliated in 1960 and replaced by the Textile Labor Association.

The predominance of personal and factional considerations in most of these splits is evident from the explanations of the trade union leaders themselves. One trade union leader who began his career as a Congressman, then formed two rival unions in succession, and eventually rejoined the Congress, attributed the splintering of the trade union movement to the "personal ambitions" of rival leaders. However, he made a careful exception in his own case, in the following words:

. . . there is nothing wrong with personal ambition when you are the best man and you don't want to work as an underling to an inferior man. My age level qualifies me to come in contact only with Yusuf [a Communist and the senior trade union leader in Kanpur]. I was General Secretary of the X union for so many years, when A was the President. But, how long could I put up with a man who can't distinguish between one loom and another, who is just a matriculate, a semi-literate. When I joined the X union, there were 200 members; when I left it, there were over 16,000. For me to work below A would be like Pandit Nehru working in an inferior position to C. B. Gupta or Kennedy working for you.[37]

The above quotation is an unusually candid, but not untypical explanation of the growth of rival unions. Most often, splits are explained in a casual manner, with less heat. Thus, another split was described by a Congress labor leader in the following way: " . . . there was a contest between me and B for General Secretary. I won and then B became independent, forming the Y union, with himself as General Secretary. . . ."[38] The matter-of-factness of such an explanation is striking. In a struggle for personal prestige, defeat is too humiliating to bear; one's prestige can be restored only by leaving the scene of defeat and building a personal organization where the possibility of defeat is eliminated.

Even when splits are attributed to differences over issues, the personal element is never absent. Honest differences of opinion over tactics and strategy are rarely admitted. Usually, a split over "issues" is described as a "betrayal of the workers" by one's opponent through a dishonest deal with management.

The struggle for personal prestige in the Kanpur trade union movement has resulted in a decline of Congress influence among industrial laborers. In the midst of the chaos of the constant proliferation of rival unions, only the Communists have consistently and persistently attended to the work of

[37] Interview in Kanpur on October 5, 1962.
[38] Interview in Kanpur on November 22, 1962.

trade union organization. Throughout most of the post-Independence period, the Communists have repeatedly called for a united front of trade unions in the textile industry. As the sole remaining heirs of the great Kanpur Mazdur Sabha, they have hoped for a return of the unity of the pre-war period and for the development of an industrial union in which they would have an important role. The opportunity came in 1954.

Trade Union unity: The Suti Mill Mazdur Sabha

Congress influence in the trade union movement, already weakened by the process of fission, declined still further in the period of fusion, of trade union unity in 1954 and 1955. The struggle over rationalization in the Kanpur textile industry is one of the most important events in the post-Independence history of the city. The details of the controversy over rationalization are not relevant to the present study. What is relevant is the fact that early rationalization proposals in Kanpur involved a threat of considerable retrenchment of the work force[39] and an intensification of workloads for those retained. The effects of the proposals upon all workers were so clear that the move for militant action came from the workers themselves, who ignored their leaders and joined together in individual mills in work stoppages, wildcat strikes, and sit-ins.

Most trade union leaders in Kanpur admit that the move for trade union unity was inevitable and that any leader who opposed the move would have been discredited. The call for unity, strangely enough, came from the INTUC union. More precisely, the call came from the leader of one faction in the INTUC union who had gained control over the union and defeated his opponent partly over the issue of the policy to be adopted towards rationalization. Whatever prestige the Congress might have gained from leading the movement for trade union unity and against the rationalization proposals was soon lost. The INTUC union which joined the united front was disaffiliated and a new Congress union was formed, which opposed militant action against rationalization. The grounds for disaffiliation this time involved an important question of policy. The rebel INTUC union had gone against national INTUC policy, which favored rationalization and opposed both strikes in general and united fronts with Communists.

Although individual Congressmen gave moral assistance to the fight against rationalization, the disaffiliation of the Congress union which participated in the united front effectively isolated the Congress among textile laborers. The Suti Mill Mazdur Sabha, formed in 1954, achieved two important victories before it fell victim to a renewal of old factional quar-

[39] Some union estimates of the number of workers who would be discharged as a result of rationalization ran as high as 13,000.

rels. The opposition unity produced by the front was extended to the 1955 parliamentary bye-election, in which a Communist-supported PSP candidate defeated the Congress with a clear majority. The second achievement of the Suti Mill Mazdur Sabha was the famous eighty-day general strike of 1955 in the textile industry, which closed most of the textile mills in the city and succeeded in forcing government and industry to reconsider and modify the rationalization proposals.

The long-term effects of this brief period of trade union unity upon party politics in Kanpur were to weaken further the position of the Congress party among industrial workers and to strengthen the Communists. Since 1955, the processes of fission and internal factionalism have been steadily eroding the strength of the Suti Mill Mazdur Sabha. Until the end of 1962, a number of non-Congress trade union leaders maintained a façade of unity. Then, toward the end of 1962, two seemingly unrelated events coincided to bring factional conflict in the Sabha out into the open—the Communists captured a majority in the mill committee elections and the Chinese invaded India. The mill committee elections reduced the bargaining power of the non-Communist leaders in the Sabha, but the Chinese aggression put local Communists on the defensive. Communist-led gate meetings were disrupted; two Communist members of the Executive Committee of the Sabha, suspected of pro-Chinese sympathies, were put in jail; and, the non-Communists in the Sabha, given a majority on the Executive Committee by the arrest of the two Communists, expelled the entire Communist contingent from the organization. The threat of a struggle between the rival groups to capture the office premises led to police intervention and the locking of the entrance by the police.

The situation was not without its irony. The two great experiments in trade union unity in Kanpur ended in exactly the same way. In 1946, a similar struggle for control over the Kanpur Mazdur Sabha ended with triple locks on the office door—one for each of the rival groups and one for the police. In 1962, the issues were similar, even some of the participants were the same. Only the locks were different.

Whether the effects of the Chinese aggression and the stalemate over control of the Sabha have neutralized the increased influence which the Communists acquired among textile workers in Kanpur remains to be seen. One Communist felt that the party had been set back fifteen years by the Chinese aggression and the opportunity which it gave to the opponents of the Communists in the city. The strength which the Communists gained and which the Congress lost among textile laborers in the period between 1955 and 1962 is nevertheless clear from the election statistics, which are discussed below.

THE 1962 GENERAL ELECTIONS:
CLASS, COMMUNITY, AND THE CONGRESS [40]

Although the Congress was able to win four out of five of the Assembly constituencies in the 1962 election and lost only one Assembly constituency and the parliamentary constituency, the decline of Congress strength in the electorate of the city has been much greater than these results indicate. Table 13 gives the percentages of votes polled by the Congress in the 1952, 1957, and 1962 general elections for Parliament and the Assembly.

TABLE 13

COMPARISON OF CONGRESS VOTE (IN PERCENTAGES) IN KANPUR CITY
IN THREE GENERAL ELECTIONS

Constituency	1952	1957	1962
Assembly			
I	42.92	47.76	46.42
II	55.77	47.23	32.49
III	71.44	51.84	39.16
IV	40.31	45.35	36.28
V	69.44	52.42	41.94
Parliament	64.91	40.11	30.97

The Congress vote has declined from 1957 to 1962, in most cases sharply, in every constituency in the city. In only one constituency has there been an over-all improvement in the Congress vote from 1952 to 1962. If the Congress is still the strongest party in the city, it is only because opposition party fragmentation is an even more important force in the elections than Congress factionalism.

After the Congress, the Communists are the strongest political party in the city. A Communist candidate defeated the Congress in the predominantly industrial labor constituency (II) of the city and Communist organization was largely responsible for the success of an independent, Communist-sympathizing candidate in the parliamentary constituency. The parliamentary constituency was first won by the opposition in the 1955 bye-election when the period of trade union unity spawned a united front of opposition parties to fight that election. Although both trade union unity and opposition party cooperation have disintegrated since then, the polarization of the electorate which was created in 1955 has been maintained in the parliamentary contest. This polarization has worked very

[40] Some of the material presented in this section has been published in Paul R. Brass, "Studies in Voting Behaviour, II: An Industrial Labour Constituency, Kanpur," *Economic Weekly*, XIV (July, 1962), 1111-1118.

much against the Congress. In the Assembly contests, local issues play a much more important role than they do in the larger constituency and opposition party fragmentation tends to blur issues. Nevertheless, it is possible to see even in the Assembly contests taken together a certain uniformity of support or lack of support among economic classes and ethnic groups for Congress or opposition party candidates. In the parliamentary contest, the divisions in the electorate become clearer and sharper. In this section, the strength of the Congress and opposition parties among various segments of the population of the city will be analyzed.

From the analysis of Congress party leadership and of the decline of Congress influence in the trade union movement in Kanpur given above, one would expect the Congress to be supported by business groups and the middle class among caste Hindus and to be weakest among industrial laborers, Muslims, and Scheduled Castes. The analysis of the election results confirms these expectations, but it is of some interest to examine the extent of support for or alienation from the Congress among various economic and social groups and to consider the reasons for such support or alienation in more detail. Table 14 summarizes the 1962 election results in Kanpur for both Assembly and Parliament by polling station.

TABLE 14

CLASS AND COMMUNITY VOTING IN KANPUR CITY, 1962
GENERAL ELECTION

| | No. of Stations | No. and Percentage of Total Pluralities[a] Won By Congress | | | |
| | | Parliament | | Assembly | |
		No.	Pct.	No.	Pct.
TOTAL	511	100	19.6	301	58.9
Economic groups[b]					
Labor	84	3	3.5	40	47.6
Business	32	22	68.8	29	91.6
Middle Class	16	6	37.5	16	100.0
Mixed	379	69	18.2	216	57.3
Community groups					
Muslim	76	1	1.3	23½[c]	30.9
Scheduled Castes	5	0	0.0	2	40.0
Refugees	13	2	15.4	3	23.1
Hindus	417	97	23.2	272½[c]	65.4

a That is, the number and percentage of polling stations in which the Congress won at least a plurality of the votes cast.

b A polling station has been classified as labor, business, or middle class if it falls in a mohalla of the city in which at least 50 percent of the population belong to the particular economic group. All other polling stations have been classified as mixed. The data are based upon the 1961 census for Kanpur city.

c The Congress and main opposition candidates polled identical votes in one polling station.

Economic groups

Labor.—Eighty-four polling stations fall in areas of the city where industrial labor forms a majority of the population. As the table indicates, the Congress position in the major labor colonies is poor. In general, the Communists are strongest in the textile industry, whereas the Congress is strongest in government-run industries, such as the defense industry and the railways. The support for the opposition parliamentary candidate, S. M. Banerji, was most impressive in that it came from all categories of labor. Originally a trade union organizer in the defense industries, he was fired from his job for participating in the 1955 textile workers' strike. He is the only labor leader in Kanpur who has mass support in more than one industry.

Some of the Congress labor workers expressed discontent at the ticket selection for the 1962 election, particularly at the fact that no INTUC leader had been given a ticket either for Parliament or the Assembly. They argued that, in the past two general elections, INTUC nominees had been given the parliamentary ticket and one Assembly ticket. In fact, factional considerations have always dominated the ticket selection for the Kanpur Congress candidates. INTUC was completely unrepresented in the ticket distribution this time because INTUC no longer has any leaders from the city who have real influence in party factions either in the local Congress or at the state level. There were two potential Congress candidates from the labor movement for the parliamentary ticket, but one had no factional backing and thus was never really in the running. The other aspirant was a non-INTUC labor leader who had recently rejoined the Congress, after a long separation, specifically to fight the parliamentary election; however, he was identified with one of the factional groups in the City Congress and lost out in the final selection. Another Congress labor worker was being considered for the predominantly labor Assembly constituency, but he too fell a victim to the factional quarrels of the City Congress. Both major groups expressed the desire to give one Assembly ticket to a Congress labor worker—as long as the ticket given fell within the domain of the opposite factional group; neither group was willing to give ground, with the result that INTUC was completely unrepresented in the ticket distribution in 1962. The selection of the INTUC worker considered for the Assembly constituency probably would have made no difference to the outcome (the seat was lost to a Communist); it was admitted by one of the older INTUC leaders in Kanpur that the man had no "mass" support and would not have made a popular candidate in this predominantly labor constituency.[41]

Business.—The Hindu commercial middle class forms the mainstay of

[41] Interview in Kanpur on February 16, 1962.

both Congress party leadership and of electoral support for Congress candidates. Opposition party candidates polled poorly and the Congress candidates well in the predominantly Hindu commercial and trading areas of
the city—particularly in the big wholesale cloth markets, in the grain, cotton, and oilseeds markets, and in other areas where the big merchants of the
city predominate.

The support of the Hindu commercial middle class for the Congress is
not difficult to understand; it derives partly from sentimental attachment
and partly from economic interest. Many of the early leaders of the nationalist movement in the city came from this class and, as has been seen, continue to occupy prominent positions in the City Congress. The big cloth
merchants of the city, in particular, contribute heavily to Congress election
funds.

Middle class.—This category comprises both the educated, professional
middle classes living in the old, Civil Lines area of the city and the upper
middle class of professional people and businessmen, living in bungalows
in the newly-developed areas of Kanpur. The difference between the
middle-class vote in the Assembly elections and in the election for Parliament is striking. The Congress polled a plurality in all sixteen of the polling
stations in the middle-class areas in the Assembly elections, but in only six
in the parliamentary contest.

Part of the explanation is in the personalities of the candidates for Assembly and Parliament. However, another reason for the opposition vote
among the educated middle classes in Kanpur was the fact that national
issues tend to be more important in the parliamentary election. For many,
the most important issue in the parliamentary contest was the need for an
effective opposition in Parliament to Congress rule. The opposition parliamentary candidate was the incumbent MP and had made a record of hard
work and vigorous opposition in his five years in Parliament. The middle-
class vote did not represent a vote for leftist policies, but rather a vote for
a hard-working politician who appealed to the growing feeling among the
educated of widely different political opinions that effective opposition in
Parliament was needed.

Community groups

Muslims.—Seventy-six polling stations in the city fall in predominantly
Muslim areas. The Muslim vote has been the subject of a great deal of
speculation since Independence, particularly in Uttar Pradesh, where the
Muslim League had a very strong base. The Communist Party in Kanpur
still has a hard core of support in the Muslim areas, which it owes largely
to its pro-Pakistan policy in the late thirties and early forties. The over-

whelming anti-Congress Muslim vote, most pronounced in the parliamentary contest, cannot be explained in terms of ideological sympathy for Communist policies.

The most striking facts about the anti-Congress Muslim vote are that it cuts across class divisions within the community and yet is not a communal vote. That is, although the opposition polled well in both Muslim business and labor areas, in only one Assembly constituency did most Muslim votes go to a Muslim candidate. In that constituency, both the Congress and the PSP candidates were Muslims, but most Muslim-dominated polling stations were won by the PSP candidate. In two other constituencies, including the parliamentary constituency, Muslim candidates polled insignificantly even in Muslim areas.

A number of campaign workers both for the Congress and for the opposition gave a simple formula to describe the voting tendencies of Muslims in the city. The formula is that if the Congress alone puts up a Muslim candidate, Muslims will vote for the Congress; if a leftist party alone puts up a Muslim candidate, then Muslims will vote for the leftist; if both the Congress and a leftist party put up Muslim candidates, then the Muslim vote will be split; finally, if there is no Muslim candidate at all, Muslims will vote leftist. The implication of the formula is that Muslims have a tendency both for bloc voting for candidates of the community and for leftist candidates generally, in about equal proportions. In fact, the alleged leftism of the Muslim voter is largely an expression of traditional anti-Congress sentiment which grew up during the tensions and communal riots of pre-partition days. Neither Hindus nor Muslims in Kanpur have forgotten the great communal riot of 1931, which arose as an indirect result of a Congress civil disobedience movement, and in which nearly three hundred persons of both communities were murdered.[42] The memories of communal strife in Kanpur, for which the Congress is held indirectly responsible, lead Muslims to vote for whatever opposition party candidates (excluding the Jan Sangh) have a chance of success against the Congress.

Scheduled Castes.—Scheduled Castes constitute a considerable proportion of the industrial labor force and are in a large minority in many of the important labor colonies. Only in two small areas, comprising five polling stations, however, are Scheduled Castes in a majority. Three of the polling stations in the Assembly contests were won by candidates of the Republican party, which is the political expression of militant anti-Congress sentiment

[42] An extensive report on the Kanpur communal riot of 1931 was presented to the British Parliament in June, 1931 and may be found under Great Britain, *Parliamentary Papers*, Vol. XII (*Reports from Commissioners, Inspectors, and Others*, Vol. III), Cmd. 3891, June, 1931, "East India (Cawnpore Riots), Report of the Commission of Inquiry and Resolution of the Government of the United Provinces."

among the Scheduled Castes. In the parliamentary contest, where there was no Republican party candidate, the Scheduled Caste vote went to the Communist-supported candidate.

The grievances of the Scheduled Castes, particularly the Chamars, against the Congress have been discussed in a previous chapter.[43] A study of factory laborers in Kanpur has noted that "the low castes were the most dissatisfied group in Kanpur." [44] Social protest against the inequalities of the caste structure has taken several forms—the two most prevalent being "Sanskritization" or the attempt by low castes to raise their status in the traditional hierarchy or, as in Aligarh, the rejection of the traditional social structure altogether, expressed in the adoption of Buddhism. Political protest takes the form of anti-Congress sentiment, for the Congress is looked upon as dominated by Brahmans and other high castes.

Refugees.—Opposition to the Congress comes from widely different sources and for very different reasons. It comes from groups like Muslims and Scheduled Castes, who are outside the fold of high-caste Hindu society. Opposition also comes from militant Hindus, particular from Kanpur's small, but highly localized population of Sindhi and Punjabi (mostly Hindu, but some Sikh) refugees from Pakistan, living in predominantly middle-class areas. These refugees blame the partition and their consequent uprooting upon the Congress. Many refugees are openly anti-Muslim and most favor a more aggressive policy against Pakistan. The refugee vote goes primarily to the Jan Sangh, a right-wing, Hindu communal party, dominated by caste Hindus and devoted to the revival of Hindu culture and an eventual reunification of the sub-continent.

Caste voting.—In general, most local politicians claim that caste is an important factor in voting behavior even in an industrial city like Kanpur. It is said of industrial workers that they remain factory workers only at the mill gates; when they go to their homes, they become subject to the influences which operate in their mohallas. Among these influences, which include local rivalries, the money-lending nexus, or simply personal influence, caste is an important element.

The influence of caste upon voting behavior operates in two ways. Members of a particular caste may vote for candidates of their own community, irrespective of party labels. Or, as in one Assembly constituency, traditional rivalry between two castes (in this case Brahmans and Kayasthas) may influence voting patterns in that members of the two communi-

43 See chap. v above.
44 Arthur Niehoff, *Factory Workers in India* (Milwaukee Public Museum Publications in Anthropology, No. 5; Milwaukee: Board of Trustees, Milwaukee Public Museum, 1959), p. 68.

ties will vote differently simply because of their opposition to each other.

On the whole, however, caste voting in Kanpur is less important than class and community voting. The minority communities—Muslims, Scheduled Castes, and refugees—each for different reasons, vote against the Congress. The caste Hindu vote, however, is much more divided along class lines. That is, Hindu laborers tend to vote for opposition parties, whereas the big Hindu traders and shopkeepers and the professional middle classes tend to vote Congress. Thus the bulk of the Congress vote comes from the middle and upper classes among caste Hindus, whereas laborers and members of the minority communities—those of low economic and social status particularly—tend to vote against the Congress. The Congress draws electoral support from the same groups in the population which provide the leadership for the local party organization.

Congress factions and the election

Congress factions played a role in the two constituencies lost by the Congress in this election. Although a united Congress probably could not have won the parliamentary seat, it is possible that a united Congress might have won the much closer contest for the Assembly seat that was lost. The Congress parliamentary candidate was considered a nominee of the Tandon group and was not supported by Congressmen of the Gupta group. However, major conflict between the two groups was not possible since most of Ram Ratan Gupta's election workers were in Gonda district, working for the latter's election there. The dissatisfaction of INTUC workers with the ticket distribution in this election was another factor, already mentioned.

The Congress candidate who lost the Assembly contest was opposed by several minor groups in the local Congress. Four other Congressmen had applied for the ticket for this seat, including an INTUC worker. Two of the rejected candidates, although they did not themselves contest against the official Congress candidate, reportedly supported independent candidates who drew over six thousand votes away from the Congress—more than enough to make a difference in the outcome.

Although factional conflict thus had some influence upon Congress fortunes in the 1962 election in Kanpur, the influence was not so great as to invalidate the general conclusions reached above about the voting behavior of various categories of voters. The vote of different classes and communities in Kanpur reflects real social and economic cleavages in the population of the city, cleavages which transcend merely factional alignments. In fact, the preoccupation of Congressmen with factional conflicts which do not reflect the major cleavages in the society is one reason for their inability to win support from large groups in the population which play no role in Congress factions—groups which have not been integrated into the factional system of the local Congress.

CONCLUSION

In this chapter, the nature of factional conflict, its effects upon local institutions, and the relationships between Congress factions and the cleavages which exist in the population of an industrial city have been discussed. In many ways, the Congress is faced with the same kinds of problems in an industrial environment as it is in the rural environments. Factionalism is the major problem of the Kanpur City Congress as it is of the Gonda, Aligarh, Deoria, and Meerut organizations. The structure of factional conflict is also similar. At the root of factional strife in Kanpur, as elsewhere, are purely personal enmities between men of different caste and social origins. Although the main protagonists in Kanpur—Shiv Narain Tandon and Ram Ratan Gupta—come from two communities which have a tradition of social and political conflict in Kanpur, the fact of their different origins is not the cause of their political differences. Neither do their supporters come from their own communities. The differing caste and social origins of political leaders make it more likely that they will come in conflict and reinforce conflicts that arise for other reasons, but caste does not cause the conflict and does not structure it.

As in Aligarh especially and in the other districts to some extent, factional conflict in the Kanpur Congress leads to the paralysis or malfunctioning of local institutions of self-government. The interference of state party and government leaders in local conflicts and the power of the state government and administration over local institutions foster this situation. In Kanpur, the separation of legislative and executive functions between a locally elected legislature and a state-appointed administration fosters the kind of fragmented authority in which factional conflict thrives.

In Kanpur, as in Aligarh, factional conflicts in the local Congress have taken place among members of the high caste and economically dominant communities. Preoccupied with internal conflicts within a narrowly-recruited political leadership, the Congress is unprepared to cope with the more important social and economic cleavages which exist in the population. Increasingly, both the Aligarh and Kanpur Congress leaderships have become estranged from large segments of the population, who have little voice in Congress affairs. The result has been, in both cases, a decline in electoral support for the Congress.

Moreover, the same groups which oppose the Congress in Aligarh oppose the Congress in Kanpur—Muslims and Chamars, on the one hand, and the most militant Hindus, on the other hand. Perhaps the only major difference, in terms of voting behavior, between Kanpur and Aligarh, are the clear class cleavages which exist in Kanpur. Among caste Hindus in the rural areas, electoral divisions tend to be based upon a combination of caste and factional differences. In Kanpur, the most important divisions among Hindus are class divisions.

Despite the decline in its electoral strength, the Congress remains the strongest political party in Kanpur. Factionalism in the Congress is more than counterbalanced by opposition fragmentation. Yet, the results of the parliamentary contest indicate that popular support for the Congress in Kanpur is at a low point.

IX.

The Substance of Congress Power:
Politics, Patronage, and Administration

Passing references have been made in the district case studies to the role of state ministers in local factional conflicts and to the relationships between Congress politicians and local administrators. In this chapter, the relationship between the Congress party organization and the state and local bureaucracies will be discussed in some detail. The chapter will be concerned both with the ability of the Congress and Congressmen to influence administration on behalf of faction members and voters and so strengthen local structures of power and with the impact of Congress factional conflicts upon state and local administration. This chapter also will be concerned with a problem in democratic development, that is, with the role which Congressmen perform in mediating between their constituents and the bureaucracy.

POLITICS, PATRONAGE, AND ADMINISTRATION IN THE STATE AND IN THE DISTRICTS

The patronage power of the ministries

In a state which is overwhelmingly rural and where the most important single program, in terms of resource allocations, is agricultural development, one would expect the development departments to be the major posts in the Cabinet. In fact, the opposite is the case. For political control in the districts, the rural development departments—Public Works, Community Development, Agriculture, and Irrigation—are the least important. This does not mean that the development departments have no patronage to distribute, but rather that development patronage—tube wells, fertilizers, seeds, and the like—is distributed in the districts. The departments have

212

great importance, but the ministers do not. Most of the development patronage must be obtained from the local administrative staff through local influence.

The ministries which are of the greatest political importance—in the sense of power and patronage in district politics—are Home, Industries, Education, and Cooperation. Of these departments, Home is by far the most powerful. One former minister, with experience in several departments in the Uttar Pradesh government, emphasized both the political significance of Home and the relative lack of power of the development departments:

Home means power. Because, under the British, this was a police state, the Home Minister was supposed to be the next officer [after the Chief Minister]. The most powerful officers in the district then and now are the District Magistrate and the Superintendent of Police. The SP is powerful because life and property are in his hands. [How is this important politically?] Every day your supporters are coercing my supporters—the only relief is through the police. Then, people can be falsely implicated in dacoities; similarly, Home can give relief to people. Home has constitutional power over the District Magistrate. [Isn't the District Planning Officer as important now as the District Magistrate?] In the district, the District Planning Officer is not powerful because he has to function according to the wishes and desires of the people. He can only offer improvements to the people, but he cannot coerce them. In general, the development departments are not important because they don't have the capacity to force and coerce people.[1]

The emphasis in this statement upon the use of force and coercion is a strikingly blunt comment upon political reality. The other powerful ministries are politically important because of the patronage available through them, rather than because of their powers of physical coercion. The Home Minister too has patronage to distribute, since the lower-level police officials are not appointed by examination.

The greatest amount of patronage, in terms of the number of people affected by it, is available to the Education Minister. If Home means power, Education is patronage. The Education Minister controls the state universities directly and the private schools and colleges indirectly. In some respects, the Minister for Education has greater leverage over the private, government-aided schools than over the universities. The vice-chancellors of the five state universities are chosen formally by a panel of judges, but informally by the Chief Minister and the Education Minister. Political control, nevertheless, must then be exercised through the vice-chancellor. The private schools are run by managing committees of local men of influence. When a grant is given to a district school, the members of the committees, the teachers, and the parents of the students are benefited. The

[1] Interview in Lucknow on May 12, 1962.

Education Minister also has scholarships to distribute and, under certain circumstances, may grant admissions to schools. Thus, if the Education Minister wants to appoint a teacher to a private school, he is not likely to encounter opposition. The managing committees themselves are often run by politicians or political aspirants. Local Congressmen associate themselves with district schools to acquire support for themselves in the community, while the members of the managing committees and often the teachers have a built-in political organization among their colleagues and students if they care to run for an Assembly seat.

The Minister of Cooperation too has direct patronage links with the district. Some evidence of the important role of the Minister of Cooperation in district politics has been given in the Gonda and Aligarh studies. The general powers of the Ministry in the district include appointments, the power of supervision and supersession of local cooperative institutions, and the granting of financial assistance to local cooperatives. Appointments are of two kinds—government nominees on local cooperative institutions and the supervisory staff. The members of the supervisory staff are appointed in addition to the regular officers of the Cooperative Department in each district. The members of the supervisory staff are actually appointed by the non-governmental Provincial Cooperative Union, but the Minister's wishes cannot be opposed since the government staff has control over the non-governmental supervisors. The latter act as advisors in helping to organize local cooperatives, in making the bylaws, and in checking the accounts. Depending upon the size of the district, there may be 15 to 40 supervisors or, in the entire state, perhaps 1,500 patronage appointments available through the Cooperative Union and the Cooperative Ministry. In addition, some of the regular officers of the Cooperative Department in the districts are patronage appointments. The most important Cooperative officer in the district is the Assistant Registrar, who is appointed by the Public Service Commission. However, there is an officer for Marketing and an officer for Warehousing in each district, both of whom are appointed by the Ministry. Finally, in the power of supersession and through its ability to grant or withhold financial assistance to cooperative societies, the Ministry has direct influence over the local units.

The Ministry of Industries too carries great patronage importance—less quantitatively perhaps than Education or Cooperation, but more "qualitatively" in the sense that a favor granted to a wealthy industrialist is worth more than favors granted to less influential people. Not all the patronage of the Industries departments is granted to men of wealth, however. The Ministry for Small-Scale and Village Industries grants licenses also to smaller entrepreneurs who wish to participate in government-financed industrial estates. The decision on the location of an industrial estate is itself an important instrument of political leverage.

The necessities of factional politics sometimes have strange effects upon the patronage power of ministries. A former Local Self-Government minister remarked that the LS-G Ministry once had considerable patronge to distribute, but that he had done away with most of it, not for the sake of political morality, but for very practical reasons: "Local Self-Government was very powerful when I took over, but I shed all the patronage. I was afraid of what would happen after I left. LS-G used to be able to nominate three persons to the municipal boards, which might make the difference of a majority or not, but I did away with nominations. Also, I made a ruling that the life of a municipal board could not be extended for more than one year. So, now LS-G does not have much patronage power left." [2] In a system of factional politics, where there is conflict and the possibility of loss of power, the party politician must be concerned not only with acquiring patronage for himself but in denying it to others.

Fragmentation of authority and responsibility among ministers

A more general consequence of factional conflict for the functioning of the state government has been not the shedding of the patronage power of the ministries, but the division of patronage by the splitting of ministries and ministerial responsibilities. This tendency reached ludicrous proportions in the last Gupta government. In order to satisfy all of his prominent district supporters and also to foster unity in the state party organization by bringing into the government some of his political opponents, C. B. Gupta formed a government of 46 members—including 17 cabinet ministers, 4 ministers of state, 11 deputy ministers, and 14 parliamentary secretaries. To accommodate such a huge Council of Ministers and also to prevent any single minister from gaining too much power, authority and responsibility had to be fragmented. One minister described the somewhat chaotic situation in some of the ministries, in reply to a question about the division of responsibilities between the Ministries of Agriculture and Community Development:

All extension work is under Community Development. The Agriculture Ministry is in charge only of research, training, education, and technical guidance, that is, of schools, colleges, and research farms. . . . The Agriculture Ministry is a very truncated affair. The process of truncation was begun under Pant and continued under both Sampurnanand and Gupta. For example, milk development is the responsibility of the Cooperative Department, but animal husbandry

---

[2] *Ibid.*

is under Agriculture. . . . Cane development is also now a separate department. Formerly, cane development was under Agriculture and marketing was under Cooperatives and Industries. Horticulture in the hills is with the Industries Department.[3]

The effects of such a fragmentation of authority and responsibility upon integrated rural development can be well imagined. In the districts, it leads to confused lines of administrative control. Thus, to take Agriculture and Community Development once again, the Agriculture Department has its officers both in the district and in the community development blocks within the district—the District Agriculture Officer (DAO) and the Assistant Development Officer (ADO), Agriculture. However, the ADO, Agriculture in the district is under the Block Development Officer who is under Community Development; the same relation is true of the DAO and the District Planning Officer.

If there has been some "truncation" of once powerful departments, there have also been some strange combinations in the process of shuffling portfolios about. Thus the Department of Economics and Statistics, which should be associated with Planning, became attached to the Forest Minister. The Government Estate Department, run by the Public Works Department, became attached to the Irrigation Minister. Finally, one Department became attached to two ministries; the Health and Medical Department remained one unit with two ministers, one for Health and one for Medical services.[4]

The bifurcation of various ministries and the division of patronage power was not done only because there were more ministers than portfolios. In fact, despite the huge government he formed, Chief Minister Gupta kept five portfolios for himself, among them the two key departments of Home and Industries. The Chief Minister was unable to find among his supporters two men loyal enough to be trusted with this much patronage.

State ministers and district politics

Conflict involving ministers in district politics is of two kinds. Conflict may arise from rivalries between two ministers in the state government whose political interests in a particular district are at variance. Conflict also arises when a minister seeks to use the power of his department to eliminate an opponent faction leader in a district.

One incident which took place in the 1950s illustrates the first kind of conflict. The incident was described by a former Minister for Cooperation:

[3] Interview in Lucknow on April 21, 1962.
[4] *National Herald*, March 19, 1962.

I tried to protect my officers when I was a Minister. There was a Supervisor in Farrukhabad district, whose brother was a *sarpanch* [President of a village co-operative society]; the two of them used to embezzle seed. The District Cooperative Officer transferred this supervisor. The *sarpanch* was a supporter of A, an MLC from Farrukhabad and a very undesirable fellow. This *sarpanch* approached A, who saw B, who was then a Deputy Minister to the Chief Minister. I was ready to transfer this Supervisor back to the District; but, in the meantime, [my] Inspector was given a good beating and this upset me, so I didn't bring him [the Supervisor] back. B was furious; he was a very good friend of the District Magistrate and the District Planning Officer was under him [administratively]. The question was how to protect my officer [against victimization from his superior officers]. In the meantime, I went to the Soviet. While I was away, B got my Deputy Minister, C, to go there [to the district]. C went to the District and came back thinking that I was ill-informed and gave a report to the Chief Minister. When I came back from the Soviet, I told the Chief Minister and everybody else that they were all wrong.[5]

This quotation reveals a great deal about political and administrative processes in state and district politics. First, it shows the three-tiered relationship of influence involved in the redress of a grievance or the satisfaction of a request. An aggrieved person in a district, in this case the *sarpanch*, approaches a Congressman in the district who, in turn, has access to a minister in the state government. Access to a minister was clearly not enough in this case, however, since the minister with the authority to redress the grievance belonged to a different group in the Congress. Minister B thus could not satisfy his group followers in the district, but he could retaliate indirectly against the Minister for Cooperation by using his officers in the district against the officers of the Cooperative Department. The number of people involved in this incident is also noteworthy. The officers of several departments in the district, three ministers in the state government, and finally the Chief Minister himself were eventually brought into the controversy.

The effects of such conflicts upon the administration of the state are obvious. Clearly, they are time-consuming, involving much of the time of several ministers in the government. Such conflicts also reinforce personal antagonisms among members of the government and make cooperation among ministers difficult. Finally, conflicts of this sort tend to politicize the local bureaucracy. District administrators are not expected merely to follow the orders of their ministers but to become involved directly in political controversies at the district level when necessary.

The politicization of the district administrative staff becomes particularly evident in conflicts between ministers and district faction leaders. The

[5] Interview in Lucknow on May 12, 1962.

involvement of state ministers in local factional struggles has been mentioned in several of the case studies. When a minister becomes involved, his staff in the district often becomes involved also. For example, it was charged by one faction in Aligarh that the staff of the Cooperative Department had been ordered by the Minister of Cooperation to implicate local factional leaders in a charge of embezzlement. In another instance in the same district, the Home Minister was charged with permitting the harassment of members of a particular faction by local police officials. The political use of a minister's right to supersede a local institution of self-government or a cooperative society also involves the district administrative staff, for the district administrators must gather the evidence and frame the charges so that the supersession order will withstand a court test.

A minister's involvement in district politics does not always center around cases of conflict. The minister is not constantly seeking to harm his enemies; he also rewards his friends and thus builds up support for himself, first in his own district, but also in other districts. One important method of building support is the "tour." The *National Herald*, a Lucknow newspaper, daily publishes the "Tour Programme" of members of the government. The "tour" of one's home district and of other districts is a continuing ritual which every minister performs several times throughout the year, in fair weather or foul. In June (the hottest month of the year in the plains) of 1963, the *National Herald* listings revealed that twenty-one members of the government had announced plans for a tour, only a few of them to the hills. Almost every minister visited his home district during these tours. One parliamentary secretary went on tour four times during the month, another three times, and six ministers toured twice during the month.

The ministerial tour is carried out to maintain contact with one's supporters, to keep informed about local quarrels, and to find out if there are any grievances to be remedied or requests to be satisfied. If the minister goes by train when he visits his home district, he will be greeted (and garlanded) at the railway station by his leading supporters, who will accompany him to a Government Inspection House, where he will stay for the duration of his visit. Here, he will hold his *darbar;* he will also go out to see some of his officers and he may make a speech in the district town or pay a visit into the interior on a special occasion. However, the visit is not designed for mass contact, but to maintain ties with local leaders. As one Congressman in a district put it during the visit of a minister in whose group he belonged, "Generally, the ministers are not so much interested in the problems of the masses; but, on account of groupism, they discuss the position of their groups and generally they favor their own men." [6]

[6] Interview in Meerut on December 14, 1962.

THE DISTRICT CONGRESS AND THE
DISTRICT ADMINISTRATION

Congressmen and administrators

The ability to influence administration in the districts has been looked at from the minister's point of view, in terms of what a minister can do in the districts and how he builds group support. The man in the district who has access to a minister is also a man of power. The man who can "get things done"—who can get permits, licenses, and loans, who can obtain house allotments, admissions of students to schools, who can influence appointments to district institutions—becomes powerful and popular in the district.

Access to a minister is only one source of power over administration in district politics. The District Congress Committee, and especially its president, has power in its own right to influence policy implementation in the district. One Congressman in Deoria district described the position and powers of the DCC and the president in the following way:

The Congress organization is the Government, so the organization has pretty good influence with the Government. Second, most organizational matters bearing on Government work are decided by the DCC President or the Executive. For example, the DCC may pass a resolution that such and such a road . . . or such and such an embankment should be built by the administration. When you manipulate these things to be done, then the people are on your side. Third, in matters of relief, e.g., flood relief, the DCC President is always consulted. . . . The DCC President has got a general supervision of the entire matters concerning the district . . . the DCC President wields greater influence on general administration than any other person.[7]

In addition to Congressmen who have access to ministers and men who are prominent on the DCC, the MLAs also have considerable influence over administration. The power of an MLA rests on his contacts with ministers in the Government and on the fact that he can table embarrassing questions in the Assembly if his wishes are not respected by local administrators. The ordinary MLA's concern is primarily with his own constituency, of course. He may want a school constructed, a road or bridge repaired, a tube well sited in places where his supporters are concentrated. Most officers will cooperate with their MLAs when requests are reasonable; conflicts arise when the technician's assessment of the economic value of a project is opposed to the MLA's assessment of its political value. An unduly recalcitrant officer may find himself transferred out of the district to Hamirpur, Banda, or Jalaun—the "Siberian" districts of Uttar Pradesh.

Villagers attach great importance to the ability of their MLAs to provide

[7] Interview in Kasia (Deoria district) on July 20, 1962.

favors and services. After three elections, most villagers have come to expect attention to their demands from their MLAs and are quick to criticize their representative if he does not perform for them. Many an MLA lost his seat in the 1962 election because he failed to "nurse" his constituency. One defeated PSP candidate in Deoria district commented on his failure to win an Assembly seat in 1962 in a PSP stronghold:

We lost the election not on any issue. The villagers want you to come to the village for trifles. In 1952 and 1957, the seat was PSP, but the PSP MLAs did not go hither and thither; they didn't recommend cement permits and this and that. [The successful PSP candidate in a neighboring constituency] got more than 200 boys appointed to the malaria department whereas, in this constituency, several times we were scolded [by the voters], "Well, we gave you two chances and you did not come, now we will give the Congress a chance." [8]

Villagers are very much aware of their rights and often do not wait for the MLA to visit their village before requesting assistance. Like voters in Western countries, Indian villagers will write to their representatives when necessary, for example, to request flood relief or in other times of stress.

A wise MLA will not wait for the villagers to write to him. One MLA from Aligarh district, who has won three elections from the same constituency, said that he toured his entire constituency three to five times each term. He goes to meet his constituents and to hear their grievances. An MLA who wants to satisfy his constituents must have broad influence over all administrative officials in the district, for the villagers have many demands and many complaints. The MLA from Aligarh remarked that, in his tours, he hears complaints against the police (not all of them genuine); against the Irrigation Department over lack of water supply, the lack of irrigation channels, the taking of bribes by irrigation employees; against schoolteachers for improper teaching or for demanding monthly tuition payments from pupils (an illegal act); against the Cooperative Credit Societies for not giving money regularly. He also listens to demands for schools or for employment. In the case of grievances against the police, the MLA must see the station officers or the Deputy Superintendent or the Superintendent of Police in the district; on irrigation matters, he talks to the irrigation engineers; on school matters, he must see the President of the Zila Parishad (District Board).

Attitudes of Congressmen and Officials Toward Each Other

The development of a relationship of mutual respect between politicians and officials, a relationship which permits some sort of balance between the dictates of administrative efficiency and the demands of politicians

[8] Interview in Kasia (Deoria district) on July 20, 1962.

on behalf of their supporters, is necessary both for economic progress and for democratic development. The nature of the relationship between Congressmen and officials has changed greatly since Independence. During the nationalist period considerable antipathy developed between Congressmen and officials, since they were continually in conflict. After Independence, many Congressmen in the districts felt that they were now superior to the officials and that the officials would have to respond to their wishes. In many districts, for some time after Independence, Congressmen succeeded in intimidating district officials to such an extent that the officials were afraid to do anything that might displease prominent local Congressmen. In recent years, relations between Congressmen and officials have stabilized somewhat and the party and government leadership have curbed Congressmen from making excessive demands upon the district staff. However, there still exist large areas of distrust in the relations between Congressmen and administrators, which may take years to work out.

In the years before Independence, the district staff had a different orientation than it has today. The district administration, headed by the all-powerful District Magistrate, performed all of the functions of Government in its area of responsibility—the maintenance of law and order, the provision of justice, the collection of taxes, many development functions, as well as the hearing of grievances and the settlement of disputes in the community. The emphasis, under British rule, was upon law and order and revenue. The District Magistrate's primary functions were to see that there were no threats to authority in the district and no communal riots and to ensure that the revenue was collected punctually and in full. The officers, though they would listen to the grievances of the people, were very much concerned with maintaining the people's respect for their authority and, thus, were always somewhat aloof and detached.

Today, the district staff has even more functions to perform than before Independence, as a result of the great increase in development activities. Also, a major change has taken place in the relations between administrators and politicians. S. S. Khera, a man with administrative experience under both regimes, has described the difference:

As a whole, the public services . . . remained screened under the old regime from the play of public opinion and public activity. In the revolutionary change from the imperial autocracy of a foreign power to an independent democracy, many of us have by and large found it rather difficult to find our footing. . . . The other side of it is that the political party which is in office today was effectively screened, under the old regime, from the administration and from administrative procedure. . . .[9]

[9] S. S. Khera, *District Administration in India* (New Delhi: Indian Institute of Public Administration, 1960), pp. 46-47.

In order to have both "good administration and good government," Khera goes on to argue that "there should be considerable interpenetration between the political party and those representing authority on the one hand and administrative function and power on the other" and that the bureaucracy "should avoid any rigid attitude about the exclusiveness of the administrative services and the administrative staffs from the play of political events."[10]

As far as Uttar Pradesh is concerned, this statement of the problem is out of date. The bureaucracy no longer contains men with "rigid attitudes" and "interpenetration" has sometimes been carried to a degree which threatens the continued existence of a neutral bureaucracy. The "penetration" of the administration by Congressmen and other politicians is a feature of democratic development which is to be expected. What has sometimes happened, however, is a real "interpenetration" in the sense that district administrators, sometimes willingly, but most often unwillingly, have actively participated in political and factional quarrels.

In the early years after Independence, considerable tension arose between Congressmen and administrators. One incident which occurred in Gorakhpur district in 1950 is typical of the problems that existed then. A Congress MLA of one faction charged in a letter to the press that government officials in his tahsil were actively participating in Congress organizational elections on the side of the faction opposed to him.[11] The District Magistrate personally came to the defense of his officers, denied the charges, and made the countercharge that the MLA was merely angry that the officers had refused to work on behalf of him and his faction. Yet, in the course of the District Magistrate's statement, it became clear that there had been considerable "interpenetration" between politicians and administrators. The controversy arose at a time when the government had urged cooperation between party workers and officers in the implementation of *zamindari* abolition. In furtherance of the government policy, administrators provided jeeps to Congressmen to travel through the district and address meetings. According to the District Magistrate of Gorakhpur, the MLA and his group used the government facilities for political purposes. The District Magistrate also charged that some of his officers in the district had been forced to work for the MLA's faction.[12]

Clearly, this kind of "interpenetration" creates bad feeling among both politicians and administrators. This particular form of participation by administrators in local factional conflicts has probably declined in the last

[10] *Ibid.*

[11] Clipping in All-India Congress Committee (AICC) newspaper file marked "N.C.," June 4, 1950.

[12] Clipping in AICC newspaper file, source not listed and undated.

decade, but there are times when the district staff cannot avoid involvement. A very common form of involvement by the district staff in local interparty and Congress factional disputes stems from the advisory and supervisory functions which the senior administrative officers must perform for local government and cooperative institutions. The District Magistrate, the District Planning Officer, the Assistant Registrar of Cooperative Societies are constantly being approached by opposing groups to decide a dispute involving a legal-*cum*-political question in their favor—to decide issues of membership, of times and dates of meetings, of election procedures, of alleged malfeasance in office of one's opponents, and so on.

For their pains, the district officers are often rewarded only with abuse and the enmity of all parties and factions. The administrative staff are abused both in the districts and by the state Congress leadership. For lack of policy differences, party factions and opposition parties too attack the government for permitting corruption and inefficiency in administration. The administration is a scapegoat in political conflicts. When the Gupta group launched its assault on the Sampurnanand government, its first thrusts were against the bureaucracy. The Gupta group opposed extension of the retirement age of government officials by three years and, as part of a scarcely veiled attack on the Sampurnanand government, passed resolutions censuring the state bureaucracy for arrogance, inefficiency, corruption, and nepotism.

On the other hand, the growth of factional conflict and the existence of a vocal, if weak, party opposition in the Legislative Assembly has, in recent years, lessened the pressure upon the district administration by Congressmen and has often made it possible for local officers to avoid direct involvement in political disputes. The increased bitterness of factional strife in the district Congress organization and the existence of sharply defined groups in the district have made administrators wary of identifying themselves with particular factions. Of course, when state ministers are directly involved, then the district staff have no choice but to obey the directives of their ministers. In fact, what has been happening in recent years is that ministers in the state government have used their officers in the district for their own political purposes but have protected them from the pressures of local Congressmen, lest local men of influence acquire too much power.

Much of the tension that existed in the relations between politicians and administrators has lessened in recent years. There is some possibility that an equilibrium will be reached eventually. Conflict continues and there is distrust on both sides, but there is also evidence that some politicians are beginning to put limits upon their demands and that some administrators are learning that an officer may be accommodating without compromising his integrity.

PANCHAYATI RAJ AND THE CONGRESS

The immediate effects of panchayati raj upon the district Congress have been to increase both the patronage power and the power over the local bureaucracy available to Congressmen. Under panchayati raj, or "democratic decentralization," the powers of previously existing institutions of rural self-government—the Zila Parishad (District Board) and the village panchayat—have been greatly increased and a new institution, the kshetra samiti (Block Development Committee) has been created on an intermediate level between the village and the district. The new system of panchayati raj in Uttar Pradesh has been introduced gradually since 1961. A gradual approach was adopted only partly because of the great administrative difficulties posed by introducing such a scheme of decentralization. The Government of Uttar Pradesh proceeded cautiously for political reasons also—to ensure that the new institutions would be controlled by Congressmen.

Theoretically, political power under the new scheme is supposed to increase at the lower levels. However, during the interim period (1961 to 1963), the Zila Parishad remained the central institution of district rural government. To ensure that the Congress did not lose control of this politically powerful institution, the Government resorted to two devices—indirect elections, and the favorite and traditional device of nominations. The original bill provided for direct, district-wide elections to the Zila Parishad on the Maharashtra model. However, most likely as a result of the continued decline in Congress electoral strength in Uttar Pradesh, both in general and local elections, and the continued increase in district party factionalism, the government decided that the Zila Parishads should be composed of a combination of *ex officio,* indirectly elected, and nominated members. Thus, the Zila Parishad is composed of five categories of members —all MPs, MLAs, and MLCs from the district; the pramukhs (presidents) of the kshetra samitis and an additional member from each samiti elected by the pradhans (presidents) of the village panchayats; representatives from other important institutions in the district—the municipal boards, the cooperatives, the secondary schools, and so on; co-opted members (women and Scheduled Castes); and, finally, three direct nominees of the state government. A body so composed ensures control from above by the state government and district party leadership and guarantees representation to locally influential rural leaders, but it effectively inhibits the direct expression of popular demands.

Whether it is democratic or not, the Zila Parishad has acquired considerable additional powers under the new scheme. The political purpose of the framers of the Act has been served also, since all but a few of the Zila Parishads in Uttar Pradesh have been controlled by Congressmen. Of course, the presidency of the Zila Parishad has been bitterly contested by district Congress party factions in each district. In effect, the state Congress government has determined that control of the Parishad and its presidency shall not be thrown open to interparty competition, but shall remain as prizes of Congress factional conflict.

The election of the kshetra samiti and its president, the pramukh, is more straightforward, but also indirect. The samiti is composed primarily of all the pradhans of the block, who elect a pramukh from amongst themselves. Direct election enters into the structure of panchayati raj in Uttar Pradesh only in the village, where the pradhan is elected by all the voters of the village or villages composing a gaon sabha (village council).

Whereas the Congress is very much concerned with having direct, formal control over the Zila Parishad, its attitude toward the lower bodies is different. Congress policy for the lower bodies is that party politics should be eliminated from them. What this means practically is that Congressmen may contest the elections for pradhan and pramukh informally, but that the Congress as a party will not participate in these elections directly. The reasons for the different approach of the Congress to these bodies is clear. The Zila Parishads are dominated by professional politicians, mainly lawyers from the towns; whereas, most of the samitis and village panchayats are composed of and controlled by locally influential cultivators, whose party ties, if they exist at all, are not strong. The Congress as a party cannot afford to identify formally with local factions which contest for control of the samitis;[13] if it did, Congress support in the countryside would be immeasurably weakened.

The Zila Parishad president controls the entire development staff of the district and has some say in the allocation of state-granted funds for development and education. All primary education in the state has been put in the hands of the Zila Parishad. In addition, the Zila Parishad has other powers and functions—the maintenance of roads, the management of ferries, the care of medical compounds, and so on.

The allocation of development funds is shared by the Zila Parishad and the samitis. Allocation of resources within each block is primarily the responsibility of the samitis, but the allocation of resources among different blocks is the responsibility of the Parishad. In general, the Parishad has supervisory powers—only experience will tell how effective they are and to what uses they will be put—over all lower bodies. Similarly, the samitis

[13] It is likely that factions within the Congress party organization will form alliances with factions in the samitis. The point here is simply that Congress leaders wisely want to keep the *name* of the Congress out of local disputes.

have general powers of supervision and some control over resource allocation with respect to the village panchayats.

If the introduction of panchayati raj has added to the powers of the district Congress organizations, it has also added another element in internal factional conflicts. The post of Zila Parishad president has become the most highly valued political office in the district after the presidency of the DCC itself. Most district Congressmen would have no difficulty in choosing the Zila Parishad presidential ticket over a ticket for an Assembly seat. The first election, in the reconstituted Parishads, of presidents to serve for the full five-year terms took place in June, 1963. A preliminary election for the transitional period, while the Zila Parishad Act was being implemented, was held in 1961 and has been mentioned in the Gonda study. In 1963, with Congress victory assured in every Parishad and with the Parishads in possession of their full powers, the elections were very bitterly contested within the Congress. Old factions split and new factions formed in each district to fight for the Congress ticket. In the 50 districts in which an election was scheduled, 165 Congressmen applied for the ticket. In one district, as many as 8 Congressmen applied.

Panchayati raj in Uttar Pradesh is not likely to arouse the enthusiasm of the whole community and its participation in development activities, as it is supposed to do. The structure does, however, very much enhance the power and prestige of the village panchayat presidents, who will now participate actively in political affairs outside their own villages. The enhanced position of the pradhans is likely to have an impact upon the internal policies of the villages and to make the position of pradhan even more desirable. It is likely also that the political parties will begin to recruit leadership from among these people.

The opposition parties face a clear disadvantage from the beginning in this new structure of rural self-government. There are several districts in Uttar Pradesh where opposition parties, singly or in alliance, could offer a serious threat to Congress dominance over rural institutions under a system of direct elections. However, as this analysis and the Gonda case study have shown, opposition parties have little chance of gaining control over the Zila Parishads. Where opposition parties are strong enough, they may gain control of one or several blocks; in Gonda district, a number of blocks are under the influence of Swatantra. At present, most blocks which are under the influence of opposition parties are led by professional politicians. As the blocks come under the control of local leaders, there may be even less opportunity for opposition parties. Local leaders who are unattached to any political party will wish to remain so for fear of antagonizing the district Congress leadership, which controls the allocation of resources from the Zila Parishad to the blocks.

It should not be inferred that opposition leaders are completely exclude from patronage. An MLA of any party can influence administration if his requests are reasonable. Moreover, every Zila Parishad has a small minority of opposition party members or independents. On local issues in the Zila Parishad, party lines are not very important. As has been demonstrated in the case studies, Congress factions may bargain with opposition party men to defeat other Congress factions. Finally, of course, ties of caste and kinship between politicians and administrators cut across party allegiances. Opposition party men can obtain patronage, but they cannot gain control over its distribution.

CONCLUSION

Panchayati raj has increased and formalized the control of Congressmen over patronage and administration in district politics. The patronage available to the Congress is a formidable weapon with which the district party organizations maintain themselves in power. A local Congress organization may lose every Assembly seat in a district and still retain its power as long as it maintains its hold over government patronage and district administration. The structure of panchayati raj is designed to make it difficult for an opposition party to transform voting power into political power in the district.

The ability of Congressmen to disribute patronage is an element in Congress power. The distribution of patronage is also a means of communication between a political party and the electorate, which draws rural people into the political process, into the competition for goods and services. In distributing patronage and remedying grievances, the Congress (and opposition parties) also perform the function of mediating between the bureaucracy and the public, lessening the distance between government and people.

If the Congress has performed a service for the electorate, its impact upon administration in the state has not been so beneficial. Recruitment to the administrative services is politically influenced to a greater or lesser degree at all levels in the state. Even if there were no political influence, administrative efficiency might have suffered from the mere fact that the size of the administrative staff has had to be increased tremendously and rapidly since Independence. In addition, many officers have been cowed into a submissive inactivity by the threats of Congressmen and by the abuses which are constantly leveled against the "bureaucracy." Finally, factional conflict among Congressmen has often worked toward the politicization of the district administrative staff. Thus, any assessment of the impact of the Congress upon administration in Uttar Pradesh must weigh the political advantages—in terms of democratic development—which have resulted from Congress rule against the economic disadvantages which flow from a demoralized and inefficient bureaucracy.

It is too soon to tell what the impact of Congress factionalism will be upon the institutions of panchayati raj. It has been demonstrated in the case studies that Congress factionalism often tends to lead to the paralysis of local institutions of self-government and cooperation. It is likely that Congress factional conflict will be intensified as the new institutions acquire more power and will be directed more and more toward gaining control over them. It is possible that immobilism and log-rolling will come to alternate in the affairs of these rural institutions. On the other hand, whatever the outcome in terms of operational efficiency and despite the defects in the structure of panchayati raj in Uttar Pradesh, there is no doubt that the system will foster increased political participation and a greater integration of politics between the village and the district.

X.

Conclusion: Congress Strengths and Weaknesses

SOURCES OF CONGRESS POWER

The Congress in its economic and social environments

The functioning of the Congress organization in Uttar Pradesh has been examined in five very different kinds of environments. Yet, as diverse as these environments are, there are some common features in the external setting of the local Congress organizations and some established patterns of accommodation between the local Congress organizations and these features in their environments. By far the most important source of Congress strength in the districts of Uttar Pradesh is the relationship that has been established everywhere between the locally dominant rural communities and the leadership of the Congress organizations. In all four rural districts studied, the leadership and the major sources of support for the local Congress organizations have been drawn from the high caste ex-tenants of the *zamindars* and *talukdars* and from the petty and middle ex-*zamindars*. Power in the countryside rests upon control of the land. The power of the Congress rests upon its network of relationships—established through its leadership and through its control of local government and cooperative institutions—with the locally influential communities in the villages, with those who control the land.

The Congress organization in the districts is the political instrument of the dominant peasant proprietors. The district Congress organizations generally are led by coalitions of "dominant castes." Only in Deoria do Brahmans alone dominate the local Congress organization; in Gonda and Aligarh, Rajputs and Brahmans jointly provide the leadership of the district Congress. In Meerut district, where Jats and Tyagis replace Rajputs and Brahmans as the "dominant castes," the former castes control the Congress.

Opposition parties, to defeat the Congress, must either win influence among the dominant peasant proprietors for themselves or they must organize alternate sources of support. In Uttar Pradesh, the moderate leftist parties, led largely by ex-Congressmen, compete with the Congress for the support of the peasant proprietary body. Other opposition parties, such as Swatantra, Jan Sangh, and the Republicans, have different social bases. Swatantra and Jan Sangh rest heavily upon the support of the ex-*talukdars* and the former big *zamindars*, whose influence in the countryside continues to be substantial. The Republicans, in contrast, draw support from the landless, the field laborers who depend economically upon the peasant proprietors. A third alternative source of support for opposition parties lies with the "backward classes" such as the Ahirs and Kurmis, who became proprietary castes after *zamindari* abolition. In many cases, these middle castes occupy a secondary position in Rajput or Brahman-dominated villages, as in the Deoria villages discussed above. In such villages, conflict tends to be organized around differences between the Rajput and Brahman ex-*zamindars* and their former tenants.

A second important element in Congress strength is its ability to form coalitions of caste and community groups. By maintaining good relations with locally dominant castes, the Congress acquires additional support from other castes which may be economically dependent upon the dominant castes or tied to them through local factional alliances. However, it is not only economic or local factional interest which unites different castes. The tremendous social diversity of Uttar Pradesh makes caste and community coalitions essential for political success. Traditionally, electoral support for the Congress has been broader than its leadership. The Congress has been able to draw support not only from the dominant castes, but from other communities as well, from Muslims and Scheduled Castes in particular. The ties of Muslims and Scheduled Castes to the Congress have, however, always been weak. Both these important groups represent potential sources of opposition support. In Kanpur, the Muslim vote has been overwhelmingly anti-Congress in two successive parliamentary elections. In Aligarh, Muslims allied with Chamars to defeat the Congress organization in the 1962 elections. Yet, in rural Meerut and elsewhere in Uttar Pradesh, the Congress has retained some support from both these groups.

The Congress operates most effectively in situations where there are no issues, where it can apply its patronage to maintain its network of influence among the locally influential and to build political coalitions. Strikes and agitations by opposition party leaders in Deoria attacking the Congress government for setting a low price for sugar cane or for reducing the quota of cane to be grown, the rationalization controversy in Kanpur, communal tensions in Aligarh—these kinds of issues and problems threaten the Congress because the Congress can be blamed for them in the minds of voters.

On the other hand, the size of Uttar Pradesh and its great social and economic diversity operate to protect the Congress from being threatened in the state as a whole by such issues. Sugar is grown over a large part of the state and sugar politics is important in many districts, but the special importance of the politics of sugar in Deoria arises out of conditions which are peculiar to Deoria and a few other eastern districts. Hindu-Muslim tension exists almost everywhere in Uttar Pradesh and riots have occurred at one time or another in most districts in the state. Yet, the Hindu-Muslim problem in Aligarh has a special setting, centering around the existence of a great Muslim university in a small Hindu town. The Aligarh riot of 1961 spread to other towns in the western districts of Uttar Pradesh, but potential outbreaks in other parts of the state were effectively checked by government action. Industrial unrest in Kanpur may hurt the local Congress organization, but Kanpur's problems are unique in the huge rural state of Uttar Pradesh.

Nonenvironmental factors

Money is an important factor in the ability of the Congress organization to maintain itself. The industrialists and big merchants in Kanpur and the sugar millowners in Deoria district and elsewhere in the state provide funds to keep the state and local Congress organizations functioning both during and between elections. Contributions to the Congress from the moneyed men in the state are expected as a matter of course. Industrialists are "taxed" according to the number of bags of sugar their mills produce or according to the number of spindles operating in their factories. Opposition parties receive some voluntary contributions from industrialists and businessmen, but the lion's share goes to the Congress, which has indispensable services to offer in return.

Even more important than money in maintaining the Congress organization is government patronage. Patronage is the cement of the Congress organization. In the districts, the men of power are those who have access to state government patronage or who control an important local government or cooperative institution. The struggle for control of local institutions—the district and municipal boards, the Cooperative Development Federations, the banks, the cane unions, and the local cooperative societies—is the essence of district politics. As long as the district Congress retains control of most of these institutions, it can afford to lose most of the Assembly seats in a district without losing its ability to function. The struggle for control of these local institutions is a continuing one within the local Congress organizations and keeps them in unceasing internal turmoil. Sometimes factional struggle for control of local institutions becomes so intense that factional rivals are unable to work together in the general elections.

On the other hand, the constant struggle gives the Congress a continuing vitality; the local Congress organizations do not sleep between the five-yearly general elections.

Another important reason for the continuance of the Congress in power in Uttar Pradesh is the fragmentation of opposition parties in the state. The Congress party polled only 35 percent of the Assembly vote in the 1962 election, but the next strongest party, the Jan Sangh, polled only 15 percent; the Congress won five times as many seats as the Jan Sangh. Opposition party fragmentation stems partly from the factional character of politics in the state; but, as has been mentioned, it also reflects the great social and economic diversity of Uttar Pradesh. Opposition fragmentation makes the position of the Congress relatively secure in Uttar Pradesh and allows Congressmen to compete among themselves, rather than against others, for the rewards of politics.

FACTIONALISM AND THE CONGRESS PARTY IN UTTAR PRADESH

The struggles of Congressmen among themselves have been the major concern of this study. The capacity of the Congress to control internal factional conflict is currently far more important for its continued ability to maintain itself than the patterns of interparty competition. Whether or not the Congress wins or loses an election in a constituency, in a district, or in the state as a whole may depend more on is ability to maintain internal cohesion than on its ability to compete with opposition parties for external support from the electorate. Organizationally, the Congress is a collection of local, district, and state factions forming alliances and developing hostilities in a constant struggle for positions of power and status in Congress-controlled institutions of state and local government. The case studies have shown that there is considerable variation in the origins of factional strife, in the economic and social bases of factions, in the characteristics of faction leaders, and in the impact of factional conflict upon the functioning of the local Congress organizations. There are also some recurring patterns in the character of factions and factional conflict in the Uttar Pradesh Congress.

The origins of factional conflict in state and district politics

A system of factional politics may develop in any society under certain objective conditions. Three conditions have contributed to the development of the factional system of the Uttar Pradesh Congress: the absence of an external threat, the presence of an internal consensus upon ideological issues, and the absence of authoritative leadership. In the state as a whole, there has never been a threat to Congress control over the legislature and government. Within the party, an ideological consensus developed in the years after Independence, following a series of controversies within the party and a number of defections from it. Gradually also, the leadership of the state Congress changed. The authoritative leaders, people who could manage conflict because of the great esteem in which they were held by all Congressmen, went to the central government, leaving the state Congress in the hands of men less skilled in the art of political management.

In the districts, similar developments took place. Few of the local Congress organizations faced a serious challenge from opposition parties in the first General Elections; in 1952, the Congress won every seat in the districts of Aligarh and Meerut and in Kanpur city; one seat was lost in Gonda district. Only in Deoria district (of the districts analyzed here) did the Congress face much opposition; here the Congress lost four Assembly seats out of fifteen in 1952. In the absence of external party competition, internal factional conflict sometimes became wholly unrestrained. The Gonda Congress was the first of the five district organizations analyzed to be affected by the disintegrative impact of factional conflict. A split in the Gonda Congress in 1955, as a result of a factional dispute, seriously weakened the organization and caused or contributed to the defeat of the Congress in eight of the thirteen Assembly constituencies in the district in the 1957 election. Similar to the experience of the Gonda Congress organization in 1957 was the defeat of the Aligarh Congress in 1962 by a combination of opposition parties, rebel Congressmen, and internal sabotage. In Meerut district in 1962, three seats were lost because of factional disputes and, in Kanpur city, one seat was lost for the same reasons.

There is some evidence—by no means conclusive, however—that factional conflict declines in intensity as external competition increases. In Gonda, faction leaders in the Congress, who normally oppose each other, were willing to combine to defeat Swatantra on the District Board and to work together in the General Elections of 1962. Factional conflict also is less intense in Deoria district, where there has been a long tradition of opposition party competition, than in Aligarh or Kanpur where there was less external danger before 1962.

Factional conflict in the districts, as at the state level, has flourished in an atmosphere of ideological consensus. Ideology was always less important in district politics than at the state level. What ideological differences did exist in the districts before Independence were solved by the splits from the Congress that occurred throughout the state after Independence. Few Congressmen in the districts are concerned with matters of ideology or even of policy; most are concerned with more pragmatic questions of how to get things done for followers and constituents.

In some districts also, a change in the character of local political leadership took place similar to the change in the state Congress. Thus, in Deoria district, factional politics was intensified when leadership passed from a saint-politician to his less saintly follower. This kind of development is not typical, however. More often, local rivalries in the Congress organization of a district were kept submerged before Independence only by the orientation of all Congressmen toward the goal of Independence; in most districts, factional conflict became open immediately after (and sometimes even before) the achievement of Independence.

The indigenous character of factions

Factional conflict requires a certain kind of environment in which to flourish. However, factions and factional conflict in India are part of the indigenous social and political order. The leader-follower relationship is a characteristic form of social and political organization in India. Loyalty to a faction is one form of loyalty which is politically important in the traditional order, like loyalty to a lineage group, to a caste, to a village, or a region. (On this point, see Myron Weiner, *Party Politics in India: The Development of a Multi-Party System*, p. 238.) Within Indian villages, politics is frequently based upon factional divisions which, like factional divisions in the Congress organizations, cut across other loyalties.[1]

To the degree to which Indian factions are traditional forms of social and political organization, they differ from factions in the American South. The essential difference politically between an Indian faction (or a Japanese faction) and a faction in the American South lies in the primacy of factional interest over party loyalty in the former.[2] In the American South, factional organization and conflict do not usually take precedence over party loyalty. Defeated factions in the South do not usually go into opposition,[3] as very often happens in India. For this reason, there is likely to be a much more direct relationship between external competition and internal

[1] For example, in a recent study, R. W. Nicholas has shown the interrelations between factions and other loyalties (caste, economic dependency, kinship, and territory) in two West Bengal villages; see his "Village Factions and Political Parties in Rural West Bengal," *Journal of Commonwealth Political Studies*, II (November, 1963), 17-32.

[2] On this characteristic of Japanese factions, see Robert A. Scalapino and Junnosuke Masumi, *Parties and Politics in Contemporary Japan* (Berkeley: University of California Press, 1962), p. 19.

[3] Key notes that the anti-Long voters in Louisiana voted for Eisenhower in 1952, but this kind of behavior is different from the behavior of Indian factions. The Louisiana factions had developed ideological and other differences so that they appeared "to possess a coherence, a continuity, and a habit of competition not sharply at variance with the two-party model." That is, the factions in Louisiana had come to resemble political parties. Factions in Uttar Pradesh sometimes become political parties. However, the kind of movement out of the Congress and then back into the Congress, which is characteristic of factions in the Uttar Pradesh Congress is less typical of the behavior of factions in the Democratic party. Citation from Key, *American State Politics: An Introduction* (New York: Alfred A. Knopf, 1956), p. 23.

cohesion in the Democratic party than in the Indian Congress party. To the extent that such a relationship exists in Uttar Pradesh politics, it may reflect the beginnings (or as likely the remnants from nationalist days) of a broader party loyalty.

Varieties of factional systems

Similarities between Indian factions and factions in the American South do exist, nevertheless. As in the American South, there are a wide variety of factional systems in the Uttar Pradesh Congress organizations. Occasionally, a single faction is strong enough to dominate a local Congress organization for a long period. A single faction dominated the Gonda Congress under the Raja of Mankapur and the Meerut Congress for a time under Charan Singh. So far, however, no faction leader has been able to build a sufficiently secure dominion to become a "boss." One important reason for the inability of a single faction to dominate a local Congress organization indefinitely is the integration of the local and state factional systems. There are always leaders at the state level who have interests in local politics which conflict with those of a would-be "boss."

At the other extreme from the domination of a single faction leader is the amorphous factional system of the contemporary Deoria Congress organization. This kind of factional system is the most fluid and is marked by a generally less bitter atmosphere than is characteristic of other systems. Leaders of strictly local influence and with very small followings join together in loose *ad hoc* alliances. The multifactional system of the contemporary Gonda Congress is very similar.

A third distinct kind of factional system, very different in structure from the above, is the bifactional system of the Aligarh and Kanpur Congress organizations. In these bifactional systems, two well-organized factions dominate the political conflict. Other factions exist, but they are subsidiary to the dominant ones and ally now with one, now with the other dominant faction. In a politics of status, bifactional competition tends to be extremely bitter. Both in Aligarh and in Kanpur, the main protagonists were motivated by extreme personal enmity for their rivals. In Aligarh, political conflict degenerated into violence and murder.

Bases for faction-building

The strength and cohesiveness of a faction depend very heavily upon the ability of the leader to distribute material benefits to his followers. Very often faction leaders in the districts bring private resources into local politics to build and maintain political support. In the countryside, the large landed proprietors or the managers of their estates have great economic resources to apply to the building of political followings. The Raja of Mankapur provides an example of how a faction may be built upon the base of a large landed estate. In the same district, the Raja's brother used his share of the family estate for the same end. Estate managers also wield great influence when the rajas themselves are not politically active. Also in Gonda, the manager of the Gonda estate is a factional ally of the Raja of Mankapur and the manager of the Balrampur estate is an important faction leader in the district Congress.

In Kanpur, the two dominant faction leaders also used private economic resources to build their structures of political power. Shiv Narain Tandon used the resources of his cloth firm to distribute patronage and Ram Ratan Gupta used the resources of his mills. Faction leaders without large resources of their own must sometimes turn to others to provide them. In Deoria, the financial support of a sugar millowner and an ex-raja was used to maintain a faction.

Another common basis for faction-building exists in the lawyer-client relationship. Lawyers do not usually have the economic resources of the merchants, businessmen, and ex-rajas. However, lawyers in the small rural towns buill up factional followings from their clients, who themselves often come from the villages to pursue village factional disputes in the law courts. Similarly, educators and teachers in the district schools often can convert their reputations among colleagues and students into political support.

A very important source of strength for a faction leader is control over a local institution of self-government or cooperation. Similarly, control over local administration and access to state government patronage through friendship with a state minister provide bases for faction-building.

Finally, a noneconomic basis for faction-building is community support. Community support is often a stepping-stone to political power. However, support from one's own community is in itself not sufficient. All faction leaders seek cross-caste alliances, for it is political power they desire and not merely the advancement of the claims of their communities.

It is important to recognize that a faction is a vertical structure of power which cross-cuts caste and class divisions. A faction is, in this sense, like a political party. A faction in Uttar Pradesh is not merely a miniature political party, however. A political party is an association of like-minded or similarly-situated people for the promotion of common interests or policies or an ideology. A faction in the Uttar Pradesh Congress is an organization based upon the ties between a leader and his followers, an economic patron and his dependents, a lawyer and his clients. These are vertical ties, some of which flow directly out of the traditional hierarchical order; others, like the lawyer-client ties are modern forms of association, based upon mutual service rather than traditional loyalties. Most factions are based upon a combination of traditional loyalties and individual interests. Factions in the Uttar Pradesh Congress link the modern political party with the traditional order; the factions themselves operate comfortably in the traditional society from which they spring and in the secular institutions of modern government.

Faction leaders: Power, prestige, and politics

The importance of the role of the leader in a faction has been sufficiently stressed in this book and a picture of the "ideal" faction leader has been drawn.[4] No Indian faction leader exactly conforms to the ideal. Every leader deviates from the ideal in one way or another, sometimes to his harm, sometimes to his advantage. Certainly the most important quality which a faction leader must have, in order to maintain his support, is loyalty to his followers. The members of a faction depend upon the leader to care for their interests. When the leader succumbs to personal temptations and ambitions at the expense of his followers' interests, his effectiveness as a faction leader is not likely to last. A faction leader is not expected to be an ascetic. The leader is expected to try to advance himself in every way possible. The only condition which his supporters will insist upon is that when he advances himself, the leader must take his followers with him.

Most faction leaders are accommodating politicians, easily accessible and quick to come to the aid of their followers and constituents. However, there are variations in this pattern. In Meerut district, Charan Singh—a highly successful faction leader—has developed the reputation of being relatively unaccommodating and uncompromising. It is not that Charan Singh will not listen to grievances or provide material benefits to his followers: but he requires that requests for his intervention be reasonable and just. Charan Singh can be relatively unaccommodating in this sense because he is loyal to his followers and because he seeks nothing for himself which he would not share with those who depend upon him.

The faction leader has needs, as his followers do. Faction leaders in the Uttar Pradesh Congress seek both power and prestige. The support of a large and cohesive group of followers is necessary for a faction leader to rise to power in state politics. His supporters also give the leader esteem. The leader receives from his followers both direct personal admiration and the indirect benefit of status in the broader society as a leader of men.

In their external relations with others, faction leaders are often motivated more by considerations of prestige than by the desire for power only. Politicians in Kanpur would rather be mayor than deputy mayor, even though the latter position is more powerful. However, prestige alone is not enough.

[4] See chap. iii above.

When a faction leader in Uttar Pradesh acquires a position of high prestige, but little power, he tries to bring prestige and power together. Conflict is likely to arise when institutions are established in which positions of power and prestige are separated.

The concern of Congressmen in Uttar Pradesh with questions of prestige introduces an element of irrationality (with respect to power goals) and unpredictability into Uttar Pradesh politics. The best example of irrational political behavior caused by a concern for prestige is the rebellion of the Raja of Mankapur against the Congress in Gonda district. The selection of an old rival for an Assembly ticket to contest an unimportant bye-election angered the Raja to such an extent that he took action which led to his loss of control over the Gonda Congress organization.

Factional conflicts in Uttar Pradesh are based not merely upon a struggle for power but upon a struggle for personal prestige. The struggle for personal prestige produces a climate of bitterness in Uttar Pradesh Congress politics. Political rivals tend to bring to politics or to develop in politics bitter and lasting personal animosities, which set the boundaries for conflicts and alliance. Personal enmity is the primary organizing principle of factional conflict in the Uttar Pradesh Congress.

The bitterness of Uttar Pradesh Congress politics is reflected in the personal accusations which are constantly being made against faction leaders. Admittedly, there is a great deal of corruption in Uttar Pradesh politics, but it is often difficult both for researchers and for courts of law to distinguish politically motivated accusations of corruption from those based upon facts. It is especially difficult to do so when forgery, perjury, and concocted evidence are common devices in the game of character assassination. Occasionally, however, the political motivations in charges of corruption become evident. A three-year course of litigation over an alleged embezzlement of an insignificant sum of money in Aligarh district is clearly a politically motivated case. Litigiousness is a well-known characteristic of modern Indian society. As is often the case with village disputes, charges of political corruption in politics are often not easily judged on their merits. Court cases such as these are often extensions and isolated events in broader patterns of local factional conflicts. They are instigated by faction rivals in attempts not only to defeat, but to discredit, their opponents.

The functions of factions

Factions and factional conflict perform both integrative and disintegrative functions for the Congress party organization in Uttar Pradesh. The disintegrative impact of factionalism upon the Congress is the more evident impact. The integrative functions which factions perform are less obvious, but may be more important in the long run.

Disintegrative functions.—In a sense, factional conflict in Uttar Pradesh cuts at the very basis of the existence of a modern democratic political party. Although a system of factional politics may develop in any society under certain objective conditions, factional conflict in Uttar Pradesh is intensified by traditional attitudes toward decision making and conflict resolution. In traditional Indian society, decision making is a long process of evolving a consensus.[5] Conflict is resolved ideally over time; if disagreement prevents a decision now, then the desired agreement may be reached later. When conflict cannot be solved by agreement and a quick decision is essential, arbiration is the only acceptable alternative. Decision making and conflict resolution in a democracy and in a democratic political party rest upon different bases. In place of consensus and unanimity, there is the doctrine of majority rule;[6] when conflict arises, formal institutional procedures are established to resolve them. However, faction leaders in the Uttar Pradesh Congress accept neither the doctirne of majority rule nor institutional mechanisms to resolve their disputes with other factions. Defeated faction leaders tend to describe an unfavorable vote as a corrupted vote, a misguided vote, or a vote of betrayal, a failure of allies to deliver promised assistance. Institutional mechanisms are perceived as unfairly constituted, dominated by one's personal opponents, from whom a fair decision is hardly to be expected. As in the traditional order, the only procedure for conflict resolution which is acceptable to faction leaders is the mediation of an impartial arbitrator. In the state Congress and in the district Congress organizations, the role of arbitration has been performed by senior Congressmen who have no factional affiliations. However, the number of arbiters has been decreasing as the internal politics of the Congress has more and more become organized along factional lines. The kind of personality who best performs the role of arbitration is rarely recruited into the Congress now, since it is the faction which now performs the recruitment function for the Congress.

Where arbitrators are no longer available to resolve conflict, a real danger exists that the party organization may split apart. In 1959, ninety-eight members of the then dissident group of the Uttar Pradesh Congress Legislature Party declared that they had no confidence in the state Congress government. Although the dissidents did not actually vote against the government, the threat to do so was obviously implicit in the declaration. In

[5] For a description of the traditional process of decision making in a village in western Uttar Pradesh, see Ralph H. Retzlaff, *Village Government in India: A Case Study* (Bombay: Asia Publishing House, 1962), p. 24.

[6] Majority rule is, of course, not the only or necessarily the primary way in which decisions are made in practice in a democracy. However, the principle of majority rule has a general legitimacy, in modern western democracies, which is lacking in Uttar Pradesh politics.

the districts, factional conflict has sometimes become so intense that local Congressmen, occupied with their own internal struggles, have failed to perceive external threats. In such cases, it is not uncommon for a local Congress party organization to lose most of the Assembly and parliamentary seats in the district, even in a district where the Congress has been traditionally strong. Where arbiters cannot mediate conflict, disaffected and defeated faction leaders may run against official Congress candidates or sabotage election campaigns from within the organization. A disaffected faction leader does not mind participating in the defeat of the entire Congress organization if this is the only way to defeat his faction rivals.

It is not uncommon for factional conflict in Uttar Pradesh to reach such an intense pitch. Factional politics in traditional societies are personal politics and status politics. Conflicts of prestige between faction leaders lead to intense factional disputes which are often in their very nature insoluble. When prestige or honor become of primary importance in politics, the possibilities of resolving conflicts are reduced, for honor cannot be shared. Factional conflicts in the Congress party in Uttar Pradesh often have an extra-political origin. They may be extensions of conflicts which arise in the society between former rivals in school or business as part of a more general struggle for personal prestige. Political disputes in Uttar Pradesh tend to be part of an interlocking pattern of disputes in which factional rivals seek status and esteem not only in politics, but in the society as a whole. Thus, political rivals may carry their conflicts into business and social life, even into such apparently petty affairs as the running of a local library and reading room. Conflicts which have such extra-political ramifications are not amenable to ordinary political solutions.

The disintegrative impact of factional conflict on the Congress party organization in Uttar Pradesh has led to a decline in Congress electoral strength in the state. The Congress polled only 35 percent of the vote for state Assembly seats in the 1962 election, making the Congress party in Uttar Pradesh the weakest state Congress party organization in India. Yet the Congress remains in power in Uttar Pradesh, with a comfortable majority of seats in the state Assembly. More important, the local Congress organizations have occasionally demonstrated their ability to regain lost electoral strength in succeeding elections. A number of features of the factional system of the Congress party in Uttar Pradesh have contributed to the ability of the Congress to maintain itself in power.

Integrative functions.—Factions perform the function of political recruitment for the Congress organization. In fact, there is a direct relationship between the intensity of factional conflict and the size of Congress membership. Factional opponents enroll primary members for the local organizations in order to acquire voting strength in the organizational elections.

Factional conflict broadens the bases of participation in the Congress organization. Not only are more members enrolled, but new caste and religious groups become politicized and integrated into the Congress organization, adding to its diversity and to its strength. Most important, factions tend to divide caste and community groups and so to free the Congress from the threat of communal politics. The integration of local caste groups into the internal factional system of the district and state Congress organizations prevents either the dominance of a particular caste or community over others in the Congress or the development of polarized conflict between large caste groups or between Hindus and Muslims.

In the contemporary factional system of the Uttar Pradesh Congress, the party organization is threatened neither by communal nor ideological issues. Ideological issues are unimportant both in the external relations of the faction leader with his rivals and in the internal relations of the leader with his supporters. Ties between leaders and followers are personal and material in character. Within reasonable limits, party leaders may follow whatever policies they choose as long as they maintain the respect of their followers and provide them with material benefits.

Another important feature of the factional system of the Congress party in Uttar Pradesh which contributes to the stability and resilience of the party organization is the autonomous character of each local factional system. The autonomy and separateness of local factional systems mean that sudden changes in the electoral strength of a district Congress organization will not affect other district organizations. In one district, factional conflict may become so intense and so disruptive that the local Congress organization cannot function. Yet Congress organizations in neighboring districts will be unaffected. In the state party organization as a whole, the disruption of one or a few local organizations is a relatively unimportant matter.

Moreover, within each district, factional conflict tends to become stabilized. After Independence, a variety of factional systems existed in the Uttar Pradesh districts. Some Congress organizations were dominated by one leading personality, others were divided into two large factions, still others were multifactional in composition. In most districts, the tendency in recent years has been towards increased fragmentation and fission of factions, so that multifactional competition has become the rule. Multifactional competition in the Uttar Pradesh Congress has been less disruptive and less bitter than other forms of factional struggle. Struggle between large and well-organized factions may lead to the total disruption of a district Congress organization. Under a multifactional system, several political leaders with strictly local influence may coexist, bargaining among themselves for positions and patronage and forming temporary alliances of mutual convenience.

The most important function which factions perform for the Congress party in Uttar Pradesh is to channel conflict and hostility within the party without endangering its stability. Although factional loyalties take precedence among Congressmen over loyalty to the party organization, faction leaders will leave the Congress only when absolutely necessary for reasons of prestige and will return to the Congress as soon as it is possible to do so with the least loss of face. The dominance of the Congress in Uttar Pradesh and the inability of opposition parties to gain control over the government in the foreseeable future are facts which all faction leaders recognize. Faction leaders will go into opposition to defeat a political opponent, but they will return to the Congress whenever it is to their advantage to do so. The looseness of Congress discipline on such matters permits the maintenance of this kind of factional system.

Dissident faction leaders are permitted by the looseness of Congress discipline to form alliances freely to replace the party leadership. When a dissident group succeeds in becoming the majority group, the process of factional alliance to replace the new leadership begins again. Under the new system of factional politics, the leadership of the Congress party is always unstable, but the party organization itself is rarely in danger.

Congress factions and social and economic change

Congress factions perform functions for the society as well as for the organization. A particularly important function which factions perform in the society is the politicization of social and religious groups in secular terms. The division of parochial social groups by factions and factional conflict aids the local Congress organizations because it prevents them from being disrupted by communal conflicts. The role which factions perform in dividing social groups is also important for the political system as a whole. Factions are well suited for this role since they are based upon a form of loyalty which is traditional, but adaptable to secular political institutions. Factions are oriented towards political power rather than towards the advancement of the goals of parochial groups. Over and over again in the case studies, it has been demonstrated that the quest for power by factions and faction leaders overcomes caste antagonisms. All factions are multicaste in composition.

The politicization of caste and community groups in secular terms is clearly conducive to the stability of the political system. It is not so clearly conducive to social change. By dividing caste groups, factions prevent the articulation of the demands of the lower castes. In other parts of India, caste associations perform this function. In Uttar Pradesh, caste associations are of little importance in politics. Disaffected low-caste groups, like the Chamars in Aligarh, cannot effectively express their demands in the Congress organization and must go into opposition to articulate their demands and express their discontent.

Factions and factional conflict in the Congress also work against the effective expression of economic demands. Factions in both Congress and opposition trade unions in the sugar industry and in the Kanpur textile industry have splintered the trade union movements and left them hopelessly ineffective. In the countryside, the unifying effect of factions is even more harmful to the expression of economic demands. Low-caste and economically weak groups participate in factions dominated by high and economically powerful castes. The powerful rural communities provide material benefits to their low-caste faction followers in return for their political support. Under these conditions, the economically deprived are divided and effectively prevented from challenging the social and economic dominance of high-caste groups.

CONGRESS FACTIONS AND POLITICAL DEVELOPMENT

The growth of strong and stable political parties is of crucial importance in the maintenance of a democratic political system. It has been argued here that, despite great internal factionalism and in some respects because of factionalism, the Congress party organization in Uttar Pradesh is a strong political organization, with considerable resiliency. Yet a certain reservation about the underlying stability of the Congress organization must be stated.

This reservation relates to the question of party loyalty, what F. G. Bailey calls a "moral" commitment on the part of party workers and voters to a political party. Bailey has argued that the absence of this commitment in Orissa reflects the failure of the parties (and the Legislative Assembly in which they function) to achieve legitimacy in the society.[7] As long as the parties lack legitimacy, a strong element of potential political instability exists.

It is probable that loyalty to the Congress organization has declined since Independence. Certainly, the younger generation of Congressmen lack the same attachment to the Congress which the pre-Independence leaders felt. For pre-Independence Congressmen, nationalism was their religion and the Congress represented their nationalism. For many Congressmen, the Congress symbolized a way of life. Few of the younger Congressmen have this feeling of attachment to the Congress. For many now, participation in the Congress organization is a purely "rational" activity, in the sense that calculations of personal advantage predominate over other motivations.

[7] See F. G. Bailey, "Politics and Society in Orissa (India)," in *Advancement of Science* (May, 1962), p. 27. Bailey's argument is developed more fully in *Politics and Social Change: Orissa in 1959* (Berkeley: University of California Press, 1963).

The absence of a commitment to the Congress party is even more evident among voters than party members. Habit, tradition, and ideology, factors which are important in the West, are relatively unimportant in Uttar Pradesh elections. In urban centers, there are educated voters who vote Congress for ideological reasons. In the rural areas, ideology is hardly a factor. Neither in urban or rural areas are there many people who vote Congress because of habit or family tradition. Partly, of course, the absence of habit and tradition as factors in Uttar Pradesh elections reflects the relative newness of elections in the state and in the country based on universal adult franchise. However even among the firmest supporters of the Congress, such as the headmen and panchayat presidents in the villages, very little attachment to the Congress as a party is detectable. The locally influential vote Congress because the Congress is the Government and one always votes for the Government; because one knows how bad the Congress is, but not how bad other parties are, so that it is safer to vote Congress; finally, one votes Congress because the Congress has done something for the village or for the voter himself.

Probably more important than the absence of ideology, habit, and tradition as factors in elections and party organization is the relative absence of organized interests. Many of the most important interests in Uttar Pradesh are unorganized or poorly organized. Peasant organizations exist in Uttar Pradesh only in memory, caste associations have declined in importance, trade unions are fragmented and ineffective. Yet, "interests" do exist in Uttar Pradesh and they are occasionally expressed very forcefully, as in the rationalization controversy in Kanpur or the organization of the Chamars in Aligarh district. For the most part, however, interest organization is local and transitory. Thus, caste and community solidarity operates in individual constituencies, but not in the state as a whole; Chamars in Deoria know nothing about the activities of Chamars in Aligarh.

The factional structure of the Congress party organization may be an inhibiting factor in the development of interest group organization in Uttar Pradesh. Factions are alternative forms of political organization to interest groups and are based upon conflicting principles. Factions are vertical structures of power oriented towards influence, that is, towards the establishment of links which will provide for the transmission of favors and services. Interest groups are associations oriented towards the promotion of the long-term interests of a generalized category in the population. Factions inhibit the organization of interests because they are based upon ties which unite opposed interests. The members of a faction come from different social and economic groups in the society, united by a desire for personal privileges.

The strength of the Congress in Uttar Pradesh lies in its willingness and in its proven ability to organize diversity. Yet the principles upon which the Congress has organized diversity do not necessarily foster the long-term goals of political development. On paper, the Congress maintains or works through a network of auxiliary organizations—trade unions, student and youth organizations, women's organizations, and the like. Organizations such as these are conceived partly to mobilize support for the Congress, but also to aid in the achievement of national policy goals of economic development. In fact, these auxiliary organizations in Uttar Pradesh are usually ineffective and are often ignored by most Congressmen. Auxiliary organizations, if taken seriously by the Congress, might recruit young people with a commitment to the party and to its policy goals. The regular district organizations do not successfully perform this function; they are concerned, as they must be, with power more than with policy. The Congress in Uttar Pradesh is successful enough at winning votes and maintaining itself in power, but it has lost much of its ability to attract enthusiastic and dedicated young people. In this respect, the Congress is much weaker than it was twenty or thirty years ago.

Appendix

THE FORMAL STRUCTURE OF THE CONGRESS PARTY ORGANIZATION

There are two main categories of members in the Indian National Congress (INC), primary members and active members. Any adult who does not belong to another political party may become a primary member of the Congress by paying an annual fee of four annas (5 cents). Primary members may become active members after two years by paying an annual fee of Re. 1 (21 cents) and collecting another Rs. 10 for the Congress Fund, by wearing hand-spun cloth, and by conforming to certain party practices and beliefs. The major difference between primary and active members is that the former are entitled only to vote in organizational elections and to become members only of the lowest units in the Congress organization. Candidates for office at all levels of the organization and for membership of the higher committees must be active members.

The primary unit of the Congress organization is the Mandal Congress Committee (MCC), which covers a population of up to 20,000 persons. Members of the MCC are elected by the primary members of the Congress. From this point on, elections become indirect, with the members of the lower units forming constituencies for the higher units. At each stage, there are other categories of committee members in addition to those elected, for example, co-opted members to represent special groups, representatives of certain organizations and institutions, past officers, and members of higher committees residing in the areas served by lower party units. Organizational elections and enrolment of members are supposed to take place every two years. Postponements are frequent, but elections are held with sufficient regularity to keep the organization always active or anticipating activity.

Above the Mandals are the District Congress Committees (DCCs) for each district and the Pradesh Congress Committees (PCCs) for each state. At the national level, the next highest organization is the delegate body of the INC, composed of all members of all the PCCs. This body meets once a year and is too big to be effective. The All India Congress Committee (AICC), composed of one-eighth of the PCC members elected from among themselves, is a more important body. However, the business of the national Congress is carried on primarily by the Working Committee (the "High Command") and by the President and his General Secretaries. The president of the INC is formally elected by the delegates to the annual session. During the prime ministership of Pandit Nehru, the president was actually chosen by the Prime Minister and his closet advisers. Two-thirds of the members of the twenty-one-member Working Committee are appointed by the President; the remainder are elected by the AICC.

Other Congress institutions of some importance are the state and central Election Committees and the central Parliamentary Board. The first two are very important organizations since they formally distribute the Congress tickets for the general elections. The Parliamentary Board is also an important body, which serves as an agency for the settlement of disputes which arise in the Congress Legislature Parties in the states.

There is a formal procedure for the selection of candidates to contest state and national elections. Mandal Committees are polled and district observers are sent from the state headquarters to investigate the credentials and prospects of potential candidates. Anyone can submit an application for a Congress ticket to the Pradesh Election Committee (PEC), however, and the selection is largely a matter of factional bargaining, involving district and state party leaders. The Central Election Committee must approve all candidates and often does change the decision of the PEC.

For further details on the formal structure of the Congress organization, see M. V. Ramana Rao, *Development of the Congress Constitution* (New Delhi: All India Congress Committee, 1958) and *Constitution of the Indian National Congress* (New Delhi: All India Congress Committee, 1962).

Bibliography

PUBLIC DOCUMENTS

Great Britain. *Parliamentary Papers.* Vol. XII (*Reports from Commissioners, Inspectors, and Others*, Vol. III) Cmd. 3891, June, 1931: "East India (Cawnpore Riots), Report of the Commission of Inquiry and Resolution of the Government of the United Provinces."

Government of India. *Census of India, 1891.* Vol. XVIII: *The North-Western Provinces and Oudh*, by D. C. Baillie. Pt. III—*Imperial Caste Tables.* Allahabad: North-Western Provinces and Oudh Government Press, 1894.

——. *Census of India, 1891. District Census Statistics: N.-W. Provinces and Oudh, Meerut Division* and *Fyzabad Division.* Allahabad: Government Press, 1896.

——. *Census of India, 1921.* Vol. XVI: *United Provinces of Agra and Oudh*, by E. H. H. Edye. Pt. I—*Report.* Allahabad: Government Press, 1923.

——. *Census of India, 1931.* Vol. XVIII: *United Provinces of Agra and Oudh*, by A. C. Turner. Pt. I—*Report.* Allahabad: Superintendent, Printing and Stationery, 1933.

Government of India. *Census of India, 1941.* Vol. V: *United Provinces*, by B. Sahay. Delhi: Manager of Publications, 1942.

——. *Census of India, 1951.* Vol. II: *Uttar Pradesh*, by Rajeshwari Prasad. Pt. I-A—*Report.* Allahabad: Superintendent, Printing and Stationery, 1953.

——. *Census of India, 1951.* Vol. II: *Uttar Pradesh*, by Rajeshwari Prasad. Pt. II-C—*Age and Social Tables.* Allahabad: Superintendent, Printing and Stationery, 1953.

——. *Census of India, 1951. Uttar Pradesh District Population Statistics 6: Aligarh District.* Allahabad: Superintendent, Printing and Stationery, 1953.

——. *Census of India, 1961. Paper No. 1 of 1962: Final Population Totals.* [New Delhi?: Government Press, 1962.]

——. Tarriff Commission. *Report on the Cost Structure of Sugar and Fair Price Payable to the Sugar Industry.* Bombay: Government of India Press, 1959.

249

Government of the United Provinces. *District Gazetteers of the United Provinces of Agra and Oudh.* Vol. IV: *Meerut,* by H. R. Nevill. Allahabad: Government Press, 1904.

——. *District Gazetteers of the United Provinces of Agra and Oudh.* Vol. XLIV: *Gonda,* by H. R. Nevill. Naini Tal: Government Press, 1905.

Government of the United Provinces. *Final Settlement Report of the Aligarh District,* by S. Ahmad Ali. Allahabad: Superintendent, Printing and Stationery, 1943.

——. *Final Settlement Report of Gonda District,* by Jai Krit Singh. Allahabad: Superintendent, Printing and Stationery, 1944.

——. *Final Settlement Report of the Meerut District,* by C. H. Cooke. Allahabad: Superintendent, Printing and Stationery, 1940.

——. *Report of the United Provinces Zamindari Abolition Committee.* 2 vols. Allahabad: Superintendent, Printing and Stationery, 1948.

Government of Uttar Pradesh. Department of Labour. *Annual Review of Activities, 1961.* Allahabad: Superintendent, Printing and Stationery, 1962.

——. *Development of Industries in Uttar Pradesh (Progress Review), 1961-62.* Kanpur: Directorate of Industries, n.d.

——. Planning Department. *Third Five Year Plan.* Vol. I: *Report.* Lucknow: 1961.

——. *The Uttar Pradesh Imposition of Ceiling on Land Holdings Act., 1960.*

BOOKS AND PAMPHLETS

Ambedkar, B. R. *Ranade, Gandhi, and Jinnah.* Bombay: Thacker and Co., Ltd., 1943.

Bailey, F. G. *Politics and Social Change: Orissa in 1959.* Berkeley: University of California Press, 1963.

Baljit Singh. *Next Step in Village India: A Study of Land Reforms and Group Dynamics.* Bombay: Asia Publishing House, 1961.

Beals, Alan. "Leadership in a Mysore Village," in Richard L. Park and Irene Tinker (eds.), *Leadership and Political Institutions in India.* Princeton: Princeton University Press, 1959.

Charan Singh. *Agrarian Revolution in Uttar Pradesh.* Uttar Pradesh: Publications Bureau, Information Department, n.d.

——. *Joint Farming X-Rayed: The Problem and Its Solution.* Bombay: Bharatiya Vidya Bhavan, 1959.

Chopra, Pran Nath. *Rafi Ahmad Kidwai: His Life and Work.* Agra: Shiva Lal Agarwala and Co., (Pvt.) Ltd., 1960.

Cohn, Bernard S. "The Changing Status of a Depressed Caste," in McKim Marriott (ed.), *Village India: Studies in the Little Community.* Chicago: University of Chicago Press, 1955.

Cotton, Evan. "Some Outstanding Political Leaders," chap. x in John Cumming (ed.), *Political India, 1832-1932: A Co-Operative Survey of a Century*. London: Oxford University Press, 1932.

Crooke, W. *The North-Western Provinces of India: Their History, Ethnology, and Administration*. London: Methuen and Co., 1897.

Dharma Bhanu. *History and Administration of the North-Western Provinces (Subsequently Called the Agra Province), 1803-1858*. Agra: Shiva Lal Agarwala and Co. (Pvt.) Ltd., 1957.

Fürer-Haimendorf, C. von. "Caste and Politics in South Asia," in C. H. Philips, *Politics and Society in India*. New York: Frederick A. Praeger, 1962.

Harrison, Selig S. *India: The Most Dangerous Decades*. Princeton: Princeton University Press, 1960.

Indian National Congress. *Constitution of the Indian National Congress*. New Delhi: All India Congress Committee, 1962.

——. *Report of the Congress Agrarian Reforms Committee*. 2d ed. New Delhi: All-India Congress Committee, 1951.

——. *Reports of the General Secretaries*. 1954-1960. New Delhi: All India Congress Committee.

Key, V. O., Jr. *American State Politics: An Introduction*. New York: Alfred A. Knopf, 1956.

——. *Politics, Parties, and Pressure Groups*. New York: Thomas Y. Crowell Co., 1952.

——. *Southern Politics in State and Nation*. New York: Alfred A. Knopf, 1949.

Khera, S. S. *District Administration in India*. New Delhi: Indian Institute of Public Administration, 1960.

Khetan, Bhagwati Prasad. *Problems of Sugar Industry in Eastern Uttar Pradesh*. Gorakhpur, 1961.

Majumdar, D. N. *Social Contours of an Industrial City: Social Survey of Kanpur, 1954-56*. Bombay: Asia Publishing House, 1960.

Marriott, McKim. "Little Communities in an Indigenous Civilization," in McKim Marriott (ed.), *Village India: Studies in the Little Community*. Chicago: University of Chicago Press, 1955.

Mehra, S. P. *Cawnpore Civic Problems: A Critical and Historical Review of City Government in Cawnpore*. Cawnpore: The Citizen Press, 1952.

Neale, Walter C. *Economic Change in Rural India: Land Tenure and Reform in Uttar Pradesh, 1800-1955*. New Haven: Yale University Press, 1962.

Nehru, Jawaharlal. *A Bunch of Old Letters*. 2d ed. Bombay: Asia Publishing House, 1960.

——. "My Father," in S. P. and Preet Chablani (eds.), *Motilal Nehru: Essays and Reflections on His Life and Times*. Delhi: S. Chand and Co., 1961.

Niehoff, Arthur. *Factory Workers in India*. Milwaukee Public Museum Publications in Anthropology, No. 5. Milwaukee: Board of Trustees, Milwaukee Public Museum, 1959.

Ramana Rao, M. V. *Development of the Congress Constitution*. New Delhi: All India Congress Committee, 1958.

Ram Gopal. *Indian Muslims: A Political History (1858-1947)*. Bombay: Asia Publishing House, 1959.

Retzlaff, Ralph H. *Village Government in India: A Case Study*. Bombay: Asia Publishing House, 1962.

Rushbrook Williams, L. F. *India in 1923-24*. Calcutta: Government of India Central Publication Branch, 1924.

Saksena, Shibban Lal. *Justice Demanded to the Sugar Workers of U.P.: Why the Fast Was Resumed*. New Delhi: 1950.

Sampurnanand. *Memories and Reflections*. Bombay: Asia Publishing House, 1962.

Sarvadhikari, Rajkumar. *The Taluqdari Settlement in Oudh*. Calcutta: Thacker, Spink and Co., 1882.

Scalapino, Robert A., and Masumi, Junnosuke. *Parties and Politics in Contemporary Japan*. Berkeley: University of California Press, 1962.

Shyam Sunder and Savitri Shyam. *Political Life of Pandit Govind Ballabh Pant*, Vol. I: *1887-1945*. Lucknow: Shailanil, 1960.

Singh, Hari Kishore. *A History of the Praja Socialist Party*. Lucknow: Narendra Prakashan, 1959.

Spate, O. H. K. *India and Pakistan: A General and Regional Geography*. 2d ed. London: Methuen and Co., Ltd., 1957.

Weiner, Myron. *Party Politics in India: The Development of a Multi-Party System*. Princeton: Princeton University Press, 1957.

———. *Political Change in South Asia*. Calcutta: Firma K. L. Mukhopadhyay, 1963.

ARTICLES, PERIODICALS, AND REPORTS

Aligarh Muslim University. *Prospectus for the Session, 1961-62*.

Bailey, F. G. "Politics and Society in Orissa (India)," *Advancement of Science* (May, 1962), pp. 25-28.

Brass, Paul R. "Studies in Voting Behaviour, II: An Industrial Labour Constituency, Kanpur," *Economic Weekly*, XIV (July, 1962), 1111-1118.

Franda, Marcus F. "The Organizational Development of India's Congress Party," *Pacific Affairs*, XXXV (Fall, 1962), 248-260.

Harrison, Selig S. "Caste and the Andhra Communists," *American Political Science Review*, L (June, 1956), 378-404.

Indian Affairs Record.

Indian Sugar.

Nicholas, R. W. "Village Factions and Political Parties in Rural West Bengal," *Journal of Commonwealth Political Studies*, II (November, 1963), 17-32.

Tyagi Brahman.

Weiner, Myron. "The Third General Elections, Studies in Voting Behaviour I: Introduction," *Economic Weekly*, XIV (July, 1962), 1107-1110.

———. "The Third General Elections, Studies in Voting Behaviour IX, Village and Party Factionalism in Andhra: Ponnur Constituency," *Economic Weekly*, XIV (September 22, 1962), 1509-1518.

NEWSPAPERS

Advance.
Citizen.
Express.
Hindustan Standard.
Hindustan Times.
Hindustan Times (Kanpur Supplement).
Leader.
National Herald.
Pioneer.
Statesman.
Times of India.

UNPUBLISHED MATERIAL

Nayar, Baldev Raj. "The Study of Voting Behavior in India," n.d. (Mimeographed.)

Pradhan, Mahesh Chandra. "Socio-Political Organization of the Jats of Meerut Division." Unpublished Ph.D. dissertation, University of London, School of Oriental and African Studies, 1961.

Reeves, P. D. "Landlord Associations in U. P. and Their Role in Landlord Politics, 1920-1937," n.d. (Mimeographed.)

Reeves, Peter. "The Politics of Order: 'Safety Leagues' Against the Congress in the United Provinces, 1921-22. 1962. (Mimeographed.)

Reeves, P. D. "Zamindari Abolition in Uttar Pradesh: An Investigation Into Its Social Effects," n.d. (Mimeographed.)

Tilak, Raghukul. "Acharya Narendra Deva as I Knew Him," n.d. (Mimeographed.)

OTHER SOURCES

Personal interviews with more than 250 political leaders and others in Uttar Pradesh. September, 1961 to January, 1963.

Election statistics by polling station from the District Election Offices in Gonda, Aligarh, Deoria, Meerut, and Kanpur districts.

Registers of active members of the Congress for Aligarh district (1959) and Kanpur City (1961).

Records from the court of the Civil Judge, Aligarh, Suit No. 24 of 1960.

Index

Abdul Bashir Khan, 105, 106
Administration, 212-228
Afghans. *See* Rohilla Afghans
Agarwal, Piyarelal, 180, 181
Agriculture, 14; in Gonda, 62; in Aligarh, 87; in Deoria, 113; in Meerut, 137-138
Ahmad Khan, Sir Syed, 20, 99
Aligarh Muslim University, 20, 88, 99-103, 104, 106
All India Hindi Sahitya Sammelan, 45
Ambedkar, Dr., 104
Andhra, 53, 163, 164
Arya Samaj, 108, 109, 147
Awasthi, Suraj Prasad, 198

Bailey, F. G., 243
Bajpai, Ganesh Datt, 171, 198
Baksar, 8
Baldeo Singh, 64, 67, 70
Banaras region, 7-10 *passim*
Banerji, S. M., 205
Bengal, 20, 21
Bharat Sewak Samaj, 74-75
Bhumidhars, 12
Bihar, 7, 8, 17, 112, 122
Bindeshwari Prasad, 64-65
Block Development Committee, 224; election of, 225
Bombay, 10, 15, 20, 104, 112, 185, 188
British: entrepreneurs, 7; policy to-

ward Oudh, 8-10 *passim*; land settlement under, 11; local self-government under, 191-192; district administration under, 221
Buddhism, and Scheduled Castes, 104, 208
Bundelkhand, 6-7, 8, 10; Congress strength in, 30

Calcutta, 10, 15, 20, 112
Cane Unions. *See* Cooperative Cane Unions
Caste associations, 16, 242
Castes, classification of, 16-18; and factions, 56-57, 210, 241; and politics in Meerut, 137-166; and leadership of the Kanpur Congress, 182-184; and voting in Kanpur, 208-209; and Congress strength, 230; solidarity of, 244
Ahirs and Ahars, 17, 18, 31, 63, 132-133, 138, 146, 156, 157, 161, 230
"Backward" castes, 132, 149, 230
Banias, 18, 43, 56, 57, 63, 138, 146, 148-151 *passim*, 158, 168, 173, 180, 182, 183, 184
Bhuinhars, 17, 18, 115, 118, 131, 132
Brahmans, 6, 16, 17, 18, 31, 44, 56, 57, 63, 71, 84, 88, 95, 107, 115, 131, 132, 133, 138, 139, 146, 147, 148-151, 158, 168, 181, 182, 183, 184,

ST. MARY'S COLLEGE OF MARYLAND LIBRARY
ST. MARY'S CITY, MARYLAND

33783